Developing expertise through experience

Edited by Alan Maley

ISBN 978-0-86355-950-1

Contents

Foreword: on the value of shared experiences

A teacher's experience of teaching the first few lessons to a class of learners is likely to be one of anxiety and discomfort, facing rows of unknown faces and wishing to maintain one's status as a teacher. The most likely response to this tension is to seek some form of protocol as protection, drawing perhaps on memories of the pattern of 'model' lessons one witnessed as a trainee, or the way one's own teacher used to sequence things in a lesson. This may then become a settled routine for one's teaching, sufficiently impersonal to reduce anxiety while fulfilling the expectations of the job. Such routines can consist of things such as following the sequence of units and tasks in the prescribed textbook, reading out and simplifying/paraphrasing pieces of text, getting the class to repeat words and sentences to practise pronunciation or grammar, and getting learners to read aloud around the class, etc. In this way, learners can complete the curriculum and teachers can claim professional experience in due course, but teachers are unlikely to be aware how much is being learned, much less develop a sense of how learning happens or how it can be enhanced.

I have come across one or two ways of avoiding such entrapment in routines. One is what is generally called the 'activities' method. I first became aware of it some 50 years ago in Madras. I was settling down to my job in the British Council as an English Language Officer and heard frequently about a 'Billows' method' of teaching English, spoken of with obvious admiration. I learned that an Englishman called Lionel Billows had been my predecessor in the British Council in Madras about a decade earlier and, many years later, I came by the typescript of an unpublished account written by him of his experience of designing and running for a while an ambitious project for strengthening the teaching of English in Madras Presidency. He had told the Madras government that 'provided the language was taught through activity and play, the earlier a start was made the better'. On a short visit to Karachi, he had taught a demonstration lesson to a class of four-year-olds 'using the various red and black marks on the foreheads of the girls as a starting point, and they had all had a romp'. A training programme, he believed, should 'give active experience and demonstration of active, co-operative and play methods of teaching to the teachers, and the team of trainers should have, besides a methodologist, people with experience in drama, visual aides and singing'.
At an army staff college in India, Billows had noticed the use of a large 'sand-table' on which lines and shapes can be traced with fingers and had quickly started to use that simple aid in language teaching. When a teacher-training course Billows was running at a place outside the city of Madras was interrupted for a few days, 'a significant result was that a deputation of stone-workers from a nearby quarry called to ask why we had stopped, as their children were teaching them in the evening what they had learned in our demonstration classes in the morning'. Billows was later to publish many of these ideas in *The Techniques of Language Teaching* (1961), parts of which still resonate today.

I have since seen and known several others who employ the activity method and have wondered what makes it more productive of language learning than systematic teaching of the language itself. I think first it brings about a kind of social relationship between teacher and learners, throwing off the entrapment in routines and creating, instead, personal feelings and relations. Learners get interested in what the teacher says and does and, if those things are specially interesting and attractive, want to get involved. A kind of mental bridge is created between teacher and learners, leading to, and facilitating, comprehension and thereby acquisition of the teacher's language.

A different way to something similar relates to my own experience. While I was doing a year's diploma in the Teaching of English at the Central Institute of English, Hyderabad, in the mid-1960s, there was a project at the institute called 'Language through Literature' to construct a coursebook of English employing short, simple and enjoyable literary texts, instead of sets of sentences representing grammatical structures. The work in progress at that time was put to and discussed with students of the diploma course in the tutorial sessions. I felt that the emphasis was entirely on making texts easy to comprehend, and very little on getting learners to make an effort to comprehend them and thereby raise their ability to read. When, about five years later, I found myself working on a similar project (called 'English through Reading'), I explored ways of getting learners to read and comprehend texts with an effort. I realised two things in that process. First, texts are not just sequences of sentences but chunks of knowledge, with facts, thought and logic woven together, with explicit as well as implicit meaning and with networks of cross-references back and forth. Understanding a piece of text therefore involves perceiving and inter-relating a variety of things from a variety of signals with different levels of effort. That makes it possible to frame questions to cater to learners of varied abilities in the same class and to gradually raise the general level of challenge as the general performance of the class improves. Second, I noticed that comprehending something with an effort is a moment of genuine pleasure for a learner in the way success in problem-solving generally is. Each instance of success raises not only, however slightly, the learner's comprehension ability but also a desire for further pleasure through further effort. Task-based pedagogy for me is essentially such effort-based learning and teaching. Such classroom activity also leads to a kind of teacher–learner bonding, perhaps similar to that between trainer and trainee in athletics.

While the activity method, as I see it, gives learners enjoyable exposure to a new language, task-based teaching creates for them what I consider an intensive exposure to the language of the text. I feel that the two forms of pedagogy, very different in form and learner level, nevertheless have something in common. Both bring about a kind of mental bridge between teacher and learner (social/emotional in one case and somewhat cerebral/intellectual in the other), and both bring about a contingent effort to make sense, little by little, of what is heard or read.

The word *contingent* is important. In neither of the two situations do the learners see themselves as trying to learn the language. They are trying to understand what is going on or looking to solve a problem for the pleasure of doing so, and understanding the language is simply a part of the process. It is not very different in kind from acquiring one's mother tongue, which can be seen as a process of making sense, bit by bit, of a whole new world and contingently making sense of what people say. This is also true of other comparable situations such as schooling in a second-language medium, or displacement to a different language community. New knowledge needs to be acquired, driven by need or desire, and the new language gets acquired with it. Language is the medium of meaning and gets decoded when there is enough effort to get to the meaning.

I am aware that I am interpreting my own experience of task-based teaching and making inferences from my perception of the 'activity method', and also going on to make some larger generalisations based on them. Such interpretation and inference are perhaps a form of speculation but they do have a ring of truth for me, so much so that I went on to carry out a five-year project of experimental teaching at some primary schools in southern India (called 'The Bangalore Project', reported in *Second Language Pedagogy*, 1987) based on the premise that 'language is best learned when the attention is on meaning', essentially trying out the somewhat cerebral task-based teaching with learners about the same age group as Billows' pupils.

While I was writing *Second Language Pedagogy*, I happened to read Vygotsky's *Mind in Society* (1978) and was struck by how well his concept of the 'zone of proximal development' captured my notion of language learning happening in a series of small steps, each with a successful effort at comprehension. Perhaps such small steps and effort are a feature of other human abilities too.

Around the same time, I also came across a short excerpt from an American educational journal, which read:

> Our coin of knowledge is not firm generalisations, but is more akin to the good measure of meanings: plausibility. In educational research, and in education as a whole, good judgement should be seen as the prized intellectual capacity. Good judgement will not yield certainty, but it can yield interpretations and analyses far more acute and powerful than even the most skilful application of the empiricist 'scientific method'.
>
> (Ericson and Ellet, 1982: 506).

I saw how well the term 'plausibility' captured my own perception of the phenomenon and have been using that term since.

Plausibility is a feeling or perception that occurs to one, not something that can be aimed at, worked for or predicted. Twenty years ago, I thought of taking it further and describing my perception of it and took a few months' leave for the purpose. All that happened was a mental block and a fading away of what perception I had.

I think, however, that a teacher can facilitate its occurrence, by shedding what I have called the entrapment of routines, developing a rapport or 'mental bridge' with learners and staying alert to events in the classroom. There tend to be moments when one feels that something is being learned or has been learned. At some subsequent point of time, such moments get recollected with a degree of clarity or understanding. Over time, various pieces of understanding that had occurred earlier begin to coalesce into a fuller perception of learning.

Plausibility is commonly seen as a state of knowledge short of certainty. But it is actually preferable to certainty in areas such as education where there is no final state of knowledge and no end of a search for it. Certainty signals an end point, while plausibility is always a stage in understanding that can change and develop indefinitely.

Plausibility is of course subjective, being an interpretation of one's own continuing experience. That, in fact, is part of its value since it gets one more and more involved in the act of teaching and makes one feel rewarded by it. However, an articulation by individuals of their personal perceptions of plausibility can lead to a shared understanding of it in the profession at large, perhaps adding to everyone's sense of self-worth as a teacher.

I see this volume as a major effort to facilitate such sharing between professionals working in different parts of the world. The aim, as I see it, is not arriving at a common or agreed perception between many individuals but rather an enlarging, sharpening or enriching of every individual's personal perception. Plausibility in pedagogy is a teacher's intuition about learning arising from her own experience of teaching. While the cognitive process of learning might be the same for all learners, the intuition felt and the perception/interpretation made of it are bound to vary among teachers depending on personal factors. Nevertheless, one teacher's perception can stimulate/make contact with another's, as happens with other forms of experience, thus influencing it in some way. Such mutual influence can advance everyone's sense of plausibility or, minimally, help to keep it alive and engaged, since perceptions can soon degenerate into unchanging assumptions. I also think that an exchange of experience among professionals is especially valuable in an area as inherently personal as a sense of plausibility, in avoiding a sense of isolation and diffidence.

The beginning of a sense of plausibility enables a teacher to emerge from a shell of routinised teaching and start making decisions and noticing outcomes in each lesson, thus starting on a process of professional growth. Reading about how a number of other teachers experienced and interpreted similar processes can help to prompt or hasten that process for oneself.

NS Prabhu
Former Head of Department of English Language and Literature,
National University of Singapore
British Council

References

Billows, L (1961) *The Techniques of Language Teaching*. London: Longmans Green.

Ericson, DP and Ellet, FS, Jr (1982) Interpretation, understanding and educational research. *Teachers College Record* 83/4: 506.

Prabhu, NS (1987) *Second Language Pedagogy*. Oxford: Oxford University Press.

Vygotsky, LS (1978) *Mind in Society*. Cambridge: Harvard University Press.

Introduction

The aim of this book is to give substance to Prabhu's (1987) concept of 'the teacher's sense of plausibility'. That is to say, to explore the ways in which teachers develop professionally and personally by building a personal theory of teaching action based upon their own accumulated experiences – and reflection on them.

Objective history is useful but perhaps more interesting are our personal histories. In this book, I invited 20 experienced professionals to link their personal histories in English language teaching (ELT) to the places they have worked in, to the personalities they have encountered, to the evolving currents of ideas and publications, and to critical moments in their own development.

By weaving together the five strands of places, personalities, ideas, publications and critical moments, it was my hope that we could demonstrate how these five strands have influenced the direction of the professionals' own continuing development of a personal theory of teaching. I suggest that this kind of reflective process can be a valuable element for inclusion within the framework of teacher development as a whole.

My understanding of Prabhu's concept (which he himself describes in the foreword to this volume) is that teachers build their personal theories of teaching and learning through a continuing process of reflection on their lived experiences. It is this process that fuels their personal and professional growth.

This conceptualisation of teacher development is significantly different from the 'training' paradigm that currently enjoys popular assent. The 'training' paradigm is broadly algorithmic in nature: 'If we give teachers X forms of training, they will emerge with Y competences.' The 'plausibility' paradigm, by contrast, is broadly heuristic: 'Whatever training we give them, teachers will adapt and transform it according to what works for them and to the belief system they have evolved, and this is forged through the experiences they undergo'. Furthermore, this is a continuing process with no defined end.

Critics may argue that this approach is unduly personal and anecdotal and lacks scientific rigour. I would respond by insisting that the act of teaching and learning is not scientific anyway but highly individual and personal to both learners and teachers. While our own 'sense of plausibility' will be different from that of other teachers, my expectation is that some valuable themes may emerge from it that are shared across the profession – and that we might do well to attend to them at least as much as we do to the more algorithmic systems of teacher education.

Coincidentally, I link this personal narrative approach with analogous movements in medicine. Oliver Sacks in *Awakenings* (2012) shows how intense focus on his catatonic, supposedly incurable, patients yielded surprising results. He was treating the patients as individuals, acting as a concerned human, rather than simply treating the disease as a scientist. I argue that it might be worthwhile helping our trainees to act in similar fashion.

The contributors

Having published articles on my own professional pathway (Maley, 2016, 2019), it seemed like a good idea to extend the inquiry to others. The guiding principle in selecting the contributors to this book was inclusivity. I have tried as far as possible to include the widest range of geographical contexts, types of teaching context, age, gender and length of experience. The unifying factor is their lives as committed professionals. One interesting finding is that, however varied their narratives, there are strong thematic similarities among them as we shall see below.

Clearly, many of the contributors are well known. But fame is not the focus: the point is to unwrap how, famous or not, their personal experiences have helped forge their values, beliefs and practices.

Contributors were given a set of guidelines. Some have followed these closely. Others have taken a more individual line, while still including the basic themes of the book.

We were concerned that this book should be written in an accessible, non-academic style – what in sartorial terms would be termed 'smart casual'. It is for the reader to judge how well we have achieved this aim.

Some common recurrent themes

The underlying theme of the book is the significance of experience. Viktor Frankl's *Man's Search for Meaning* (2004), based on his experiences in Auschwitz and Dachau, claims that we must deal with whatever life throws at us with dignity and resolution. Even the worst atrocities should be valued as part of our experience. *Was Du erlebst, kann keine Macht der Welt Dir rauben* ('What you experience no power on earth can take from you'). We should value it accordingly. So, it behoves us in our teaching to offer experiences that matter – to us as well as to our learners.

The chapters that follow trace enormously varied life paths by equally diverse personalities. But a number of thematic threads weave the narrative together. The following are the most striking and possibly the most important for future work in teacher development:

- The power of early language-learning experiences to affect later attitudes to foreign languages and cultures.

- Learning new languages is good for us. It keeps the mind active. It shines new light on the human condition. It affords infinite pleasure.

- We need to be aware of the total context of our teaching – geographical, political, sociological and material – not just the linguistic context.

- The influence of key teachers and other 'mentors'. We can learn a lot alone but can profit from timely and appropriate intervention by teachers or mentors.

- The importance of learning from peers is as important as formal instruction. Friends and colleagues are one of our most valuable resources. It is often in free-ranging 'learning conversations' when new ideas and insights are sparked.

- Hence, forging relationships and participating in a learning community is key. This entails building a learning community in which trust and good-humoured playfulness are paramount, and where praise and blame are largely irrelevant – what Wajnryb (2003) calls a 'storied class'.

- Professional groups, such as teachers' associations and special interest groups, are crucial in offering psychological support, in sharing information and in developing solidarity.

- The need to be constantly open to change and new ways of operating. Risk-taking can be the springboard for learning for teachers as well as for students. To avoid risk is to avoid learning. We need to learn to say 'yes'. In improvisation (Johnson, 1989, 1999; Poynton, 2013) and clowning, this is termed 'to accept the offer'.

- At the same time, we need to be sceptical of the claims of published materials, trendy ideas and academic research.

- Creating a space and time for reflection is necessary for us, if we are to think in a concentrated way about what we do.

- The essential role of persistence in the face of adversity: 'I never promised you a bed of roses.'

- The need for constraints as well as freedom. Wine tastes better from the confines of a glass.

- Preparation and planning are important but we must be ready to throw them away as unforeseen learning opportunities occur. We need to learn to go spontaneously with the flow (Csikszentmihalyi, 1996).

- We can effect significant change by making small, manageable changes to the way we teach (see Chapter 2).

- Large, ambitious projects for change, designed and administered from above, are generally doomed to failure. Real change usually happens from below with the willing participation of teachers in classrooms.

- Our job is to provide 'compelling' content, to offer engaging activities and to provide useful feedback and support to students. By 'compelling', I mean things that really matter to our students – and to us. Teachers need to listen and observe closely so as to tailor their responses to learners' emerging needs (see Chapter 20).

- It does not help to teach harder: learning is done by learners, not by the teacher. Learning to 'non-teach' is important (see Chapter 6). There is no need to teach anything that learners can find out for themselves. Language cannot be taught, only learned.

- We need to teach the person(s) in front of us, not just the language as a subject.

- We should never underestimate the capacity of our students to surprise us. And we must give them the space and time to unlock their creative resources.

- There is no best method (Prabhu, 1990), there is only what best suits a particular group at a particular moment.

- All students are individuals with different needs and diverse ways of learning. It is easy to say this but dealing with it in practical terms is always problematic.

- A massive amount of reading is one of the keys to learning, sustaining and developing another language.

- Reading widely, outside the ghetto wall and beyond the narrow confines of our professional literature, is equally important. We can learn a lot from 'feeder fields'. Reading in foreign languages is also beneficial. As Francis Bacon said, 'Reading maketh a full man'.

- Keeping our own first language in good condition is also important.

- The importance of setting language learning and teaching within a wider educational framework, especially the awareness of global issues (Maley and Peachey, 2017).

- The aesthetic dimension is highly significant, both in life and in teaching (see Chapters 4, 12, 15, 17 and 20). We need the expressive dimension as well as the purely referential function.

- We teach who we are, not just the language. Hence the importance of self-knowledge. *Zhi ji zhi bi, bai zhan bu dai* (知己知彼, 百战不殆 – 'Know yourself, know your enemy: a hundred battles a hundred victories') (Sun Zi, 2005).

- Teachers should be role models and show their practical commitment to what they do. They must also be willing to engage in the tasks they set their students.

- Part of being a role model is to show that we too are constantly learning something new – a new language, a new skill, and so on.

- Hard work helps – but we also need to be intellectually and psychologically alert so that we notice what opportunities happen along the way.

- Luck is important, including being in the right place at the right time. But we also make our own luck through our attitudes and decisions. It is not just what happens to me but what I decide to do with it that counts (see opening poem, 'Events'). And it helps to be prepared to work with what happens. There is no right way. We have to find our own. In the words of the Spanish poet Antonio Machado (1912), *Caminante, no hay camino / Se hace camino al andar* ('Traveller, there is no road / You make the road by walking it').

How might we include this in training and development programmes?

1. We could draw on a number of published sources and make space for discussing them. They include Lew Barnett's *The Way We Are* (1988), a collection of teachers' reports on their histories as teachers. Esther Ramani's 'Theorizing from the classroom' (1987) is an early example of looking at teachers' conceptualisation of their practices. Ephraim Weintraub's concept of 'ghosts behind the blackboard' in his interview (1989) highlights the way we are all in some sense replicating the way we ourselves were taught. There is also the classic account of a language teacher's life in Appel's *Diary of a Language Teacher* (1995). Pickett's (1978) survey of experienced language learners' personal accounts is also suggestive and could be replicated. My own account of teacher creativity might also be the starting point for further work (Maley and Kiss, 2018: 161–201). Floris and Renandya's recent collection of teachers' stories (2019) accompanied by reflective activities also offers a rich resource. There is an interesting ongoing project in China run by Richard Young, which should yield useful results (Young, 2016; Sun, Wei and Young, 2019).

2. We could create space for discussion of trainees' personal histories, key turning points, highs and lows, and current areas of interest and growth.

3. We could focus on the importance of spontaneity and improvisation in teaching (Maley and Underhill, 2012; Underhill, 2014). This would highlight the insufficiency of preparation (planning) in dealing with unpredictability (preparedness).

4. We could take a selection of the themes above as the focus for further discussion.

5. We have also suggested a range of possible continuing professional development (CPD) activities in the e-link at (www.teachingenglish.org.uk/sites/teacheng/files/e-file.pdf).....

Concluding remarks: So what...?

In this book we have tried to amplify Prabhu's notion of 'the teacher's sense of plausibility' with reference to our own histories in language and language teaching. But why bother to do this?

Socrates reportedly said, 'The unexamined life is not worth living.' We believe that retrospective reflection on our professional development can be highly revealing. It can help strip away unexamined suppositions and prejudices and this can feed into changes in our current practice.

As mentioned above, I believe that there is an over-emphasis on teacher training as an algorithmic system, and that not enough attention is paid to the human, personal side of learning and teaching. Regular group sharing and discussion of individual 'senses of plausibility' can be highly rewarding as part of a teacher-training or development programme.

I conclude with Young's comments in his study proposal (2016): 'Very few previous studies in applied linguistics have addressed the synergy between the personal history of teachers and learners and the discourse of language learning in the classroom.'

It is time to change that.

Alan Maley
Co-founder of the C group (Creativity for change in language education) and author of many ELT materials

References

Appel, J (1995) *Diary of a Language Teacher*. London: Heinemann.

Barnett, L (1988) *The Way We Are*. Barcelona: ESADE.

Csikszentmihalyi, M (1996) *Creativity: Flow and the Psychology of Discovery and Invention*. New York: Harper Perennial.

Floris, FD and Renandya, WA (2019) *Inspirational Stories for English Language Classrooms*. Jakarta: TEFLIN.

Frankl, VE (2004) *Man's Search for Meaning*. London: Rider.

Johnson, K (1989) *Impro: Improvisation and the Theatre*. London: Methuen Drama.

Johnson, K (1999) *Improvisation for Storytellers*. London: Faber and Faber.

Machado, A (1912) *Campos de Castilla* (no. 29 of Proverbs and Songs). Madrid: Renacimiento Press.

Maley, A (2016) The teacher's sense of plausibility revisited. *Indonesian Journal of English Language Teaching* 11/1: 1–29.

Maley, A (2019) The power of personal experience. *HLT Mag* 21/3.

Maley, A and Kiss, T (2018) *Creativity and English Language Teaching: From inspiration to implementation*. London: Palgrave Macmillan, 161–198.

Maley, A and Peachey, N (eds) (2017) *Integrating global issues in the creative English language classroom: With reference to the United Nations Sustainable Development Goals*. London: British Council.

Maley, A and Underhill, A (2012) Expect the unexpected. *English Teaching Professional* 82/4–7.

Pickett, D (ed) (1978) *The Foreign Language Learning Process*. London: British Council. Available online at: https://www.teachingenglish.org.uk/sites/teacheng/files/F044%20 ELT-43%20The%20Foreign%20Language%20Learning%20Process_v3.pdf

Poynton, R (2013) *Do/Improvise/Less push. More pause. Better results. A new approach to work (and life).* London: The Do Book Company.

Prabhu, NS (1987) *Second Language Pedagogy.* Oxford: Oxford University Press.

Prabhu, NS (1990) There is no best method – why? *TESOL Quarterly* 24: 2.

Ramani, E (1987) Theorizing from the classroom. *ELT Journal* 41/1: 3–11.

Sacks, O (2012) *Awakenings.* London: Picador.

Sun, C, Wei, LL and Young, RF (2019) *Cognition in Chinese EFL Teachers.* Unpublished article.

Sun Zi (2005) *The Art of War* (trans. Thomas Cleary). Boulder, Shambhala.

Underhill, A (2014) Training for the unpredictable. *The European Journal of Applied Linguistics and TEFL* 13/2: 59–69.

Wajnryb, R (2003) *Stories.* Cambridge: Cambridge University Press.

Weintraub, E (1989) An interview with Ephraim Weintraub. *The Teacher Trainer* 3/1:1.

Young, R (2016, ongoing project) *History in Person: Moments of language teaching in the personal histories of teachers.* Wuhan: Central China Normal University.

1

The development of my sense of plausibility and its implications

Robert Bellarmine

My understanding of the 'teacher's sense of plausibility'

Inspired by the proposal of this notion by Prabhu (1987, 1990), the discussion of *Practical Theory* by Dorovolomo (2004) and the description of the development of his 'teacher's sense of plausibility' (TSOP) by Maley (2018), I have described below my own understanding of the TSOP.

Overall, it is a personal theory of learning and teaching. It is a value and belief structure. Its elements are not only beliefs and values but also concepts, principles, rules of thumb, truths and metaphors. Between some elements there can be tension but not conflict.

Being open-ended, its development is continual. It is created and developed through personal experience, reflection, intuition, common sense, experimentation in the classroom, interaction with mentors, students, specialists and colleagues, exposure to books and articles, teacher-training and teacher-development activities, and critical incidents in life. One's TSOP is continuously revised according to the value, power and plausibility of the new inputs.

Its application and diffusion are subject to professional ethics and personal morality. When encountering specialists', trainers' or colleagues' TSOPs or a method, one does not automatically apply the purest form of one's TSOP, in certain cultures and contexts. The application and diffusion of TSOPs depend on factors such as the believers' professional freedom, risks involved when applying their TSOPs in their purest forms, need for changes in methods in vogue, power structures, and the specific role one is required to play, such as promoting a method.

The development path of my own TSOP

The following narration is neither exhaustive nor strictly chronological.

My TSOP began when I was in Standard IX. It grew through my college days when I experienced English as an instructional medium. It developed further when I prepared for my MA in English Literature as a private student. It matured when I taught chemistry through English for three years and English as an L2 for ten years.

Next came my training as a teacher of English at the Central Institute of English and Foreign Languages (CIEFL), now the English and Foreign Languages University (EFLU), Hyderabad, followed by the opportunity to pursue my MSc in Applied Linguistics at the University of Edinburgh, where I developed more as an academic than as a teacher or trainer.

My TSOP developed most significantly when I was first a trainee and later a trainer at CIEFL. That was thanks to my interaction with reputable Indian specialists in ELT, a number of classroom practitioners from various parts of India, and NS Prabhu of the British Council Division for South India.

Another period of significant growth was the 11 years I served as English Studies Officer of the British Council Division, South India. Important for me were interactions with a number of visiting British specialists who demonstrated the value of activities and games in contrast with the ineffectiveness of the presentation-cum-practice techniques of the structural approach then in use in India.

This was also the time I observed how readily and effectively English was learned in subject classes in good English-medium schools.

Another strong and obvious influence on my TSOP were the library resources at CIEFL, at the University of Edinburgh and in my home. Books are not dead – not yet anyway.

Yet another important influence was the mixed bag of presentations, debates and discourses by literary, religious and management gurus. Under their influence, I explored the various aspects and types of communication, especially classroom communication. That reinforced my faith in humour, questioning, presentation strategies, interaction with the audience, use of visuals, especially realia, appeal to emotion and Krashen's 'compelling comprehensible input hypothesis' (Krashen, 2011, 2018).

How some elements of my TSOP developed

Belief in motivation

This began when I was in the first year of high school. By this time, I had become aware of the urgent need to do well in education, especially in English language learning. My family desperately needed to escape poverty and the oppressive, sectarian 'majoritarianism' practised in the administration of our village – and I was their escape route.

The earliest form of motivation was extrinsic and instrumental. However, it soon turned into the integrative and intrinsic kind, in the following circumstances. My exposure to North American culture happened around that time via the English magazines lent to me by the director of the orphanage in my village. More importantly, I observed first hand the US government's generous charity to the orphanage and the schools attached to it, in the form of wheat, vitamins, milk powder, dehydrated egg, cottonseed oil and clothes. This predisposed me to an affection for this foreign culture.

Integrative and intrinsic motivation matured later when, as a teacher, I prepared for my MA in English Literature exam. The books prescribed for this degree exposed me to several aspects of English literature, language and life in England. It was then that I started to admire British literature, culture, democracy and public sense of fairness. This was mainly through the works of literary giants such as Shakespeare, Milton, Dryden, Blake, Wordsworth, Keats, Shelley, Tennyson, TS Eliot, Dickens, Jane Austen, Thomas Hardy, Bernard Shaw and GK Chesterton. Trevelyan's *English Social History* (1946) had a tremendous effect on my attitude to the people of England. All this helped turn my motivation into the integrative type.

Exposure via reading

As early as Class IX, I realised that the three books prescribed for detailed and 'non-detailed' study were seriously inadequate for effective exposure. I was in a Tamil-medium school, where in one academic year English was taught only for 160 periods of 40 minutes' duration.

What is more, in my village, English was spoken only at school in the English classes. Therefore, my exposure to spoken English was limited to reading materials until I went to college. Luckily, I got plenty of these materials, believe it or not, from a grocer. He bought second-hand books when the school year ended and used them as waste paper to wrap items such as tamarind. Fortunately, he allowed me to exchange my siblings' as well as my own books for other students' English books. After studying them, I exchanged them for more books.

I would also walk to the library in the neighbouring town to read the English-language dailies. I read them intensively, and took down new words and the sentences I liked. Incidentally, it was then that I felt acutely the need for a bilingual dictionary, which came my way via my sister, after she got through her school final exam.

Exposure to spoken English via the BBC

Around the same time, I pressured my father to get a cheap radio assembled from cannibalised parts. One day, I happened to receive BBC Radio, when it was announcing its schedule. From that day on, I listened every single day to the BBC's *English by Radio* programmes, news bulletins, interviews, book reviews and talks from 4.30 to 7.30 in the morning. My listening was always very active, my attention fully focused, and was accompanied by learning activities such as noting down useful/interesting words, correct pronunciation and idiomatic expressions and repeating new words after the teachers on the programmes. I am sure a lot of others around the world were doing exactly the same thing!

Exposure via English films

When I went to college, I had the opportunity to watch English films and developed a taste for movies with lots of conversation. Immediately after the shows, I used to repeat useful words such as 'hell drivers' and 'This way please!', idioms and memorable dialogues. I used to watch three to four films every weekend.

Relation between motivation and exposure

Thus, thanks to my experience of acquiring English effectively through my motivation and exposure, my faith in these factors became unshakeable. This was later confirmed for me when pundits in applied linguistics such as Corder (1973) observed that, given motivation and exposure, second language learning was automatic. But my extreme view is this: 'Given motivation, exposure is automatic'. Well, maybe!

Lack of faith in isolated sentences

In the schools and the college I attended, the syllabuses required the study of large amounts of explicit grammar. But I attended to grammar only as far as the exams required. For isolated sentences did not seem useful to me. Later, when advocates of the structural approach presented isolated sentences and then contextualised them, I was not impressed either. To me, this was as senseless as sticking lifeless flesh to dry bones.

Value of 'context-arousing' sentences

However, I did value and memorise certain types of seemingly isolated sentences. These were sentences, such as the illustrative sentences in Hornby's dictionary (1948/1974), that aroused appropriate contexts, pictures or scenes in alert learners' minds.

Metaphorically, these sentences are 'inverted doughnuts', in which the core is hard and around which lies a halo. In a context-arousing sentence, the core is the seemingly isolated sentence, the halo being the context, picture or scene it arouses. Here are some examples of 'inverted doughnuts' from India's number one grammar book at the time (Wren and Martin, 1935/1960).

All that glitters is not gold.
The darkest cloud has a silver lining.
A live ass is stronger than a dead lion.
Hunger is the best sauce.

Two of my guiding lights

Impact of Prabhu

My face-to-face interactions with Prabhu, though brief and infrequent, were extremely useful. Besides, I attended all his returned study fellows (RSF) seminars and the seminars CIEFL organised for Prabhu and UK specialists in the 1980s.

As his analyses, observations and questions were always insightful and provocative, he had an indelible impact on me. At an RSF seminar held in the early 1980s, his presentation 'Exposure is necessary, but is it sufficient?' struck me in two contrasting ways. First, it included his masterly analysis of 'Exposure', which we use loosely as a linguistic holdall. In a one-page tree diagram, he first split its features into five groups: 'quality', 'means for achieving comprehensibility', 'what was selected primarily', 'means to achieve systematicity' and 'means to achieve effectiveness'. He then split each group of features into its manifestations or varieties. All told, the five types of exposure were analysed into 32 manifestations or varieties. Thus, on a single page, Prabhu captured comprehensively the types of exposure employed by the methods developed in the last five centuries (see pages 20–21 for a copy of the diagram).

Second, neither in the handout nor in his presentation did he mention motivation even once. Motivation being *the* most critical factor for L2 learning in my view, I was provoked. Therefore, I asked him why he avoided talking about motivation. Pop came his reply: 'It's a fuzzy concept!' He also once said, 'Motivation is the name of the unknown.'

However, a few years later, I got a slightly less evasive answer, in his *Second Language Pedagogy* (Prabhu, 1987: 55–56), where he states: 'Learners' immediate motivation in the task-based classroom derives from the intellectual pleasure of solving problems, in addition to such traditional sources as a desire to do well at school, to win the approval of the teacher, or to gain the admiration of one's peers.'

EXPOSURE IS NECESSARY but is it sufficient? Is it the best one can do?

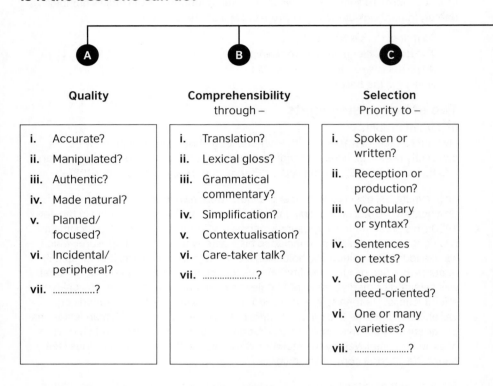

A Quality	**B** Comprehensibility through –	**C** Selection Priority to –
i. Accurate? ii. Manipulated? iii. Authentic? iv. Made natural? v. Planned/focused? vi. Incidental/peripheral? vii. ....?	i. Translation? ii. Lexical gloss? iii. Grammatical commentary? iv. Simplification? v. Contextualisation? vi. Care-taker talk? vii. ....?	i. Spoken or written? ii. Reception or production? iii. Vocabulary or syntax? iv. Sentences or texts? v. General or need-oriented? vi. One or many varieties? vii. ....?

Notes

1. The need for exposure to the target language is **the only thing we are sure about**; the rest is and has always been a matter of probability, speculation and inconclusive investigation.

2. The different methods/approaches can be seen to be (i) concentrating primarily on **particular features of exposure** (e.g. the structural approach concentrating on systematicity in terms of grammatical and lexical grading; the direct method concentrating on comprehensibility through contextualisation) and (ii) selecting **particular means of making exposure successful** (e.g. one form of the communicative approach: functional systematicity + simulation of real life + texts, not sentences + language 'made natural'). As a result, certain features (means) are crucial to certain methods/approaches while others are not (e.g. avoidance of translation was crucial to the direct method, while systematic grading was not; authenticity is crucial to some ESP (English for Specific Purposes) approaches; care-taker talk is crucial to acquisition-based approaches, while translation is not). The centrality of syllabus or method (product or process) is also the result of which aspects of exposure are seen to be crucial.

D
Systematicity
in terms of –

i. Grammatical/ lexical grading?

ii. Semantic/functional sequencing?

iii. Natural/built-sequence?

iv. Grading by cognitive content?

v. Learner-controlled grading?

vi. ....?

E
Effectiveness
through –

i. Repetition or practice?

ii. Meaningfulness?

iii. Interest/enjoyment?

iv. Systematic correction?

v. Simulation of real life?

vi. Perceived relevance to real life?

vii. Mind-engagement?

viii. Interaction?

ix. Receptive state of mind?

x. ....?

3. **This is only one particular way of relating varied issues in ELT.** Alternative (or improved) charts are welcome on the seminar, as are arguments against such 'global' statements or demonstration of its imperfections/distortions.

4. Expositions on particular features/means or a tracing of them through different methods/approaches/periods of history can form the bases of presentations as well.

(Emphasis added)

Impact of Michael West via PT George

The training course I pursued at CIEFL, Hyderabad, introduced me to Michael West as the father of extensive reading and author of the *General Service List* (1953), famous for listing 2,000 key English words. However, thanks to George, I went much beyond that.

West struck me as the first ELT specialist to carry out action research, searching for answers for practical questions such as 'In the context of reading extensive readers, at what difficulty level in terms of lexis do learners become frustrated?' He himself wrote the extensive readers his learners needed. As for the overall value of his work in West Bengal, when Oxford University denied him a DLitt for his work in India, the Indian government collected all his writings as a report titled *Bilingualism* (1926). Even today, this is an important reference for ELT administrators as well as ELT specialists in India.

If I can borrow one of West's famous phrases, for 'teaching English in difficult circumstances', he introduced the *New Method Readers* (1927) and *The New Method English Dictionary* (1941). Mainly because of him, the concept of graded readers became an important part of ELT curriculum in those days.

Further, he never missed the essential point that in ELT as well as education, the central factor is the learner. This is why, though he opposed the direct method for exclusively emphasising speaking, at the learners' request he wrote a dictionary and some special textbooks for spoken English too.

West struck my TSOP poignantly with his two-fold message to the Teacher Training College in East Bengal: 'You should keep on experimenting, and ... the greatest handicap to learning is an excess of teaching' (West, 1968).

Critical incident one

One day the students announced a 'total boycott' of classes. Allegedly, Father Principal Warden was adulterating the milk supplied to them, and was having an affair with the gardener's wife. Refusing to conduct any enquiries, Father Principal Warden required the teachers to ensure that students attend classes at any cost.

I immediately spread the message that on that day I would teach how to use modal verbs effectively in a brief letter to the Principal on the subject of the boycott. I assured the students that the letter would:

- describe their charges against the warden
- specify the action Father Principal should take
- explain why their protest should be condoned
- mention the steps students would/could take to restore normality.

Responding to my promise, the students came to my class. After quickly revising my earlier sessions on modals, I divided the students into five groups: four for the four parts of the letter, and one group of bright students to go around the class with me as 'language consultants'. The drafting was followed by a presentation. To the satisfaction of the students, the session was closed with suggestions for finishing touches.

The lesson I learned from that incident was this: to achieve effective learning, teaching should have 'compelling content' connected with learners' lives.

Critical incident two

One evening at the CIEFL, in the middle of a practice teaching session held in the evening, the city's power grid broke down. Still, my fellow trainer, Jayashree, offered to conduct a spoken English lesson in complete darkness!

Calling her activity 'The Chinese Whisper', she lined up five learners for its first part. Then she whispered something into the first player's ear and asked him to whisper what he had heard into the next learner's ear. The next three students continued the whisper chain. When the fifth learner received the whispered message, he spoke it out loudly: 'What noise, noise. Important monster'. Jayashree smiled a suggestive smile. As she had expected, the original message had been badly distorted and reduced. She then spoke aloud the original, whispered text: 'What annoys an oyster most? A noisy oyster annoys an oyster most.'

On hearing this, all of us burst into laughter. Jayashree then explained why the five students failed to get the whispered text. They were ignorant about the key features of spoken English and the words 'annoy' and 'oyster'.

That incident was the first to convince me that the activity-oriented approach was much more effective than the approaches CIEFL had been advocating: the structural, the language through literature and the dialogical lecture approaches.

Impact of books and articles

I have been deeply influenced so often by these resources that I cannot do full justice to them in the limited space available here. However, they are too significant to ignore completely.

Two radical books

Teaching as a Subversive Activity (Postman and Weingartner, 1969) and *Pedagogy of the Oppressed* (Freire, 1970) fell into my lap in the early 1970s. Fortuitously, they were most appropriate to the institution where I was teaching at that time, named after St Baptist De La Salle, who strove to educate the poor. The college had been dedicated to the socio-economic liberation of the people in the area. Further, although these books dealt with general education, I found in them some classroom techniques usable in language teaching.

Another inspirational book

From Communication to Curriculum by Barnes (1976) came my way ten years later. It inspired me with its strong plea for classroom interaction and students' questions, with memorable expressions such as, 'learning floats on a sea of talk' and 'the centrality of talk (dialogue) for active learning'. Prospectively, it prepared me for Prabhu's 'Bangalore Project', which placed classroom interaction at the centre of his approach.

Collections of tasks, activities and games

Again, these are too many to cover exhaustively here. What are uppermost in my memory now are as follows.

- Prabhu's tasks (unpublished) tried out on his 'Communicational Teaching Project' in 1981–82, and collections or discussions of tasks by Jane Willis (1996), Dave Willis (2007), Nunan (1989) and Ellis (2003).
- Maley and Duff's (1978) drama techniques.
- Davis and Rinvolucri's (1988) dictation activities.
- Rinvolucri's grammar games (1984/2006).
- Klippel's (1984) communicative activities for spoken English.
- Sanderson's (1999) activities using newspapers.

In the last 15 years, I have been using a few tasks/activities from each of the above resources in my teacher training and general or business English classes. Let me offer a sample from each of the above resources.

While I got only cognitive tasks from Prabhu's collection, I was able to draw other affective types of tasks from authors such as Willis. From Maley and Duff, I have repeatedly borrowed 'The Alibi'. I have often borrowed from Davis and Rinvolucri – the dictation involving the text titled 'Toys of War'; the dictation using a hand-out containing broken lines proportionate to the length of the words of the text to be read out at a speed controlled by the class; and the dictation captivatingly called 'Students Dictate to the Teacher'.

Another favourite activity is Sanderson's 'Unpacking', which requires students to tease out all the simple sentences embedded in the first paragraph of a news item, which contains one long, complex sentence.

I have drawn the largest number of activities from Klippel's *Keep Talking* (1984).

An overview of my TSOP

The key elements of my TSOP are as follows.

Current beliefs/values about English

- English is a language of opportunity.
- It is essential for many learners for their freedom from oppression.
- It is not inherently difficult to learn.
- It is a rich language with rich vocabulary, enormous morphological potential and users who are highly open to creating new words.
- Its literature is the richest, arguably next only to Tamil literature. (Do not accuse me of bias, please!)

Beliefs and values about learning/teaching English I gained as a *learner*

- Keen motivation is the most important factor for learning English successfully.
- Exposure is the second most important factor.

- Radio and cinema are extremely effective means of exposure.
- The books usually prescribed for teaching English as a subject rather than as a medium are woefully inadequate.
- Texts may be memorised but only after a reasonably good understanding, even though it is not always necessary to fully understand the text you are exposed to.
- Learning English is a long and arduous process.
- The dictionary is not only a storehouse of meanings of unfamiliar words but also a treasure-house of memorable, context-arousing, illustrative sentences, valuable idioms, standard pronunciation and useful etymological information.

Beliefs acquired after becoming a *teacher* of chemistry and then English

- Good teachers of English transcend the prescribed texts and bring in stories, anecdotes and the like connected with the texts and classroom incidents.
- Most good teachers have or develop a sense of humour.
  (They need it to survive!)
- Teaching English grammar is necessary only at advanced levels.
- Writing is the most difficult of all the four language skills.
- Teaching writing develops clear thinking, active vocabulary and syntax.
- Writing has the vital qualities of permanence, authenticity and authority.
- The 'teacher talk': 'student talk' ratio in the classroom should be about one-third/two-thirds.
- The procedural syllabus consisting of cognitive tasks is much more effective than the communicative, functional and structural syllabuses.
- A judicious mixture of cognitive, aesthetic, literary, affective and even physical activities can be more effective than exclusively cognitive tasks.
- Learners' language errors are excellent evidence of their learning effort, not sins of commission/omission.
- Teachers should correct learners' errors only selectively and incidentally.
- When the form of the language is learned, paradoxically, learners' conscious attention should be focused on meaning.
- 'Language awareness' need not be taught at elementary and intermediate levels.
- The most effective and efficient way to teach a second language is to use it as a 'medium' and its literature as the 'message'.
- An L2 teacher must be at least proficient enough in the target language to manage the class in it.
- The source of the problems of teaching English in state-run schools in countries such as India are primarily political, ethical and managerial, not educational.

References

Barnes, D (1976) *From Communication to Curriculum*. Harmondsworth: Penguin.

Corder, SP (1973) *Introducing Applied Linguistics*. Harmondsworth: Penguin.

Davis, P and Rinvolucri, M (1988) *Dictation: New Methods, New Possibilities*. Cambridge: Cambridge University Press.

Dorovolomo, J (2004) Teachers' practical theory: Personal articulation and implications for teachers and teacher education in the Pacific. *Pacific Curriculum Network* 13/1&2.

Ellis, R (2003) *Task-based Language Learning and Teaching*. Oxford: Oxford University Press.

Freire, P (1970) *Pedagogy of the Oppressed*. New York: Continuum Company.

Hornby, AS (1948/1974) *Oxford Advanced Learner's Dictionary*. Oxford: Oxford University Press.

Klippel, F (1984) *Keep Talking*. Cambridge: Cambridge University Press.

Krashen, DS (2011) The compelling (not just interesting) input hypothesis. *The English Connection* (KOTESOL) 15/3: 1.

Krashen, DS (2018) The conduit hypothesis: How reading leads to academic language competence. *Language Magazine*. April.

Maley, A (2018) The teacher's sense of plausibility revisited. *Indonesian Journal of English Language Teaching* 11/1: 1–29.

Maley, A and Duff, A (1978) *Drama Techniques in Language Learning*. Cambridge: Cambridge University Press.

Nunan, D (1989) *Designing Tasks for the Communicative Classroom*. Cambridge: Cambridge University Press.

Postman, N and Weingartner, C (1969) *Teaching as a Subversive Activity*. New York: Dell Publishing Company.

Prabhu, NS (1987) *Second Language Pedagogy.* Oxford: Oxford University Press.

Prabhu, NS (1990) There is no best method – Why? *TESOL Quarterly* 24/2: 161–176.

Rinvolucri, M (1984/2006) *Grammar Games: Cognitive, Affective and Drama Activities for EFL Students.* Cambridge: Cambridge University Press.

Sanderson, P (1999) *Using Newspapers in the Classroom.* Cambridge: Cambridge University Press.

Trevelyan, GM (1946) *English Social History.* London: Pelican Books.

West, M (1926) *Bilingualism.* Calcutta: Government of India, Central Publication Branch.

West, M (1927) *The New Method Readers.* Calcutta: Longmans.

West, M (1953) *A General Service List of English Words, with Semantic Frequencies and a Supplementary Word-list for the Writing of Popular Science and Technology.* London: Longmans.

West, M (1968) Untitled message on the sixtieth anniversary of Teachers' Training College, Dacca in Teachers' Training College, Dacca (eds) (1969) *Dacca Teachers Training College Annual, Sixtieth Anniversary Issue, 1968–69.* Dacca: Teachers' Training College.

West, M and JD Endicott (1941) *The New Method English Dictionary.* London: Longman, Green.

Willis, D (2007). *Doing Task-Based Teaching.* New York: Oxford University Press.

Willis, J (1996) *A Framework for Task-Based Learning.* London: Longman.

Wren, PC and Martin, H (1935/1960) *High School English Grammar and Composition.* Bombay: Maneckji Cooper Education Trust.

For CPD activities, visit e-file link: www.teachingenglish.org.uk/sites/teacheng/files/e-file.pdf

2

My quest to understand learning and teaching

John F Fanselow

My earliest experiences of language learning and education that have affected my current views and practices

I went to a Catholic elementary school. I wanted to be an altar boy. One requirement was that we were able to say the responses in Latin. In this case 'say' meant recite the words even if we did not understand what they meant.

The person in charge of training altar boys said my accent was not good enough to be an altar boy. Yet in studying to recite the words, I found the juxtaposition of the Latin sentences and the English renditions fascinating. So rather than give up, I applied to be a choirboy. The choirmaster asked me to read a few lines from the 'Gloria' in Latin and he said fine.

My experiences with Latin fed my curiosity about languages, so when I went to secondary school and was told I could take at least one year of a foreign language, I was thrilled. I took Spanish because more people spoke it than French and German, the other two languages on offer.

Discovering that there were such things as feminine and masculine nouns and adjectives, among other differences, was exciting. To this day I am fascinated by word origins in English.

Language teaching around the world I, believe, would be greatly enhanced if languages were not required and there were no external commercial examinations. As Paulo Freire (1976) among others has said, 'We are wired to learn!' 'Can I do this? Can I do that or the other thing?' These questions represent our constant odyssey. It is ironic that the origin of 'curious' is related to being careful!

My greatest influence was my experience as a Peace Corps Volunteer at a teacher training college in Nigeria

I was about to graduate from college with a degree in Spanish and English, and eager to get a high school teaching job, when President Kennedy established the Peace Corps. He wanted to send Americans to other countries to learn about other people, return to the US and share what they learned with fellow citizens and, in the meantime, maybe do some good, but for sure no harm.

I had no particular country in mind but my spoken Spanish was not great, so I applied for a position in Latin America thinking it would be a way to refine my Spanish. But there were no positions there in 1961. So, I accepted a position in Nigeria, teaching English, saying bye-bye to improving my Spanish.

I was assigned to a teacher training college to teach language and literature and supervise practice teachers. Two problems: first, the teachers I was supervising each had more experience than I had, from four to 20 years; and second, they were teaching Nigerian history and geography, and the currency system adopted from England – pounds, shillings and pence, before decimalisation, and British systems of measurements such as poles, rods and perches – information that was all new to me.

Fortunately for me, in the primary schools where the teachers were practice-teaching, there were two Primary 1 classes, two Primary 2 classes, all the way up to Primary 6. Also, the timetable mandated that each stream study the same subjects at the same time each day.

I decided that the only way I could be the least bit useful would be to observe the first 20 minutes of the first period in one stream and the second 20 minutes of the first period in the other stream. I wrote down as much as I could of what each teacher and some of the students said and did, with the intention of sharing what the teachers did with each other and what their students produced.

At the end of the day, when I met the two teachers teaching Primary 1, for example, I would say, 'Okon, Benedict wrote the date and all the directions on the board and had the students copy them as they looked at the board. You said the date and had the students look at the board, then look only at their notebooks and write what they remembered. So, Okon, tomorrow do what Benedict did. And Benedict, please do what Okon did.'

Key people who have left an enduring mark on my life, beliefs and practices

You will recall that the practice teachers I was supervising had more experience and knowledge of what they were teaching than I did.

Although telling teachers who taught the same classes to try out activities that were slightly different made me feel mildly useful, the range of activities that we tried was very limited. I thought that the teachers I was charged with developing were being short-changed because of my ignorance.

Fortunately for me, the British Council had posted an English Language Officer in Enugu, the capital of the Eastern Region, where I was teaching. He was charged with visiting schools and introducing books and lessons to teachers. Just as I was thinking how I was short-changing the teachers, he visited me.

He visited the primary school where my practice teachers were teaching and demonstrated some alternative activities. He gave me books by Michael West (1960) on read and look up; Hornby (1961) on ways to teach structural words and sentence patterns; French (1960) on ways to use sketches and give dictations, to name just some of the many activities he suggested; and Gurrey (1955), who introduced me to the nine types of questions, including yes/no, either/or, question words about facts in the text and inferences from the text or personal experience.

The fact that he taught my classes to demonstrate what these books suggested became one foundation of my professional life: do not just read but also do. Crucial as reading can be, we have to act in order to learn.

Key ideas and publications that have helped form or change my beliefs and practices

While I was teaching at Teachers College, Arno Bellack and colleagues there had published *The Language of the Classroom* (1966). They had asked social studies teachers to teach a speech on free trade by John F Kennedy. They told the teachers they could use whatever methods they wanted but they all had to use the same text.

In the event, each teacher focused on a totally different section of the text. But all spent most of their time asking factual questions. So, the content that was supposed to be the same was in fact different in each class – but the methods the teachers used were the same.

Imagine all the possibilities

Since my time in Nigeria I have read many other descriptions of classrooms. Almost every analysis of classroom interactions shows that the number of activities done in classrooms is extremely limited. Factual questions predominate. As in Dickens' satire in *Hard Times* (1854), Mr Gradgrind's 'Facts alone are wanted in life' was the mantra.

In Nigeria, I thought having a teacher write the directions rather than say them was a big step forward. But having observed classrooms through the years, I have seen that the options available are much broader and more numerous. Yet in our teaching we often fail to remember this fact.

As we know, the number of radii in a circle is infinite. But the narrow range of activities represents around 25 per cent of those available. Here is just one way to expand the activities beyond the 25 per cent by making just a small change.

Students in many countries erase mistakes they make during a dictation. One teacher asked her students to write 'I like ice cream'. In both her classes at the same level, she said the sentence three times. After saying the sentence, she wrote it on the board. But in one class she asked the students to keep their erasers in their pencil cases.

She discovered that in the class where students could not erase and correct their sentences, only ten out of 40 had written the sentence correctly. 'I ice', 'I cream', 'I spring' were among the renditions.

I was introduced to Douglas Barnes (1976), who had analysed classroom interactions from various perspectives. At the same time, so-called designer methods were being introduced. When I saw Caleb Gattegno teach a class without saying a word and Charles Curran teach a class eliciting the language students wanted to learn in their first language and then writing what they wanted to say in English, I thought: 'Wow, substituting written directions for spoken directions and not using erasers are nothing by comparison!'

Reading how Sylvia Ashton-Warner (1963) had Maori children draw sketches of experiences they had in their homes and then wrote lines for them to match their emotional experiences, I felt even more keenly how limited my practices had been.

But when I read Frank Smith's books on reading (1971) and later on learning (1988), I began to see how the designer methods and Barnes and Ashton-Warner, who were out of the mainstream, all had two similar messages: nurture natural curiosity and, following Plato, remind people of what they already know.

Important publications in my personal and professional development

Reading literature in university provided crucial lessons for my development as a teacher and a person. One relates to ways of analysing literature and the other to the message that authors try to convey.

When we discussed a poem, a play or a scene from a novel each of us tended to have slightly different interpretations. 'Why was Antonio sad in the opening lines of *The Merchant of Venice?*' Some gave opinions before reading no more than the opening scene. Others shared their reasons after reading more scenes. A few had opinions picked up from reviews of the play in production. Therefore, I found one-dimensional comments that are common in discussions of teaching hard to accept after studying literature.

When we re-read a poem or lines from a play aloud we tended to stress different groups of words, conveying some novel emotions and employing distinct gestures. So, when I discussed videos of teachers and students, I would ask viewers to speak the teachers' lines with different emotions, to remind them that carrying out even such a regular activity as giving directions can be engaging, off-putting, boring or a waste of time, depending on small changes in how we express ourselves.

When I re-read parts of *Don Quixote* years after college, I realised that his seeing windmills as dragons, through his knight's visor, was no different from each of us seeing an activity in a particular way – useful, not useful, challenging, boring – depending on our perception. I have substituted a pair of huge sunglasses for Don Quixote's visor to remind teachers that we all wear a particular pair of glasses and, until we substitute other pairs, we cannot see what we observe in new ways.

On a course in film, one of the films we analysed was *Rashomon*, directed by Kurosawa. In the film, various characters give conflicting accounts of the same event.

Without these themes from Cervantes, Plato, Dickens, Kurosawa and others in my literature classes, I doubt I would have written *Breaking Rules* (1987), *Contrasting Conversations* (1992a), *Try the Opposite* (1992b) and *Small Changes in Teaching, Big Results in Learning* (2018).

Walt Whitman developed many themes in *Leaves of Grass* – equality, individuality, acceptance of differences, to name a few. I have quoted the following, which is in tune with John Dewey, Frank Smith and others who remind us that we can learn only by predicting and experiencing ourselves, not by being told or talked at.

> *I lead no man to a dinner table, library, exchange,*
> *But each man and each woman of you I lead upon a knoll, [...]*
> *My right hand pointing to landscapes of continents and*
> *The public road. Not I, not anyone else can travel that road for you.*
> *You must travel it for yourself.*

Critical incidents/epiphanies in life and work, which have given me new insights

After my film course, when *Rashomon* opened my eyes, I started to ask teachers to bring in clips of favourite movies and television programmes that they thought had scenes we could learn about teaching from. One teacher brought in a clip from *Witness for the Prosecution*. In the film Charles Laughton is the defence attorney. He asks many 'yes/no' questions. After each one, the witness continues to talk after saying 'yes' or 'no'. The judge intervenes to tell the witnesses that they have to limit their response to 'yes' or 'no'. Many teachers too have been deluded that responses to 'yes/no' questions are limited to 'yes' or 'no'.

My focus on literature, film and television goes along with two other influences on my thinking: botany and the Dewey Decimal System.

We were required to take one science lab course in college. I chose botany because I loved gardening and as a Boy Scout I learned a lot about how Indians used plants and how trees were important to support the lives of insects and animals.

An integral feature of my botany class was the taxonomy of plants. When I discovered that roses and strawberries were related, I was blown away. I mean, if you asked a hundred people what a rose and a strawberry have in common few could state any connections. So, discovering that plants are grouped on the basis of multiple characteristics – number of stamens and pistils, configuration of leaves and type of roots, etc. – was stimulating. Bellack (1966) grouped student and teacher communications in the same way that botanists group plants – by looking at multiple characteristics. I found this connection very exciting.

In high school, I was fascinated by how the books were arranged in our library using the Dewey Decimal System: 300 social studies and 307 communities, as a subcategory of social studies; 500 science and 550 Earth sciences as a subcategory. Dewey reminded me that categories were insufficient; we need to use subcategories. So, in my coding system I described in *Beyond Rashomon* (1977), I point out that we communicate linguistically, non-linguistically, paralinguistically and through silence. But I then indicate that each of these mediums can appeal to our ears, our eyes and our feelings.

So, there are two Deweys in my influences: Melvil (1876), the founder of the first school of library science in the US, and John (1938), the professor and educator!

Themes emerging from my chapter

I missed Prabhu's writings while developing my own ideas about preparing teachers. But reading him now, I resonate with his thinking. He reminds us of the importance and power of joint exploration. One of my themes has been to jointly develop with teachers ways to constantly explore. As we jointly explore, I remind teachers that they should accept suggestions from others only if they fit the situations they are in – and to have faith in their beliefs based on their experiences. These ways to explore are suggestions I have been making for decades, with a nod to John Rogers, my British Council Mentor in Nigeria, among others.

Technology had a big impact on my development as a joint explorer. When video recorders became easier and easier to use, the teachers in my classes and I started to make recordings of interactions. As a result, we could transcribe and look at the data together rather than just at my notes, as had been the case in Nigeria. Over time we involved the students in the exploration as well.

Working as a peer rather than an expert was not done in a heartbeat. Initially, some teachers baulked at jointly transcribing: 'We are too busy to write what we and our students say and do in the recordings.' After transcribing for decades, of course I understood their concern. So, I suggested first that they transcribe exchanges that fitted on one sheet of A4. Second, I suggested they ask their students to transcribe the same exchanges, again just those that would fit on one sheet of A4. Even this amount of transcribing takes from 15 to 30 minutes.

Again, technology had a big impact. More recently, I have had students record their interactions with their mobile phones and take pictures of pages from their notebooks and information on the whiteboard. The availability of the new technology has made it possible to have teachers and their students more engaged in the joint non-judgemental analysis of what they do. The initial resistance faded as teachers saw that they could use the transcriptions as the basis for planning their subsequent classes.

Not only did they generate alternatives from what they analysed but they saw what language they needed to work on with their students, based on the errors they noted as they transcribed. The students also began to notice their errors. Teachers discovered that the transcripts eliminated the need to prepare, administer and grade tests.

All of the joint exploration that I have learned to do over the years has increasingly exemplified Prabhu's 'sense of plausibility'.

Given the state of teacher preparation, it seems that, tragically, many others also missed Prabhu's discussion of 'a sense of plausibility'. Most MA programmes, as well as Trinity and other certificate programmes, are one-size-fits-all, with a focus on learning from the experts. Few if any invite teachers to record and analyse transcriptions of their teaching nor develop with them ways to non-judgementally analyse what they say and do. Every service industry except teaching reminds us when we call that our call might be recorded so that the service company can better understand the needs of their clients – in our case, students.

My beliefs about languages, and teaching and learning them

Languages, like music, dance, art, mathematics and all other forms of communication, enable us to create new worlds for us and others to experience. Not all the worlds we create bring joy but all enrich us.

To me, teaching, whether languages or any skill or subject, is reminding people of what they already know and nurturing natural curiosity. The dialogue in which Socrates teaches geometry to a slave in Meno's house is the classic example of how we can prompt a person to make use of what they do not realise they know.

I believe that learning is predicting, solving problems and seeking answers to questions. If we do not have a question we want to explore answers to, we cannot learn. We cannot get through even a few minutes without making predictions. When we enter a building, we have to determine whether the door opens inwards or outwards or slides to the left or to the right. When we see something we have not seen before, such as a butterfly, we ask questions such as, 'Why is it yellow and black? How long will it live? Where did it come from?' Ignorance is the beginning of knowledge and understanding.

Learning is doing as well as predicting, though they work well in unison. As a Boy Scout, I learned how to tie knots by watching others tie knots, looking at sketches in the *Boy Scout Manual* and playing with rope. I later read John Dewey's *Education and Experience* (1938) and was thrilled that ways I had learned to tie knots had the backing of a widely respected philosopher.

John Dewey did not limit his idea of learning-by-doing to manual skills such as knot-tying, though. Nor do I. In learning languages we have to manipulate bits of language, experience the relationships between the sounds of the language, make the symbols that represent the sounds on paper with pens or touch-typed on a computer screen, say the bits of language, read them and relate them to our experiences.

All forms of communication – language, art, etc. – are creative acts. Whether learning geometry, knot-tying or anything else, we bring something new into being for ourselves and often for others, too.

The importance of small changes

A central conversation I have with teachers is to remind them of the complexity of interactions. The idea that A causes B is widespread in all fields. 'We declare a war on drugs' has been a theme of many US presidents. All the evidence shows that decriminalising drugs has more positive outcomes than having a war on drugs. But for whatever reasons, the leaders of many countries believe that A causes B, in spite of the overwhelming evidence that this is a fallacy.

'You can change the world, but please don't unless you know what you are doing!' is a comment I heard in a talk at Teachers College by James Garbarino about bullying and school shootings in the US. It resonated with me because it is a central theme of my latest book, *Small Changes in Teaching, Big Results in Learning* (2018).

Ministries of education and publishers believe in the same myth – that A causes B, whether they want to stop bullying, control drugs or tackle all other complex problems with a simple solution. 'We have a new series of textbooks that will lead all students to be proficient. We have tests to check their progress.' In my experience, big changes, new programmes and textbook series stultify teacher creativity and initiative. They also fail.

These institutional dictates not only fly in the face of Prabhu's sense of plausibility but are ineffectual too. Test scores on standardised commercial tests are closely related to the ability of students to take tests, to the educational level of their parents and to the family income. How can new texts and programmes move the test scores if these other variables are so powerful in determining success?

From a transcription of a three-minute recording of students and their teachers, both can learn more about what they need to learn than being given a score on IELTS of 15 in grammar and 17 in vocabulary or scores of 300 or whatever on TOEIC or TOEFL. The fact that only 25 per cent of students could write 'I like ice cream' in my earlier example could not be captured in a thousand years by standardised tests.

When students and teachers see what they have said they are often surprised. But a moment's thought reminds us that if we have even ten students in a class, much less 40, we cannot hear what they are saying. Couples misunderstand each other all the time. I was once walking with a couple who had been married 50 years. We saw two food trailers next to the path: one selling curry and one coffee. Marge asked, 'Ken, would you like a cup of coffee?' Ken replied, 'It's a bit early for curry.'

I focused on small changes initially because I was ignorant of what to do. But through the years I have seen that if we make small changes, they are easier to implement than large ones. If they are upsetting or not useful it is easy to stop using them. We can see the consequences more easily than if we make large changes involving many variables.

Two final thoughts

First, checking claims

My quest to understand teaching and learning, discussed in this chapter, focuses on two deficiencies in the preparation not only of teachers but of everyone: *scepticism* and *an admission of ignorance*. My ignorance of what the teachers I was supervising knew led me to much new learning.

Unless we follow Socrates and act like a gadfly, we cannot understand how far what we do, what we want to do and what we think we do are in tune. We have to question whether what we do that we think is useful might not be, and whether what we do that we think is not useful might be useful.

Second, the teacher as a human being

I have been analysing excerpts from lessons with teachers and students for 56 years. As part of the analyses, I have encouraged teachers I visit to ask their students to comment on their teaching. Here is a comment from one of my students from a secondary school in an affluent suburb of Chicago. Teachers I have learned with through the years have received similar comments.

> I feel you are more of a human being than a teacher. You understand the students; therefore you communicate with them better than the teachers that set themselves up on a pedestal!

To what extent can analysis aimed at expanding the range of engaging and useful activities lead to this type of reaction from our students? To what extent can we recruit people into teaching who will elicit this type of reaction? To what extent can we retain teachers who elicit this type of reaction? Provide experiences that enable teachers to develop a sense of plausibility! If we work with teachers as fellow humans not from up on a pedestal, it is more likely that the teachers will treat those they work with in the same way.

If claims were checked not only about our teaching but about the war on drugs, hundreds of thousands of lives would be saved and millions of people would learn more and in more satisfying and engaging ways. And the multibillion-dollar scam perpetrated by commercial standardised-test companies would be out of business.

In a way, thinking about being human is similar to being sceptical: in both cases we remind ourselves of our ignorance.

References

Ashton-Warner, S (1963) *Teacher*. New York: Simon & Schuster.

Barnes, D (1976) *From Communication to Curriculum*. Harmondsworth: Penguin.

Bellack, AA, Kliebart, HM, Hyman, RT and Smith, FL (1966) *The Language of the Classroom*. New York: Teachers College Press.

Dewey, J (1938/1970) *Experience and Education*. New York: Collier Books.

Dewey, M (1876) *A Classification and Subject Index for Cataloguing and Arranging the Books and Pamphlets of a Library, Forgotten Books*. (Original publisher not known.)

Dickens, C (1854) *Hard Times*. London: Bradbury and Evans.

Fanselow, JF (1977) Beyond *Rashomon* – conceptualizing and describing the teaching act. *TESOL Quarterly* XI/March. (Reprinted in Allwright, R (ed) (1988) *Observation in the Language Classroom*. London: Longman.)

Fanselow, JF (1987) *Breaking Rules: Generating and Exploring Alternatives in Language Teaching*. White Plains: Longman.

Fanselow, JF (1992a) *Contrasting Conversations: Activities for Exploring our Beliefs and Teaching Practices*. White Plains: Longman.

Fanselow, JF (1992b) *Try the Opposite*. Tokyo: SIMUL Press.

Fanselow, JF (2018) *Small Changes in Teaching, Big Results in Learning: Videos, Activities and Essays to Stimulate Fresh Thinking about Language Learning*. Tokyo: The International Teacher Development Institute.

Freire, P (1976) *Pedagogy of the Oppressed*. New York: Continuum.

French, FG (1960) *English in Tables: A Set of Blue Prints for Sentence Builders*. London: Oxford University Press.

Gurrey, P (1955) *Teaching English as a Foreign Language*. London: Longmans.

Hornby, AS (1961) *The Teaching of Structural Words and Sentence Patterns*. London: Oxford University Press.

Smith, F (1971) *Understanding Reading: A Psycholinguistic Analysis of Reading and Learning to Read*. New York: Hold, Rinehart and Winston.

Smith, F (1988) *The Book of Learning and Forgetting*. New York: Teachers College Press.

West, M (1960) *Teaching English in Difficult Circumstances: Teaching English as a Foreign Language with Notes in the Technique of Textbook Construction*. London: Longmans, Green.

For CPD activities visit e-file link: www.teachingenglish.org.uk/sites/teacheng/files/e-file.pdf

3

Reflections

Thomas SC Farrell

Earliest experiences of language learning and education that have affected my current views and practices

One of the important early influences in my life in terms of learning a second language was on a family trip to Spain and France when I was six years old – an amusing incident when my mother and I got lost in Spain and used a lot of body language when trying to explain to a Spanish policeman the location of our hotel. I was to have similar experiences in the Middle East and throughout Asia when I arrived to teach English as a foreign language in 1978. Such experiences laid the foundation for my beliefs about second/foreign language learning – that the process is not really about words or sentences but about people.

From childhood through to high school, the influences that were to shape me as a teacher and teacher-scholar were sometimes negative. For example, I decided that I would never teach the way many of my grade-school teachers went about teaching me. For the most part, I was taught in teacher-led classes, but especially while learning foreign languages and English language. In English class we would read aloud and not have any idea what the text was about. In Spanish class we memorised grammar rules but never practised speaking the language. We memorised vocabulary and wrote essays that followed formulas. In the Irish language class we were punished if we did not complete fill-in-the-blank exercises correctly with the right grammar test item. I was consistently reminded of the failure of these teaching methods by frequent trips to Europe with my family, when I noticed the ease of communication young German or Dutch students my age had when interacting with me in English.

University life in Ireland in the 1970s did not change my views much and after graduation I went into teaching. I had no real opinion about my career move until my first week in a secondary school during my teaching practice. After graduating, I studied for a Higher Diploma in Education at University College Dublin. One of its requirements was practice teaching for four hours per week in a secondary school for each week of the academic year. I was placed in a typical neighbourhood school in south Dublin. One incident in class early in the year made me reflect on my own educational experiences and the anti-system mode I was to adopt as a teacher at that time in 1977, and later, as a teacher-scholar.

Influences arising from places/institutions in which I have lived and worked

Several incidents occurred in my professional career that shaped me both as a language educator and as a teacher-scholar. The first was my development as a foreign language educator in South Korea. My initial readings in a very new field called TESOL and applied linguistics brought me under the influence of Stephen Krashen's (1982) work on second language acquisition theory. I read his work from a language educator/practitioner point of view as I wanted to be able to directly apply his principles or theories to my teaching. I found myself in survival mode in South Korea once again, in the sense that the context and culture were both very new to me. Of course, like many others, I found it difficult to apply his theories directly to real second language classrooms but they were very attractive to me at that time.

Indeed, at that stage of my development as a language educator I realised my theories were coming from my practice and that was a good realisation for me because, as Bullough (1997: 20) has noted: 'unless theories come from practice, they will not apply to practice'. Also, I noticed that most of the research and content in the field of teaching second or foreign language education in the 1970s was under the influence of the field of applied linguistics, itself a very young field; topics such as error analysis, second language acquisition, syllabus design (especially the functional/notional approach) and the like influenced my practice and reflections. But I found Krashen's work most seductive at this time in my professional career because I realised that I could (and probably should) make my own classroom applications of whatever theories of language learning and teaching I came across.

It was then, in 1986, that I really started to reflect on my practice. This meant questioning these earlier scientific/research conceptions of second language acquisition (SLA) that I had accepted and also the theory/values-based conception of the communicative approaches that were just appearing in the field. I realised that I was moving into a more art/craft approach when I conceptualised my practice approach (Freeman and Richards, 1993). This to me was a process where my context in general and my classroom in particular were most important in terms of creating an effective learning environment. So, I began to look at all aspects of my professional life. This reflective curiosity brought me back to graduate school in the US and a PhD. This intense period of reflection resulted in a dissertation on the topic of reflective practice, and I have been researching, presenting workshops, and publishing papers and books ever since on this topic. When I first met John Fanselow at a conference in Seoul in the early 1990s, he graciously read my dissertation and commented that I would have enough material on the topic of reflective practice for my whole career. He was correct.

I first became what I call a 'teacher-scholar' while director of English as a foreign language programmes at Yonsei University, South Korea. My previous job was director of a language centre at the university where I was teaching. At this centre I was not involved in teacher training or education but simply in charge of placing students at their correct level of English proficiency in the centre and finding teachers to teach them. As director of all the foreign language programmes at Yonsei, by contrast, I gave many workshops to teachers on various topics on teaching a foreign language, professional development and developed course syllabi for all of the 24 part-time, non-native teachers in these foreign language programmes. So, in the late 1980s, I began to read in the field again and was interested to see a change of direction away from hardcore linguistics as a guiding light to the field, to greater recognition of second language teacher education, teachers and teaching itself. Freeman (1989: 17) best expressed my thinking at that time when he said that TESOL was 'fragmented and unfocused due to the different disciplines competing for control: Applied Linguistics, Methodology, SLA, while overlooking the core, teaching'. He acknowledged that all those fields contributed to teaching but are ancillary to it and as such should not be the primary subject matter of second language teacher education. It was then that I became fully motivated to devote my career to developing TESOL as a field in its own right.

In 2004 I started teaching in the Department of Applied Linguistics, Brock University, Ontario, Canada, where I have continued my work as a teacher-scholar in the area of applied linguistics and TESOL. Since then, I have continued to conduct research in the field of L2 reflective practice with pre-service, novice and in-service teachers on a wide range of issues: novice language teachers' transition in first year; importance of reflective practice in TESOL teacher education programmes; international perspectives on English as a second language (ESL) teacher education; expectations and reality during the practicum; teacher beliefs and role identities; competences and teachers' expertise associated with effective teaching; framework for TESOL professionals (Farrell, 2015); development groups and collaborative discussions; reflective writing; teaching the four skills; mapping conceptual change through critical reflection; Dewey and Schön's contributions; reflective practice in action for busy teachers; reflective practice in both research and practice ...

Key people who have left an enduring mark on my life, beliefs and practices

In addition to Krashen, some other key people within TESOL have had a strong influence on my ideas and practices: in particular, John Fanselow, Donald Freeman, David Nunan and Jack Richards. These people have emphasised the 'T' or 'teacher' in TESOL. This 'T' has not received the respect within language education that I believe is necessary.

It was Fanselow's work that influenced my thinking and many of my early workshops (on the use of video, testing, the place of grammar and group work). Fanselow takes the view that teachers should be responsible for their own classrooms, so he encourages them to explore their classroom practice by analysing the communication patterns that occur in it. One of his salient quotes is:

> Whereas the usual aim of observation and supervision is to help or evaluate the person being seen, the aim I propose is self-exploration – seeing one's own teaching differently. Observing others or ourselves to see teaching differently is not the same as being told what to do by others. Observing to explore is a process; observing to help or to evaluate is providing a product.

(Fanselow, 1988: 115)

Further, his idea that small changes in teaching can lead to big results still resonates with me, and his idiosyncratic style in general was a refreshing approach for teachers who are interested in teaching rather than creating academic empires around themselves. John is a teachers' teacher for me.

Donald Freeman is a major scholar in the field of TESOL. He has had a large influence on my understanding of the field of second language teacher education (SLTE). Freeman has always approached his work from the perspective of a teacher, as well as his development as a language teacher educator over the years, and was one of the few scholars at the time, along with Richards, Fanselow and Nunan, to put the 'T' back in TESOL. In other words, he looked at applied linguistics and TESOL from the other side of the desk than most others at the time: those who saw 'classroom-based research' as what the learners do to the exclusion of the teacher. Arguably, he, along with Richards, Fanselow and Nunan, really introduced the field of TESOL for the first time to what we now know as SLTE.

David Nunan is another real teachers' teacher. When meeting him many years ago in Asia I was impressed that he was so focused on bettering teachers' lives and work. His edited book (with Kathleen Bailey), *Voices from the Language Classroom* (1996), really reflected his deep sense of finding space for the teacher's voice that too often goes unheard in academic circles. He has demonstrated this interest in the lives of teachers over the years as he has tirelessly given his time to speak at many teacher-focused conferences. I have come to know David personally and he has always shown me that the person behind the teacher (educator) is very important: he is always down to earth and has always been accessible.

Another strong influence on my understanding of language teaching is Jack Richards, one of the pre-eminent scholars in the field of SLTE and development. I am fortunate to have been able to work with him on the topic of professional development for language teachers. This led to co-authoring a book on this topic (Richards and Farrell, 2005) as well as a book on practice teaching (Richards and Farrell, 2011). I learned a lot from working with Jack about his depth of knowledge about SLTE and language teaching and most of all about the technicalities and care involved in writing such books.

Pivotal ideas that have helped form or change my beliefs and practices

I take a constructivist approach to teacher education in my classes, for I believe that these pre-service teachers will make sense of the theories and ideas that I give them in their own way. I agree with Williams and Burden (1997: 2) when they say that 'Each individual constructs his or her own reality'. I believe pre-service teachers of English have a personal framework of beliefs about how languages should be taught before they come into training. Therefore, whatever theories they read about or hear about in classes are incorporated into their personal frameworks. In other words, pre-service teachers actively construct their own representations of teaching and try to assimilate new theories into existing beliefs. As Kaufman and Brooks (1996: 324) state, 'Constructivist teachers look for and value the students' points of view. Understanding the students' point of view helps the teacher determine where and how instruction can facilitate learning.' My role as teacher educator is to make explicit these usually tacitly held prior beliefs to my pre-service teachers, and then to prompt them to challenge any inconsistencies between previously held beliefs and new knowledge gained from the course. This can be achieved by reflective activities such as reflective assignments and journal writing to raise their awareness of who their students are and who they themselves are as teachers.

This constructivist approach to teacher education is in direct opposition to the way I myself was educated as a teacher in the old behaviourist way, where the content of the course was rigidly defined by the institution as a set of discrete teaching skills, which I, as a pre-service teacher, had to conform to. I was then evaluated on my mastery of these behaviours in the form of a checklist of discrete items and 'passed' as a teacher. My opinions were never solicited and my attempts to protest that the context in which I was teaching (secondary school in Dublin, Ireland) was not amenable to some of the recommended teaching methods were ignored. I have taken a very long time to reach a constructivist approach to teaching and teacher education and I was only able to attain this awareness with a deep, and sometimes painful, period of reflection. I now strongly believe that I, as a language teacher educator, must first try to ascertain where my pre-service teachers are coming from before I try to attempt to shape their beliefs. As such, I have developed the following guiding principles:

- What pre-service teachers bring to the course in the form of prior experiences is very important. I start all my classes trying to get the students to articulate these experiences.

- Pre-service teachers learn by doing. Unless theory comes from practice, teachers will not apply this theory to their practice. Therefore, methods, courses and assignments should involve actual practice teaching.

- Reflection is the key to teacher survival and development. Teacher education programmes should give these pre-service teachers the tools to enable them to continue to develop as teachers after the teacher education course. This can be accomplished by collaborative assignments, self- and peer-observation, case studies, action research, journal writing and teacher development groups.

Important publications in my personal and professional development

I have mentioned a few already but here are some books that have contributed fundamentally to my professional development as a language teacher and as a teacher educator.

Parker J Palmer's *The Courage to Teach* (1998) has been a very important book for me because I read it when I first started to reflect seriously on myself as a teacher educator, wondering what direction I should take. I had just moved to Singapore in 1997 (the book appeared in 1998) to take up a position as teacher educator in the National Institute of Education in Singapore. This was a big change from the previous 18 years in Seoul. I was wondering how my research on reflective practice and teaching approach would be viewed in such a different context – and this book helped me look more deeply into myself as a teacher educator. It takes us on a journey through the inner landscape of teachers' lives. As such, it was perfect for my own professional reflections. As Palmer noted, 'Knowing myself is as crucial to good teaching as knowing my students and subjects' (1998: 3) and 'Good teaching cannot be reduced to technique; good teaching comes from the identity and integrity of the teacher' (1998: 10). The main word here is *integrity* because without that, we cannot really serve our students well. Second language teaching in my view has suffered from a lack of integrity, especially in respect to the textbook industry (perpetuated by the conference circuit where publishers fund their authors as speakers) that has developed over the years. Unfortunately, some have exploited this to make money, as students are 'encouraged' to buy many levels of books that have a questionable impact on their language development, but lots of development for the author's bottom line.

Another important book for me was John Fanselow's (1987) *Breaking Rules*. This book influenced, and still continues to influence, my thoughts on teaching and teacher education. I had been thinking about preconceived notions of what 'good' teaching is ever since my experiences as a trainee teacher – and I continue to do so today. John's ideas about looking for multiple alternatives are always useful in any age of teaching. And we can do this by carefully analysing our teaching (his way was through a system he called *focus* that is a bit elaborate but generally very useful) and then we can try to do the opposite. Sometimes we get stuck in our routines of teaching and fail to see how we are blocking opportunities for our students to learn. By generating alternative ways of looking at teaching issues and practices, John suggests we may be able to provide more opportunities for our students to learn – surely this is why we all teach. Fanselow continued this theme in a later book called *Contrasting Conversations* (1992), which was to be equally important for my development; I still dip into both these books today when I am looking for inspiration.

Donald Freeman's recent book, *Educating Second Language Teachers* (2016), also had an impact on me as it presents Donald's perspective on his own journey and is illuminated with wonderful personal narratives that keep reminding us that 'teachers matter', although he does not use these words. I first learned the words 'teachers matter' from another inspiring language teacher educator, Michael (Mitch) K Legutke, over tea at a conference. Mitch was adamant that unless teachers explore and become aware of how they learn, they will continue to teach as they were taught, not as they were taught to teach. I totally agree with him, as does Donald Freeman in this book. (Legutke and Thomas' book *Process and Experience in the Language Classroom* (1991) is also illuminating.) But this is more than a book that takes a journey down SLTE memory lane. It also presents us with a new doorway at the end of the journey, through which we are invited to enter Freeman's vision of the future of SLTE. This doorway is Freeman's 'design theory', which he claims 'ought to provide a reasoned basis on which to evaluate, to reform, and to innovate in educating second language (as well as other) teachers' (2016: 252). It does. Indeed, my own journey was somewhat similar (albeit a few years behind Freeman's). He was the trailblazer (along with Richards and Nunan), which is why I found this book so intriguing, enlightening, illuminating and delightful.

Critical incidents/epiphanies in life and work that have given me new insights

The first important critical incident for me was during my first year of teaching in Ireland in 1978. One morning, as a student teacher on my teaching practice assignment in a high school in Dublin, I was teaching a business English class to junior high school students. A student suddenly shouted out: 'Teacher you are stupid!' I was astonished, and had no idea how to respond. I was in shock for a few moments, then I told the boy that he should not say this to me, his teacher or any teacher, and that he should write a letter of apology to me before I would let him back to my class. I then asked him to leave for the remainder of that lesson. Just before class the following day, he handed me a letter. In that letter (which I still have today) he wrote the following reason for saying what he had said: 'Teacher, I called you stupid because you were stupid because you gave us the same homework the day before and that is why you are stupid.'

When I read that note, I realised that he was correct. I had indeed mistakenly given the class the same homework. I also realised that, even though we may think that our students may not be listening to their teachers, in fact, they are. Unfortunately, the student concerned was actually deemed a 'problem' student by his regular teachers. He was always at the centre of any disruptive activity that the teachers had difficulty controlling. However, I had always had a good relationship with him, probably because he reminded me of myself at his age. I have never forgotten this 'critical incident' and now, after many years working within the topic of reflective practice, I realise it was my first introduction to Schön's (1983) reflection-in-action (my immediate response to the student's statement) and reflection-on-action (my later responses). Over the years, I have had many more occasions where I have experienced both reflection-in-action moments and reflection-on-action examples in different classrooms, contexts and countries. However, it was that early classroom example that has stayed with me for many years, although I had no real understanding of its true meaning until I began to read Schön's (1983) seminal work on reflective practice.

Another series of incidents that were to influence my approach to classroom observation as a language teacher educator (especially later while teaching in a university in Singapore) occurred during the same practicum experience (Farrell, 1996). As a student teacher I was supposed to be observed and evaluated three or four times during the year by a supervisor/teacher educator from the university. I was actually observed teaching three times during the academic year and each time I became progressively more nervous during those observed classes but did not know why. I realise now that having had no pre-observation discussion (the supervisor was already in the classroom each time seated at the back of the room giving me 'The Look' of the expert: 'Show me what you can do') and having had no post-observation conference simply fuelled my anxiety. The only feedback was my evaluation as the final grade (pass) sheet at the end of the year. After that incident, I decided that as a supervisor myself, I would always ask a student teacher what would be a good day to come and observe or call ahead rather than just show up unannounced. That is clearly unhelpful to real teacher learning or development. When I was a teacher educator later in Singapore, I always called ahead before I visited a teacher in a school so that the student teacher was comfortable for the classroom observation. This seemed to work well for everybody concerned.

Themes emerging from my chapter

Probably the most significant theme emerging from reflecting on this chapter is the simple statement: 'Who I am is how I teach!' The general purpose of engaging in reflection for all teachers is to get some kind of awareness of who we are as teachers, what we do and why we do it. Becoming more aware of who we are as teachers means exploring our own inner worlds through contemplation so that we can become more mindful of what we do. Mindfulness is the opposite of mindlessness – and unfortunately our world gives us too many examples of the latter rather than the former. Recently I have developed a framework for reflecting on practice in SLTE that can help language teachers and teacher educators to become more mindful of who they are and how they teach (Farrell, 2015, 2018). As Freeman (2016: 208) maintains in his recent book, reflection offers a way into the 'less accessible aspects of teachers' work', and my framework offers such an accessible way into all aspects of a language teacher's work.

This framework differs from many other approaches because it offers a holistic approach to reflection that focuses not only on the intellectual, cognitive and meta-cognitive aspects of practice that many other approaches are limited to, but also on the spiritual, moral, emotional and non-cognitive aspects of reflection that acknowledge the inner life of teachers. Teacher educators can encourage pre-service (and in-service) teachers to use the framework as a lens through which to view their professional (and even personal) worlds, and what has shaped their professional lives as they become more aware of their philosophy, principles, theories and practices, and how these impact issues inside and beyond practice. Pre-service (and in-service) teachers need to be encouraged to think about themselves and their teaching in ways that include activating their feelings and emotions, or the affective side of reflection, so that they can develop the inner resources to meet future challenges in the profession. I believe that implementing a holistic approach to teacher reflection produces more integrated second language teachers with self-awareness and understanding, able to interpret, shape and reshape their practice.

A brief statement of my beliefs/values about language and about learning languages

Learning a language has little to do with learning grammar, vocabulary or phonology, but everything to do with learning about other human beings' ways of life. The pace of how we learn a language will match the pace of how much we want to know about others.

References

Bailey, K and Nunan, D (1996) *Voices from the Language Classroom*. Cambridge: Cambridge University Press.

Bullough, RV (1997) 'Practicing theory and theorizing practice in teacher education', in Loughran, J and Russell, T (eds) *Teaching about Teaching: Purpose, Passion and Pedagogy in Teacher Education*. London: Falmer Press, 13–31.

Fanselow, JF (1987) *Breaking Rules: Generating and Exploring Alternatives in Language Teaching*. White Plains: Longman.

Fanselow, JF (1988) 'Let's see': Contrasting conversations about teaching. *TESOL Quarterly* 22/1: 113–130.

Fanselow, JF (1992) *Contrasting Conversations*. White Plains: Longman.

Farrell, TSC (1996) 'The Look': Some observations on observation. *The Teacher Trainer* 21: 11.

Farrell, TSC (2015) *Promoting Teacher Reflection in Second Language Education: A Framework for TESOL Professionals*. New York: Routledge.

Farrell, TSC (2018) *Research on Reflective Practice in TESOL*. New York: Routledge.

Freeman, D (1989) Teacher training, development, and decision-making: A model of teaching and related strategies for language teacher education. *TESOL Quarterly* 23/1: 27–45.

Freeman, D (2016) *Educating Second Language Teachers*. Oxford: Oxford University Press.

Freeman, D and Richards, JC (1993) Conceptions of teaching and the education of second language teachers. *TESOL Quarterly* 27/2: 193–216.

Kaufman, D and Brooks, GJ (1996) Interdisciplinary collaboration in teacher education: a constructivist approach. *TESOL Quarterly* 30/2: 231–251.

Krashen, S (1982) *Principles and Practices in Second Language Acquisition*. Oxford: Pergamon.

Legutke, M and Thomas, H (1991) *Process and Experience in the Language Classroom*. London: Longman.

Palmer, PJ (1998) *The Courage to Teach*. San Francisco: Jossey-Bass.

Richards, JC and Farrell, TSC (2005) *Professional Development of Language Teachers*. New York: Cambridge University Press.

Richards, JC and Farrell, TSC (2011) *Teaching Practice: A Reflective Approach*. New York: Cambridge University Press.

Schön, D (1983) *The Reflective Practitioner: How Professionals Think in Action*. New York: Basic Books.

Williams, M and Burden, R (1997) Psychology for Language Teachers: A Social Constructivist Approach. Cambridge: Cambridge University Press.

For CPD activities, visit e-file link: www.teachingenglish.org.uk/sites/teacheng/files/e-file.pdf

4

Dressed in borrowed robes: Telling our stories in a foreign language

Claudia Mónica Ferradas

It is 1966 in a working-class neighbourhood in the outskirts of Buenos Aires. I try to get a glimpse of the low-flying planes by peering between the louvres of the closed window shutters, but I am not tall enough. My parents say there has been a coup: *un golpe*, which in Spanish also means a 'blow'. I wonder who has hit whom, what caused the fight.

A month later, Dad loses his job on what will be known as the 'night of long sticks': five schools of the University of Buenos Aires have been taken over by the Federal Police using long batons to hit students, professors and graduates. I look at Dad's bruised forehead and think I now know what *golpe* means.

My grandparents whisper in German, or broken Polish, or Ukrainian, thinking I don't understand. My elder cousins use Yiddish when I am around. But my memories' soundtrack is in English: the Monkees' first two singles, which I listen to again and again, muffling the worried conversations. 'If only I could sing those songs!' I think.

On my birthday the following January, the Monkees' second album is released. I want no other present but this LP, which takes weeks to arrive. My aunt takes me to the capital on the train and buys me an imported magazine with articles on the band and lots of pictures of Davy Jones, the lead singer. The magazine is in English. My crush on Davy Jones and my dream of becoming a singer blend to form an intrinsic-motivational cocktail that encourages me to learn a language that is not spoken at home.

Ten years later, Dad asks me to take several books to the shed at the bottom of the garden, digs a deep hole in the ground and buries them 'just in case'. I keep my two heavily underlined anthologies of short stories – after all, they are in English. Three months later, my first class at teacher training college will have to be postponed: there has been another coup.

Down memory lane

So, what happened in the ten years between one coup and another – or between my becoming a student of English and becoming an ELT trainee teacher? My parents made sacrifices to send me to classes with the English teacher in the *barrio*: a well-meaning woman with lots of teaching experience and hardly any English. We sat around the table and studied the lessons in LG Alexander's *New Concept English* (1967) books. I was the teacher's pet: I did all the readings and exercises, repeated all the drills, dutifully sat for annual exams in the prestigious evening classes centre run by the National Teacher Training College. However, I could never understand why I got such good marks in written exams but lower marks in the oral ones. I was even more worried that I could not understand the songs by the Monkees and other bands and sing them properly, which had always been my aim.

When Dad was able to afford a cassette player and the cassettes of the Alexander series, I could hear the difference between my teacher's performance and the native speakers on the tape: it was time to change teachers and unlearn my bad habits. I would fall asleep with my headphones on, playing *Developing Skills* units again and again. With the new teacher, we chatted over tea and used no textbooks – only anthologies of short stories with tapes that I found as beautiful and intriguing as the songs I started to learn. After class, I would sing in English with her children. I passed the entrance exam to the National Teacher Training College and promised myself my students would never have to unlearn what I taught them.

I did my teaching internship just as the communicative approach reached our shores. I had studied the language with the audio-lingual method, then been taught to use it as a trainee only a year earlier. Now I was forced to unlearn something once again: no more drills. Instead: communicative information gaps, authentic texts … Once again, there were exams to pass, lesson plans to write following the 'new methodology'. I did. I passed with flying colours. I was a teacher of English.

Telling our stories

In my first year as a language teacher, I got a job teaching adults. One of my classes was a group of intensive-care doctors at a hospital. Surely they needed 'authentic texts' to help them read the latest medical publications and share their research at conferences? Anything else would be a waste of time. So, I did what an English for specific purposes (ESP) teacher is supposed to do. They sometimes read specialised texts before class, but sometimes were too busy to bother and we trudged through texts in our class time.

One afternoon, the head of the intensive care unit was late. When he finally arrived, he burst into the room shouting 'Ita is dead'. I could hardly believe he had a smile on his face as he announced the sad news. Was Ita a patient? Was she young? Patients died every day at the unit and they never said a word about it. I could hardly understand what this was all about, and why all the others were commenting enthusiastically on the news. But then I remembered Ita was a character in a popular soap opera. Doctors would watch the soap when they were on duty and tell each other the bits of the episodes they missed. Ita had been sick for several episodes. They all had something to say about the verisimilitude of the plot, the way producers had manipulated the illness for dramatic effect … After that, we worked on the soap until it came to an end; no more medical papers for a couple of months. Yes, medical vocabulary was revised incidentally, the right pronunciation was practised, but above all there was a playfulness that allowed them to look forward to the class as a break from their terribly demanding jobs … and they had a lot to teach me.

I already knew students could learn in spite of the teacher, in spite of the textbook, if their motivation was strong enough and they could access samples of the language that were meaningful and interesting. However, in spite of the successful results, I still felt guilty that I had taken the narrative line of a soap opera in our mother tongue into class. It was hard to leave behind my own learning habits as a trainee. It was also hard to challenge the models I had learned from my teachers and specialised bibliographies. Was I using 'authentic material'? If so, what was the communicative purpose of the activities? Could I evaluate what items my ESP students had acquired?

Fortunately, having my experience as a language student so close behind me helped me develop my own 'gut feeling' approach, a sort of principled eclecticism based initially on three questions: 'Where does each student want to go? Where are they up to? What materials can help make their aims achievable?' But I still felt under pressure to teach what was supposedly useful, to plan lessons on the basis of the notions and functions to be taught on the syllabus ... until I discovered John McRae's *Literature with a Small 'l'* (1991), an important publication in my professional development. McRae (1991: 3) advocates the use of texts whose 'literariness' empowers students to go beyond the merely referential use of language, i.e. 'language which communicates at only one level, usually in terms of information being sought or given, or of a social situation being handled'. He claims that once language learners need to express their own meanings and interpret other people's beyond the merely instrumental, then representational language is needed: 'language which, in order that its meaning potential be decoded by a receiver, engages the imagination of that receiver ... Where referential language informs, representational language involves' (McRae, 1991: 3). The 'literariness' of the soap opera had empowered my students in this respect.

By then, I had opened my own language school with a colleague. We made sure we designed communicative activities and later welcomed task-based learning and aimed at tasks whose outcomes would be meaningful for each class. Of course, grammar and vocabulary were necessary and students were eager to learn to make sense of the task before them. Textbooks helped us with that. But what was real fun was to find resources outside the textbook and turn them into made-to-measure teaching materials that encouraged 'procedural abilities to make sense of discourse' (Widdowson, 1983, in Brumfit and Carter, 1985) and creative textual intervention (Rodari, 1973; Pope, 1995). And one day there was VHS. And then DVDs, CDs and the internet. And students could now hear native speakers with different accents, check the lyrics of their favourite songs, access newspapers on the day they were published anywhere ... I had to change my role, scaffold their own search, give them space and, above all, continue learning with and from them.

Throughout the process, whatever methodology and resources were in vogue, what mattered was telling our stories: what was happening in our lives, what we needed and were aiming at, how we felt about what we were learning. Decades have gone by. I do not remember clearly what levels and contents I taught, but I still remember the storyline in the *Access to English* series by Michael Coles and Basil Lord (1995) and the gaps it offered to be filled in with our own interests. I remember who was interested in music, who wanted to read cookery books, who loved science, acting, singing, sewing or designing. We could learn about anything together. We just had to find the texts, songs, films in English ... as my teacher had done when we chatted over tea, read and sang. We told each other our own stories, responding to those in the textbooks and videos, and that revealed what was relevant to each individual one of us. I made a point of bringing to class content my students were not acquainted with. I also learned from the content they brought. Each class was a voyage of discovery.

Implications for teaching and training

The reality of the classroom hardly ever fits the lesson plan model – in which you have language aims (grammar, vocabulary and functions), and perhaps some attitudinal objectives, and decide on materials and procedures exclusively on that basis. As an experienced Argentine teacher educator has recently written, based on Bruner, if any narrative involves constructing a world, and '"world making" is the principal function of mind, whether in the sciences or in the arts' (Bruner, 2004: 691, in Casamassima, 2017: 31), we need to stop working on predetermined lists of objectives as the basis of our didactic strategies, and construct a lesson plan as a narrative instead. This means a change of focus in teacher training: 'The plan as narrative entails the co-construction of a story, with the trainee becoming a writer rather than a planner' (*ibid.*: 31).

> With the exception of teacher training situations, objectives are sometimes written down to comply with school requirements and then forgotten about. Narrative goals are meant to be ... the living expression of what the trainee aims to achieve ... We will not wish to narrate a story about grammar because grammar, however relevant it may be, is meant to have a subsidiary role in the story ... At times, [grammar, vocabulary discourse, and phonology] may come to the foreground, but only on the condition that they contribute something to the plot and not for their own sake ... our interest in the unit is to go beyond language because language is an instrument.
>
> (*ibid.*: 49)

But far from suggesting we think of a narrative as linear, Casamassima invites us to think of a cubist painting metaphor, 'showing an object in its many facets, all at the same time' (*ibid.*: 76). Planning a lesson or a unit of work thus resembles the design of a webpage, with the possibility to move backwards and forwards from one or more foregrounded narratives (always content-based, related to the final task we aim at) to one or several background narratives (the grammar and vocabulary we need, the strategies to be developed, etc.) or from one parallel narrative to another.

This is an oversimplified view of a complex model that readers are invited to explore, but I would just like to make a point of the need to abandon the straitjacket of linear planning based on predetermined abstract objectives. Instead, I would like to focus on the exciting prospect of approaching a topic of interest and relevance to our students from multiple perspectives, in whatever order we may need in specific contexts and circumstances, with learning outcomes in mind but enough flexibility to make room for diversity. In this way, singing popular song lyrics is an aim that can be achieved and there is room for soap operas as well as academic texts, ensuring that students' motivation does not fade but leads to productive engagement.

Ourselves – in English

The texts by McRae and Pope mentioned above legitimated my approach, guided my research and helped me to rethink my practice, but my student experience as an MA student at Norwich Institute for Language Education (NILE) in the UK would lead to new insights.

Our MA class in 1997 included several Argentinians and Uruguayans. As we tend to do locally in several countries in Latin America, at breaktime my classmates would pass around a gourd filled with dry leaves on which one of them poured hot water out of a thermos flask to make a kind of tea. Both the drink and the cup are called 'maté'. The leaves are called 'yerba maté'. Drinking maté involves sucking on a metal straw (called 'bombilla') that has a filter to avoid getting a mouthful of yerba mate particles when you suck on it. The other end has a gold-coloured spout which stays cool enough to touch with your lips. Drinking maté is a symbolic sharing ritual, as the cup is passed on from one person to another and they all drink using the same straw. It is rude to refuse a maté, as the offer is a sign of friendship derived from the tradition of pouring a maté for a guest even if the host has nothing else to eat or drink in the house.

I often found myself explaining that I do not like maté and rejecting it politely with all sorts of excuses. One of our classmates, from Saudi Arabia, saw me reject the maté and join the queue at the coffee machine at breaktime. She approached me and asked me what my fellow Argentinians were having and how I had managed not to become addicted to that 'drug'. I found myself trying to find the words to explain what it was all about (the words I have written above) and, to my shock and embarrassment, I found myself as inarticulate as any pre-intermediate student. I had never before had to explain my own cultural habits in English! Even if I found the words, some of the explanatory gestures I used were evidently quite shocking for my interlocutor and the presupposition that maté was some kind of addictive practice was hard to refute – after all, my classmates seemed unable to stop passing the gourd round every time they had the chance.

It was this experience that took me back to my research on literariness and the design of representational materials, now focusing on the aim of using English to communicate across cultures. It is no coincidence that Michael Byram's foundational text, *Teaching and Assessing Intercultural Communicative Competence* (1997), was published that year. The process of globalisation and the impact of technology meant rethinking language teaching: intercultural communication would no longer be an aim restricted to business travellers. From then on, guided by my supervisor in the MA class, Alan Pulverness, my practice, my research, the INSET sessions for my school staff, my academic publications (2003a, 2003b, 2006, 2009, 2010, 2013, 2016) and materials design would all focus on this central concern.

In 2001, just as I had submitted my MA dissertation, the publication of the *Common European Framework of Reference for Languages: Learning, Teaching, Assessment (CEFR)* established an 'intercultural approach' as a new paradigm in language teaching:

> In an intercultural approach, it is a central objective of language education to promote the favourable development of the learner's whole personality and sense of identity in response to the enriching experience of otherness in language and culture.

(Council of Europe, 2001: 1)

The curricular design for foreign language teaching in the city of Buenos Aires, published in the same year, proposed the same approach, so that my inquiry was inscribed within both an international and a local context.

Since then, thousands of academic articles, books and teaching materials have been published on the topic. Among others, I have followed Michael Byram's research (1997, 2008, 2017; Byram et al., 2016) on interculturalism and the challenges posed by the model outlined in the CEFR. I have also reflected on Bonny Norton's (2000, 2013) considerations on language and identity, particularly on the question of immigrants' attitudes to the language of the host country and how this can affect language acquisition and first language loss. Claire Kramsch (1993) provides food for thought on the links between language and culture, as do Holliday et al. (2004). With the classroom in mind, John Corbett (2003, 2010) opens a treasure chest of activities to contribute to the development of cultural awareness. Publications by Argentine researchers such as Silvana Barboni (Barboni and Porto, 2013) and Melina Porto (Porto and Byram, 2017) have also informed my practice as a teacher educator from a Latin American perspective.

All these considerations question the notion of the 'native speaker' as an ideal construct in the wake of Peter Medgyes' work (1994, republished 2017). Workshops and webinars advocating the inclusion of World Englishes in classes where English is taught as the language of international communication have become more common. What varieties of English should find a place in our classrooms? How can our choices in teacher education affect future teachers' beliefs in this respect?

Being a trainer on the British Council's Connecting Classrooms and Core Skills programmes has allowed me to work with trainers from a wide range of countries and social contexts. We have explored a context-based approach to the adaptation of global materials. However, wherever I go I still find teachers planning on the basis of discrete grammar points, believing that the intercultural approach consists of adding an international touch (such as food from different parts of the world) or an occasional lesson on festivals or traditional costumes for festive occasions. The tendency towards standardisation, with its hunger for quantitative data to assess progress and achievement, hand-in-hand with the washback effect of international examinations, conspires against the central aims of intercultural learning. Teachers end up replicating the models based on the teaching and assessment of discrete linguistic items, often afraid of the challenge of becoming intercultural mediators. What is more, innovative materials often generated locally, or even globally produced materials adapted for a local context, can be rejected by teachers and educational authorities on the grounds that students need to learn about the English-speaking world, not about their own context.

I believe all this has clear implications for teacher education. Unless trainee teachers can see themselves as cultural mediators beyond the anecdotal and integrate intercultural considerations transversally within the narratives of their class plans, students will continue to be disempowered, because the jobs they will be doing – and even their daily communication – will largely depend on having the words to ask about others and talk about themselves, with a respectful attitude towards difference, in search of the commonalities that make effective communication possible.

In short, the experiential pathway described has led to constant reflection and revision of my own practice. It has meant unlearning the habit of following predetermined methods modelled by trainers and specialised publications. It has involved listening to my own narrative and those of my students to develop mutual trust and ownership of the language. No matter how often we emphasise the need to be flexible to change, we will be working in the opposite direction if we continue advocating a fixed framework to plan a class.

Appropriating a second or foreign language involves finding ways to express our own worldviews in a language often used to express different worldviews. Trainee teachers have to find their own creative ways to respond to students' needs (and their own) in this respect. It is my contention that texts in which different contexts, customs and beliefs are presented, i.e. literature and other narrative arts, as well as our own anecdotes and personal narratives, have a huge contribution to make.

Only developing self-confidence to experiment within changing scenarios can help teachers achieve the resourcefulness required as cultural mediators, especially in vulnerable contexts. This makes a case for greater agency in their own training and opportunities for hands-on experimentation with content-rich texts.

Back to the future

The recent publication of texts such as Paran and Robinson (2016) seems to suggest that there is renewed interest in exploring further the potential of literature in the language classroom, already mooted in the 1980s and 1990s (Carter and McRae, 1996; Lazar, 1993; Maley and Duff, 1989). Literature is now enhanced by its dialogue with film and digital media, which challenges it and redefines it, often as part of cross-media and transmedia projects (Jenkins, 2006). In turn, song lyrics, always productive resources in language classrooms, can also be exploited because of their literariness and cultural texture (Ferradas, 2003), which the Nobel Prize awarded to Bob Dylan seems to confirm.

Besides, the ever-growing production of texts (printed and digital) in English in different parts of the world opens questions derived from the appropriation of English, not only in postcolonial contexts, but by writers who use English as the language of international communication. Is there a 'world literature'? Can local varieties be accepted by publishers? Is there such a thing as 'international English'? Now that digital readers are also producers, can self-published texts (blogs, webpages and postings on social media) be considered texts for intercultural language education?

In this constantly changing scenario, the ownership of English and its role as mediator in intercultural communication should be a central matter of discussion in teacher education, as it is at the core of a narrative that keeps redefining the role of language teachers (native speakers or not).

Through all the changes I have witnessed in my long experience as a language teacher and teacher trainer, some certainties remain: I still want to know the words of songs in a language that is not my own, but I also need to make them the soundtrack of my own experience. I need to learn the words to tell my story – where I come from, how we do things back home and what I am looking for. A never-ending story.

References

Alexander, LG (1967) *New Concept English Series: Developing Skills*. Harlow: Longman.

Barboni, S and Porto, M (eds) (2013) *Language Education from a South American Perspective – What does Latin America have to say?* La Plata: Dirección General de Cultura y Educación de la Provincia de Buenos Aires.

Brumfit, CJ and Carter, RA (1985) *Literature and Language Teaching*. Oxford: Oxford University Press.

Byram, M (1997) *Teaching and Assessing Intercultural Communicative Competence*. Clevedon: Multilingual Matters.

Byram, M (2008) *From Foreign Language Education to Education for Intercultural Citizenship. Essays and Reflection*. Clevedon: Multilingual Matters.

Byram, M (2017) *Intercultural Communicative Language Teaching and TCSOL*. Foreign Language Teaching and Research Press.

Byram, M, Golubeva, I, Hui, H and Wagner, M (eds) (2016) *From Principles to Practice in Education for Intercultural Citizenship*. Bristol: Multilingual Matters.

Carter, R and McRae, J (1996) *Language, Literature and the Learner*. London and New York: Longman.

Casamassima, M (2017) *Planning as Narrative. A Cubist View on Planning Units of Work for English Language Teachers*. Buenos Aires: Dunken.

Coles, M and Lord, B (1995) *Access to English Series*. Oxford: Oxford University Press.

Corbett, J (2003) *An Intercultural Approach to English Language Teaching*. Clevedon: Multilingual Matters.

Corbett, J (2010) *Intercultural Classroom Activities*. Cambridge: Cambridge University Press.

Council of Europe (2001) *Common European Framework of Reference for Languages: Learning, Teaching, Assessment*. Cambridge University Press. Available online at: https://rm.coe.int/1680459f97

Ferradas, C (2003a) 'Rocking the classroom: rock poetry materials in the EFL class', in Tomlinson, B (ed) *Issues in Developing Materials for Language Teaching*. London and New York: Continuum.

Ferradas, C (2003b) Meeting the Other, Learning about Ourselves: Cultural Awareness in the Language Classroom – Closing plenary. *Proceedings of the FAAPI 2003 Conference: Humanising our Teaching Practice*. Salta, Argentina: FAAPI/ASPI/ The British Council, September 2003.

Ferradas, C (2006) Reading across cultures – developing intercultural awareness through unconventional approaches to literature. *English: The British Council Magazine for Teachers of English in Portugal.* Spring 2006.

Ferradas, C (2009) 'Enjoying literature with teens and young adults in the English language classroom', in British Council, *BritLit: Using Literature on the EFL Classroom.* Barcelona: Associació de Professors d'Anglès de Catalunya (APAC) and London: British Council. Available online at: https://www.teachingenglish.org.uk/article/britlit-using-literature-efl-classrooms

Ferradas, C (2010) 'Outside looking in: intercultural and intermedial encounters in ELT – Closing Plenary, IATEFL Cardiff 2009', in Beaven, B (ed) *IATEFL 2009 Cardiff Conference Selections.* Canterbury: IATEFL, 16–20.

Ferradas, C (2013) *Communicating across cultures: encounters in the 'contact zone'.* Plenary at the FAAPI 2013 Conference – Roots and Routes in Language Education. How do languages cultures and identities interact in 21st century classrooms? Buenos Aires, Argentina: FAAPI/APIBA. September 2013.

Ferradas, C (2016) Reflexiones sobre el enfoque intercultural en la enseñanza de lenguas: Más allá de la teoría. *Revista Lenguas Vivas* 12 (November): 15–23.

Holliday, A, Hyde, M and Kullman, J (2004) *Intercultural Communication.* London: Routledge.

Jenkins, H (2006) *Convergence Culture: Where Old and New Media Collide.* New York: New York University Press.

Kramsch, C (1993) *Context and Culture in Language Teaching.* Oxford: Oxford University Press.

Lazar, G (1993) *Literature and Language Teaching.* Cambridge: Cambridge University Press.

Maley, A and Duff, A (1989) *The Inward Ear.* Cambridge: Cambridge University Press.

Medgyes, P (2017) *The Non-Native Teacher.* Third edition. Callander: Swan Communication Limited.

McRae, J (1991) *Literature with a Small 'l'.* London and Basingstroke: Macmillan.

Norton, B (2000) *Identity and Language Learning: Gender, Ethnicity and Educational Change.* Harlow: Pearson.

Norton, B (2013) *Identity and Language Learning – Extending the conversation.* Clevedon: Multilingual Matters.

Paran, A and Robinson, P (2016) *Literature*. Oxford: Oxford University Press.

Pope, R (1995) *Textual Intervention*. London: Routledge.

Porto, M and Byram, M (2017) *New Perspectives on Intercultural Language Research and Teaching: Exploring Learners' Understandings of Texts from Other Cultures*. London: Routledge.

Rodari, G (1973) *Gramática de la Fantasía: Introducción al Arte de Inventar Historias*. Mexico: Comamex.

For CPD activities, visit e-file link: www.teachingenglish.org.uk/sites/teacheng/files/e-file.pdf

5

Developing a sense of plausibility in language teaching and teacher education

Christine CM Goh

Introduction

I am an English language teacher and teacher educator. My field is second language and bilingual language education, and my special interest is in the use of oral language for thinking, learning and communication, and metacognition (learners thinking about their own thinking and learning). Language, to me, is an indispensable tool for academic and social learning. It is still the pre-eminent medium for connecting affectively and cognitively with our fellow human beings. Learning a language takes effort and attention, yet this can be enjoyable and engaging at the same time. I believe that learning a second or additional language should begin with listening and be supported by oral interaction, just as infants and toddlers learn their first language. And I believe everyone has the potential to be bilingual. We should help all children to achieve proficiency in at least two languages.

This last belief stems from my own experience of growing up in a home environment where my father spoke both Cantonese and English to the children, while my mother spoke Cantonese, Mandarin, Hokkien and Malay. My father also spoke Malay and some Japanese, and he was proficient in both written and spoken Chinese and English. Growing up with several languages, and later learning the Malay language when I entered primary school, made learning multiple languages seem like a natural thing to do. For certain, I have enjoyed the social and academic benefits of being multilingual. I relish the idea that scientists believe that bilinguals have more efficient executive functioning in our brains because of the need to switch constantly from one language to another.

In my first job, as a secondary school teacher, I tried my best to inspire my students with the goal of being proficient in at least two languages. I wanted them to achieve high proficiency in English because of its status as an international language. It was at that time that I first developed an interest in helping learners improve their speaking and listening skills. I remember a group of boys from one of my classes who were weak in English. They did not speak up much in class and, when they did, they always made it into a joke because they were not confident that they were speaking correctly. Things started to change, however, when they took part in a school concert. They sang the song 'More than Words' well and received an overwhelming response from the audience. After the concert, they became more confident in speaking up in class. As I organised more speaking activities, where they had a chance to prepare and rehearse first, I began to see their willingness to participate. Their self-image as English learners improved dramatically. Experiencing small successes in classroom skits, mini-debates and singing competitions had helped them to see themselves as speakers of English, and not merely observers of what went on in an English lesson.

My first big idea

Over the years of my professional growth, my learning occurred in both formal and informal settings. I learned on the job, in postgraduate studies, during in-service workshops and on courses; I learned from colleagues and I learned on my own. Moreover, I had the good fortune of meeting people at various stages of my professional life whose ideas and professional dispositions helped me continually to refine and develop my own.

As an undergraduate I took English studies, which consisted mainly of literary works from the canons of British and American literature, as well as works by great Commonwealth writers, such as VS Naipaul, Chinua Achebe and Lloyd Fernando. I had always wanted to pass on my love for English literary works to my students, but I felt their proficiency level was too low to allow them to enjoy literature. Several years after I began teaching, however, I was introduced to one of the first ideas about teaching that I still hold on to today – using literature for language teaching and learning (Duff and Maley, 1990; McRae, 1994). I attended courses and workshops over a period of two years to learn more about it. The thought of using literary texts excited me so much that I spent a great deal of time and effort looking for new ways of using the various literary genres to supplement my English textbooks. Subsequently, reflecting on my practice, I published an article in the Regional Language Centre (RELC) teacher journal, *Guidelines*, on using literary texts for the language classroom (Goh, 1994).

Changing paradigms

When I began my teaching career as a secondary school teacher, English lessons focused very much on reading comprehension and composition writing, but the influence of communicative language teaching was starting to find its way into the English syllabus (Johnson and Morrow, 1981). My job was to develop students' understanding and use of communicative notions and functions so that they could develop their communicative competence in addition to the traditional literacy skills. This was quite different from the way I had learned English in school, when the syllabus was structural, and audio-lingualism was the instructional approach. I recall distinctly a page in my lower primary school English textbook. On the page were two drawings, one of which was of a pencil. Below the picture were several sentences, the first being: 'This is a pencil.' Things have certainly changed since then!

As I went through my primary school years, I was often confronted by pages with tables containing parts of a sentence. I had to substitute one word for another to form new sentences through different permutations of words. I completed numerous grammar exercises, or 'drills'. Although I do not believe this is the best and most meaningful way to learn grammar, at that time it did clarify a great deal of my knowledge about grammar and gave me a metalanguage with which to talk about it. This knowledge eventually became very useful when I became an English teacher and subsequently teacher educator.

Becoming a student of applied linguistics

When I was an undergraduate, applied linguistics was not a developed field of studies in universities in many parts of the world, especially South-East Asia. It was only several years later, when I studied at RELC in Singapore on a SEAMEO scholarship, that I first encountered the field. The Certificate in Language Syllabus and Language Teaching course introduced me to different aspects of applied linguistics, providing me with useful knowledge and skills for curriculum and syllabus design. My studies at RELC were soon followed by a master's degree at the University of Birmingham, on a Chevening scholarship from the British government. There I encountered several important ideas that have continued to influence my own work.

I learned the importance of studying real, 'authentic' texts, not ones contrived for teaching purposes, in order to understand the way language is structured and used in real communication. Linguists such as John Sinclair and Michael Hoey helped me to explore actual language use, despite its inherent rich 'messiness' compared to the 'tidiness' of most language teaching texts. Sinclair (1991) showed that the study of collocation by investigating large collections of real texts (corpora) revealed previously unnoticed lexical and grammatical patterns. Hoey (1991) demonstrated that even simple children's stories can reveal patterns in the way language is used.

The recognition that it was discourse and not isolated sentences that typified communication was another important idea, not just for linguists but also for language teachers who wanted to teach their students how to understand and use language in natural contexts. The concept of discourse was important not only for written and spoken texts, but also at the level of supra-segmental features of intonation. David Brazil's (1985/1997) model of discourse intonation consisting of stress, tones, key and termination was a simple and elegant model. Being a language teacher, Brazil developed a model of annotations and representations of the intonation system that was easy for teachers to understand and use. Applying his model to analyse hundreds of utterances for my master's dissertation showed me that linguistic theories can be robust yet simple. That was another epiphany for me: important ideas can be communicated simply, and if my work was to have any impact on teachers and language learners, I must find a way to convey my ideas plainly and clearly.

Dave Willis, a classroom teacher at heart, taught me how to use real texts for teaching grammar and vocabulary in a contextualised manner. His work on the lexical syllabus (Willis, 1990, 2004) reinforced these ideas and offered me a new way of thinking about how stages in lessons could be structured. I still believe that it is more useful to have students first try out a language task before teaching them the language, than to pre-teach language and hope that they will use it when doing their task. When I applied this in my English for Academic Purposes (EAP) classes, I could see the justification for it because the students became more interested in language after they had tried the task and realised where the gaps were in their own language use. This idea became even clearer for me in the work of Jane Willis on task-based language teaching (Willis, 1996). The ideas that I learned at Birmingham – real texts, a discourse approach and task-based teaching – became some of the key tenets in my own teaching.

Learning to be learner-centred

The ideas acquired at RELC and at the University of Birmingham became useful several years later when I moved into a new role as a university instructor and director for an EAP programme, preparing foreign students through intensive English instruction to begin university studies. Moving into the university was a watershed in my professional career. I became aware of the need for students to learn how to learn. This steered my approach from teacher- and lesson-centred to learner-centred. I began to focus on specific language learning problems that foreign students had and how I could help them to deal with these problems.

It was at this time that I developed a strong interest in not just teaching but also researching oral language skills. My students from China had told me that their biggest problem was oral communication and that listening was the harder of the two skills. I taught a course in oral communication and focused on teaching listening as a discrete skill even though it was common to teach the two skills in an integrated manner. The problem I found with not differentiating the two oracy skills was that students tended to pay more attention to speaking because it was something they could control, whereas listening was a problem they had very little control over.

This was also the time when I started trying out new ways of explicitly teaching listening. Rather than relying on some well-known listening coursebooks, I began increasingly to use videos and authentic audio recordings, often with 'messy' texts. I moved away from focusing exclusively on the outcomes of my students' listening, (for example, the number of questions they were able to answer), to planning listening lessons that guided them through the listening process. I wanted to demystify the cognitive processes that were going on in their heads when they listened. I got students to talk about their own listening experiences and behaviours to one another, and had them write short reflections on specific listening events in and outside the classroom. I asked them to share their reflections with one another so that they could learn from each other and help to give advice. I prepared self-directed listening guides for them to use when they engaged in extensive listening after class. I wanted them to move away from a 'homework' mentality where they listened to or watched a recording in order to answer questions or write summaries. I wanted them to learn how to listen.

At that time I was also writing my doctoral thesis on strategic processing in second language listening, and had the benefit of reading many scholars' work in this area. The seminal work by Gillian Brown (1986, 1990) and cognitive psychologists such as JR Anderson (1995) gave me an interdisciplinary approach to understanding second language listening. I translated this knowledge into my everyday teaching to help my students unpack the cognitive and social processes in their own listening. At that time, language learner strategy use was a current topic and I was particularly drawn to the work by Anita Wenden (1991, 1998), as I saw its relevance to teaching learners how to listen. Reading Wenden led me to study the earlier work of John Flavell (1976, 1979) on metacognition. I was convinced that being able to harness their metacognition was what learners needed, but a systematic approach to understanding and exploiting their metacognition was missing, particularly in second language listening.

My students were already demonstrating their metacognition (thinking about the way they listened) in my lessons. I had led them to reflect on their listening by breaking down listening into parts and helping them to introspect at each stage of the listening task. By doing this, students felt they could 'slow down' their process of listening and learn from what they discovered about their own listening processes and problems, and from one another. As a teacher, I had intrinsic knowledge, a hunch, a lead, and I followed it and developed teaching materials and activities. When I researched the topic, I found concepts and terminology that represented and refined what I was doing and thinking. My own sense of plausibility for listening instruction became stronger each day as I was able to draw connections between my own beliefs, my practice and my increasing knowledge of the topic of listening derived from others.

Learning with my peers

The time spent in RELC was a pivotal point in my learning and work. It gave me confidence in leading learning among my peers. I began to take an active role in sharing my new-found knowledge with colleagues. I organised sessions where English language (EL) teachers in my school could come together to learn at several levels: teaching buddies or partners who co-planned lessons and shared teaching materials, peer-observers who attended and commented on each other's lessons, members of small groups that discussed strategies that worked – and learner problems. It was some years later that I found out that a grouping such as ours was referred to as a 'community of practice'. I found much later from teacher learning literature that other formal terms reflected some of the things we were doing: 'critical friends groups', 'teacher inquiry seminars', 'study circles', 'teacher study groups', 'action-research groups', 'learning teams' and 'lesson study groups'. Not knowing the terminology for what we were doing did not hamper our desire to get together to learn from one another. It was our teachers' professional instinct that told us that it was the right thing to do. Our experience led many of us to believe that professional development situated within our own work environment and socio-cultural contexts was meaningful and powerful.

Searching for new professional knowledge and understanding

As I moved through new roles and work contexts, I continued my commitment to helping language learners develop oral skills. As I moved further into teacher education, I had opportunities to work with pre- and in-service school teachers of all levels. Being in a multidisciplinary education institution, I also had many opportunities to interact and learn from colleagues in general education studies, as well as in specific subject instruction such as science education and mathematics education. Talk was an important aspect of all classrooms, regardless of subject. I realised many L2 learners were actually studying in such classrooms in English-medium schools in Singapore. My search for knowledge and materials led me to the concept of 'oracy', which was more than just another word for oral skills. I was strongly influenced by the work of Andrew Wilkinson, the education professor who had earlier coined the word oracy. I began tracking down out-of-print publications by Wilkinson (Maclure, Phillips and Wilkinson, 1988; Wilkinson, 1965) and in the process also came across other educators' work. Apart from Wilkinson's writing, I began to study the works of Douglas

Barnes and his colleagues who examined the talk of schoolchildren (Barnes, 1988; Barnes and Sheeran, 1992; Barnes and Todd, 1977), and more recently the work of Neil Mercer on interthinking, i.e. people thinking together through talk (Mercer, 2000).

This personal learning pathway helped shift my attention and understanding of oral skills from viewing them simply as a communication tool to viewing spoken language as a tool for learning and engaging with others in the world. The concept of oracy as a foundation for learning, thinking and communication shaped my own work in teaching English, educating pre- and in-service teachers and pursuing new lines of language learning research. It also sealed my belief that the twin skills of listening and speaking, while connected, need to be taught explicitly and systematically. The development of oracy skills should be given emphasis in its own right and not done in the shadow of reading and writing instruction. Oracy and literacy have mutually supportive roles (Goh and Doyle, 2014). These ideas about oracy became important themes in the workshops and master's seminars I ran for teachers, and formed the basis for many of my published articles. My beliefs and knowledge about oracy as well as metacognition, discourse perspectives, and cognitive models of listening and speaking further coalesced in my books on teaching L2 listening (Goh, 2002; Vandergrift and Goh, 2012) and speaking (Goh, 2007; Goh and Burns, 2012).

Learning from different sources

My 'sense of plausibility' about what works developed over years and is the result of interlocking layers of learning. As all practitioners tend to do, I relied a great deal on my everyday experience of planning and delivering lessons, and seeing the outcomes of my students' language learning and motivation. Teachers can learn by reflecting on their own teaching and deriving better lessons from this, but they still need to learn from other experts. My enacted beliefs would not have been enough to sustain my teaching, much less help me to become a better teacher and teacher educator. I am fortunate to have had the opportunity to learn from my peers as well as experts who offered me new lenses with which to examine language and my own practice.

Teachers' learning does not stop after initial teacher preparation programmes and being certified to teach. On the contrary, that is just the beginning of a lifelong journey of learning teaching and a constant search for higher quality in what we do as teachers. Through learning from different sources, EL teachers will continue to hone their craft, strengthen their teacher identity and develop their professionalism. The availability of various professional development opportunities has been a huge contributing factor to my professional growth. This recognition has led me to value each opportunity I have had with teachers who wanted to learn from me at workshops, seminars and courses.

The goal of all teachers is to teach well so that our students can learn, and in this regard teachers must first have 'powerful learning opportunities' and 'have access to serious and sustained learning opportunities at every stage of their career' (Feiman-Nemser, 2001: 1,013–14). Such learning opportunities allow teachers to experience new ideas through discussions, discovery and deep learning that enable them to make connections to their context, work and students. Through the process of learning, applying and re-applying my learning, I became even more deeply committed to enacting my beliefs and knowledge about EL teaching and, specifically, to the teaching of oracy and metacognition in language learners.

As my experiences and embodied knowledge continued to expand, I also developed a deeper sense of professional identity and expertise in the routine execution of classroom lessons and plans. Furthermore, I experienced a constant deepening and broadening of my own understanding in the areas that I was specifically interested in. Teacher identity is not a stable construct. It changes as teachers move through different experiences and phases of growth. It is, however, a key factor that influences our personal commitment and teaching effectiveness. My own experience tells me that the main reason I managed to sustain mine was because I managed to learn from different sources:

- formal and certificated learning, such as further studies, workshops and courses
- contextualised and work-based learning with peers or other experts
- personal and self-paced learning from the print and non-print resources around us.

All three played an important part in enabling me to deepen and align my knowledge with my practice and beliefs, thereby strengthening my resolve to pursue certain directions for teaching English, particularly listening and speaking skills. On its own, each form of learning would have achieved limited effects on my professional experiences but, by pursuing my interest through all three forms of learning and in a sustained manner, I was able to consolidate, review and apply my learning in ways that were personally powerful and meaningful.

Exercising agency in professional development

I took on three roles that were critical to my own professional development journey: as learner, leader and designer of learning. These roles put me at the heart of my own learning, made me take ownership of it and gave me opportunities to refine and apply my personal theories of teaching and learning. As a learner, I acknowledged my limited knowledge and sought new understandings. After qualifying as an English language teacher, I had to deepen my own understanding of the English language, and the nature of language acquisition and development. My sociolinguistic knowledge caused me to become sensitive to contexts of language learning and use as I planned lessons and helped others do so. At the same time, through formalised learning, I became attuned to new theories and shifting paradigms in ELT.

Taking on the role of a learner was about what I needed to learn, and it was about *how* I learned. I developed new learning skills and strategies so that I could participate in innovative opportunities. These opportunities enabled me to engage in professional discourse and critical conversations, use analytical skills and tools to work with classroom data, and systematically approach reflection on practice and learning. I also learned new skills to tap technological affordances for learning. Learning some of these new skills took me out of my comfort zone. Like my learners, who needed to develop autonomy and metacognitive awareness, I needed to develop relevant abilities, habits of mind and dispositions that enable powerful learning to take place.

I was also a leader of my own professional learning and that of my younger peers. As I gained more experience, I mentored and coached younger teachers and led action research and facilitated professional dialogues within my own community of practice. Together we took ownership of our own learning by finding out what and how we would like to learn to achieve our professional goals. We worked together to examine our current practice and read articles, and applied what we had theorised or adopted in class. As I took on this role, I was developing new skills in presenting my own understanding of teaching and learning to my colleagues. I became a leader of my own learning by developing skills and tools to explore and challenge my own beliefs. For example, I had challenged my own beliefs about why I thought students should learn a standard variety of English and not a reduced set of language features that some scholars had said would be better for them. My own appreciation of the English language and my success as a language learner gave me the confidence that other learners could achieve similar outcomes. More importantly, I traced it back to my deep belief that each language was beautiful in its own way and any person learning a language should aim to go beyond the cold functional aspects of communicating and not miss the opportunity to enjoy its beauty.

Finally, I was also a designer of my own learning. Teacher professional development programmes are often criticised for their lack of relevance. One possible reason is that teachers attend courses and workshops when they are nominated by their schools. Professional development activities can, however, have high relevance if they are chosen by teachers themselves. This was my experience. I knew areas that I was specifically interested in: using literature to teach English, listening and speaking skills, oracy and thinking, metacognition, spoken discourse – and I sought ways to plan and structure my own learning. I registered for programmes and courses, watched talks and videos, read books and articles, participated in webinars, and sought out like-minded colleagues to learn together. Teachers can also co-design formal professional development opportunities by discussing with experts and consultants what we want to learn and how to learn it. When the initiatives for professional development are bottom-up, teachers will be more willing and interested in translating what they learn into their everyday teaching.

Conclusion

Moving through the continuum of teacher learning, teachers can develop greater self-efficacy, agency and motivation, but some may experience doubts and anxiety. Often we can lose focus on our own professional growth or the reasons we took up teaching as a career in the first place. We are just so caught up in the everyday tasks of teaching and administration. This is why it is important that teachers should pause and tell the stories of our professional learning. This is for our own benefit as much as it is for others. Writing this chapter had just such an effect on me, causing me to pause and revisit why I am who I am and do what I do today. Recalling my professional journey caused me to think more deeply about how I can support teachers in their journeys. It was not easy piecing together experiences that appeared fragmented. Yet, the exercise of recalling these somewhat fragmented experiences helped me to see the thread that ran through them and how I came to believe in the things I do when teaching English and especially when teaching oracy.

Prabhu (1990) spoke about teachers engaging with their 'sense of plausibility', stating that their pedagogical actions can influence their beliefs. This is a powerful way of conceptualising teacher learning and enactment of beliefs. It is nevertheless important to recognise that teachers also need to learn beyond their own communities and themselves. Introspecting on my own journey of professional growth and change, I could see the importance of two kinds of knowledge that have influenced my beliefs and practice. One is documented knowledge, knowledge acquired through the certified formal courses of my professional development as well as my own access to formalised knowledge found in books, in journals and on the internet. The other is practical knowledge, knowledge that I co-constructed with my peers and my students in my daily enactment of teaching and learning in the workplace.

Through both kinds of knowledge, I learned new ideas that would have been impossible to get from just being a teacher in the classroom. No doubt, my pedagogical actions in my school and university teaching contexts would have continued to shape, strengthen and entrench my beliefs of what good teaching was, or conversely what constituted poor teaching. However, these actions would not have enabled me to move beyond the realm of my own experience. As a result, I would not have been able to innovate in my teaching, even though I might have become more and more of an expert in the work I did routinely every day. My own experience has therefore convinced me of the importance to teachers of learning from different sources, and of teachers taking on active roles to lead and manage their own learning. This gives me the affirmation that I'm doing useful and important work as a teacher educator: work that is continually evolving.

References

Anderson, JR (1995) *Cognitive Psychology and Its Implications*. Fourth edition. New York Freeman.

Barnes, D (1988) 'The politics of oracy', in Maclure, M, Phillips, T and Wilkinson, A (eds) *Oracy Matters: The Development of Talking and Listening in Education*. Philadelphia: Open University Press, 45–56.

Barnes, D and Sheeran, Y (1992) 'Oracy and genres: speech styles in the classroom', in Norman, K (ed) *Thinking Voices: The Works of the National Oracy Project*. London: Hodder & Stoughton.

Barnes, D and Todd, F (1977) *Communicating and Learning in Small Groups*. London: Routledge.

Brazil, D (1985/1997) *The Communicative Value of Intonation in English*. London: Longman.

Brown, G (1986) Investigating listening comprehension in context. *Applied Linguistics* 3: 284–302.

Brown, G (1990) *Listening to Spoken English*. Second edition. London: Longman.

Duff, A and Maley, A (1990) *Literature*. Oxford: Oxford University Press.

Feiman-Nemser, S (2001) From preparation to practice. Designing a continuum to strengthen and sustain teaching. *Teachers College Record* 103/6: 1013–1055.

Flavell, JH (1976) 'Metacognitive aspects of problem solving', in Resnick, LB (ed) *The Nature of Intelligence*. Hillsdale: Lawrence Erlbaum Associates, 231–235.

Flavell, J (1979) Metacognition and cognitive monitoring: A new area of cognitive development enquiry. *American Psychologist* 34: 906–911.

Goh, CCM (1994) Language learning tasks for literary texts. *Guidelines* 16/2: 91–103.

Goh, C (2002) *Teaching Listening in the Language Classroom*. Singapore: SEAMEO Regional Language Centre.

Goh, CCM (2007) *Teaching Speaking in the Language Classroom*. Singapore: SEAMEO Regional Language Centre.

Goh, CCM and Burns, A (2012) *Teaching Speaking: A Holistic Approach*. New York: Cambridge University Press.

Goh, CCM and Doyle, P (2014) 'How do speaking and writing support each other?', in Silver, RE and Lwin, SM (eds) *Language in Education: Social Implications*. London: Bloomsbury Academic, 142–165.

Hoey, M (1991) *Patterns of Lexis in Text*. Oxford: Oxford University Press.

Johnson, K and Morrow, K (eds) (1981) *Communication in the Classroom*. London: Longman.

Maclure, M, Phillips, T and Wilkinson, A (eds) (1988) *Oracy Matters: The Development of Talking and Listening in Education*. Philadelphia: Open University Press.

McRae, J (1994) *Literature with a Small 'l'*. Oxford: Macmillan Education.

Mercer, N (2000) *Words and Minds: How We Use Language to Think Together*. New York: Routledge.

Prabhu, NS (1990) There is no best method – why? *TESOL Quarterly* 24/2: 161–176.

Sinclair, J (1991) *Corpus, Concordance, Collocation*. Oxford: Oxford University Press.

Vandergrift, L and Goh, C (2012) *Teaching and Learning Second Language Listening: Metacognition in Action*. New York: Routledge.

Wenden, A (1991) *Learner Strategies for Learner Autonomy*. Hertfordshire: Prentice Hall.

Wenden, A (1998) Metacognitive knowledge and language learning. *Applied Linguistics* 19: 515–537.

Wilkinson, A (1965) *Spoken English*. Education Review Occasional Publications Number Two. Birmingham: University of Birmingham.

Willis, D (1990) *The Lexical Syllabus: A New Approach to Language Teaching*. London: Collins ELT.

Willis, D (2004) Towards a new methodology. *English Teaching Professional* 33: 4–6.

Willis, J (1996) *A Framework for Task-Based Learning*. Edinburgh: Longman.

For CPD activities, visit e-file link: www.teachingenglish.org.uk/sites/teacheng/files/e-file.pdf

6

The more I have, the less confidence I feel about myself as a teacher

Yueguo Gu

Introduction

As of writing, it is my 37th year in my teaching career. In that sense I am a veteran teacher of English. My seniority will go beyond any doubt if my informal, ad hoc teachings are taken into account. That will exceed well over 40 years. Settled in my rocking-chair, in my study, with a whole wall-size window showering sunshine on me, I find myself lost quite cosily in reflective thoughts about this long teaching career.

The deeper I dig into myself, the more conscience-stricken I become. Officially I should have retired a couple of years ago, but I was offered a postponed retirement for some special expertise. 'You have everything!' my colleagues will tell me. Some have even labelled me *taidou ji daka* (泰斗级大咖 – super-expert). Yes, I have everything in terms of living conditions; I am well paid in terms of salary; and, furthermore, I have lots of publications and honorary titles. Yet oddly, the more I have in other areas, the less confident I feel in my career as a teacher. This is not a gesture of false modesty. I am reporting a fact of my mental state. This loss of self-confidence first struck me when I visited a kindergarten, and then a centre for children with autism spectrum disorder (ASD). Advice was eagerly sought from this 'visiting expert', but I found myself tongue-tied!

Early experiences

My reflection begins with my first experience of my first teacher, which puts my memory clock back 56 years, to the year 1962 in a rural area in Jiangsu Province, China. The village allocated a part of a mud building as its only school, the usable space being about 30 square metres. The teacher, one only, led pupils to make their own desks using the sticky mud, which was locally available everywhere. All the pupils had to bring their own stools from home and leave them in the school until the end of semester. The only teacher arranged the pupils into four functional rows, each representing a grade. That is, the teacher had to teach four grades in turn and in the same classroom, covering Chinese, numeracy, calligraphy/writing, music and sports. In a sense the teacher had almost nothing, but had to teach everything!

It is this teacher I revered – and my memory of him is still dear and vivid. Surely one's first memory of anything may endure, but my memory of him is extraordinary and exceptional. He has been my mirror, my reference model in a special sense of the term. The school was an impoverished one by any standards. It was that poverty-stricken state that rendered his dedication to teaching: his fatherly care for pupils, all of them, his tenacity against all odds and his ingenuity in instructing pupils to make their own learning aids – these shine out and cast us into shadow. He even organised us to raise silkworms and collect tree nuts during vacations to make some spare money to cover school fees.

I had another 'teacher', not in its official sense but in my personal regard. From 1974 to 1977, I was an 'educated youth' receiving 'further education' from farmers through doing farm labour with them. I was labelled 'educated' but was actually just a senior middle-school graduate. This is the period I started learning English by listening to the radio. It so happened that there was a former diplomat who, for his 'counter-revolutionary' ideology, was dumped in the same village for reform. I once went to his shabby shelter for help, but missed him. Being told by one of the neighbours I was looking for him, he returned my visit, but sadly we missed each other again. He left me a note in beautiful handwriting, which became carved in my memory: 'I hope your English will improve day by day, year by year!' When I returned home from the field, I read the note with awe and at the same time was puzzled: 'Why day beside day, year beside year?' I murmured to myself. I had no dictionary at the time. I had no idea that 'day by day' and 'year by year' were idioms!

This incident left a lifelong scar on my self-esteem. I felt ashamed later to learn that these simple words actually made idioms that I didn't know! At the same time it gave birth to my lifelong motivation for compiling textbooks for self-taught learners of English as I was then. This motivation materialised many years later in 1996 when I led a team, under British Council sponsorship, to compile a *Help Yourself with Advanced English* series. One of its avowed goals was to make the series 'teacher-proof' by incorporating the teachers' voices into the flow of the learners' learning process. The series turned out to be a big success and was later digitalised and turned into a series of web-based courseware in 2000, still in use today.

University experiences

Making teaching my lifelong career did not occur to me until I was in my second year of undergraduate studies. At this stage I thought of teaching as attractive mainly because it allowed the job-holder lots of 'free time'. That is, so long as some fixed contact hours of teaching per week were done, the remaining time was mine, with two annual vacations into the bargain. Note that the teaching job I craved for was not like my first teacher's. That was too hard! I sought after a lecturer's post in the tertiary education sector. For this, I had to undertake postgraduate studies with good academic grades. I achieved a postgraduate diploma in English literature and officially started my teaching career as a university lecturer in late 1981.

Interestingly, the university where I taught English was a 'Normal University'; that is, it specialised in producing teachers for primary and secondary education. Yet I, a staff member, had no teaching certificate myself! At that time, the Chinese education system made no clear distinction between academic achievements and qualifications for a profession. So, I was quite all right, and turned out to be 'quite popular' – I was honoured with the title of 'model teacher' once – with my students. As China embarked upon one reform after another, and opened its doors ever wider to the outside world, everyone, particularly those working in universities, experienced increasingly the pressure to 'publish or perish'. I was lucky enough, after three rounds of tests, to win a British Commonwealth scholarship so I found myself at Lancaster University 1984 doing an MA in language studies, and was awarded MA with distinction the following year – the first overseas student ever awarded this honour in the department. Later I won the prestigious Overseas Research Student Award, which enabled me to finish my PhD in 1987 in pragmatics and rhetoric at the same university.

Emergence of self-reflection, and urge for professionalism

I was considered the luckiest guy by my former classmates as well as my colleagues. I thought about myself in the same way, career-wise, but not profession-wise. My studies at Lancaster University threw me into some serious mental turmoil. As part of my academic credentials to back up my application to Lancaster University programmes, I had a couple of publications, which I regarded as evidence of my research potential. Now the revelation came to me that they were at best summaries of some literature I had read. They could be accounted as background preparations for undertaking research. By themselves, they were no research!

Another revelation struck me after exposure to the teaching practised by some outstanding professional teachers: to name but a few, the late Professor Geoffrey Leech (my MA and PhD supervisor) and Michael Short. It dawned on me that my previous so-called 'model teaching' was derived from observational apprenticeship. That is, I taught my students in the way I had been taught. Understandably it is a path normally taken in craft-learning. What had been missing in my teaching at the Normal University was constant critical reflection as a built-in ingredient in my professional development. I had been an amateur at best. There was a wide gulf between me and professionalism!

My urge for professionalism was acutely felt when I was asked to show my teacher's certificate. This took place quite by accident while I was a visiting scholar at the University of Hong Kong in 1994. One of the faculty staff took ill, and I was approached by the head of the department to fill the vacancy and teach two courses. I was asked to go to the general office to complete the paperwork for the official appointment. After displaying copies of two diplomas and two degrees, I was requested to show my teacher certificate. 'Pardon? What certificate?' 'Teacher certificate!' The head came and could not believe that I, the head of the second English department of a prestigious Chinese university, did not have a teacher certificate. There was total embarrassment all round!

Efforts towards professionalism

Ever since, teacher professionalism has become my holy grail. The late Mary J Willes and I collaborated for four years (1997–2000) on a project to develop teacher professionalism in Chinese tertiary education, the outcome of which was a textbook entitled *A Guide to Success: Professionalism* (1998). Several reprints followed. Teacher professionalism as I understood it at the time included four essential components: applicable knowledge, classroom performance, high standards and teacher ethics. So, a teacher with professionalism possesses a great deal of applicable knowledge, delivers excellent classroom performance, maintains high standards in student evaluation and conducts himself or herself morally and ethically. The achievement of these four, so I believed, would uplift me from amateurism to professionalism.

Since 2000, I have conducted numerous short-term teacher training courses. I was often amused with the feedback I received: 'Professor Gu's teaching methodology is very good, but it does not work with my students.' At first, I didn't take it seriously. But repeated hearings triggered a dual reaction. I reflected upon my own performances, and at the same time fielded observations of some trainees' classes. This led to another revelation, namely that critical self-reflections by both trainers and trainees in tandem hold a key to success. As a consequence I launched a chess-master model of teacher professional development (Gu, 2012).

My chess-master model, drawing inspirations from Wallace's *Training Foreign Language Teachers: A Reflective Approach* (1991), is built on insights from the Chinese chess game of Go. A novice plays with a master. What the former learns most from the latter is the play-back, in reverse order, receiving move-by-move comments from the master. It is a sort of learning from hindsight under the master's help. Analogously, a novice teacher records audio-visually his or her classroom performance and plays it back to re-live the experience with a master teacher over the shoulder. A master teacher on the other hand must not be so arrogant as to assume that his or her teaching is perfect, and faultless. Each session is new, for it creates a unique experience of learning on the student's side, and teaching on the teacher's side. A method or strategy, proven to be quite successful last time, does not necessarily bring about an effective learning experience this time. Pre-planning and improvisation *in situ* play an equally important role in achieving good classroom performance.

My chess-master model consists of four components:

1.   The *design phase*, prototypically including the design of teaching a session (e.g. 50 minutes long); the design of activities, tasks and methodologies; and the formation of hypotheses regarding the previous two designs (teacher + instructional designer).

2.   The *performance phase*, i.e. the real-life implementation of the lesson design, and experimentation regarding the hypothesis embedded in the lesson design (teacher + performer + experimenter).

3.   The *reflection phase*, i.e. the multimodal text analysis of the videotaped classroom performance. The analysis will provide evidence for (a) evaluating the design and hypothesis in the first phase, and (b) the performance in the second phase (teacher + multimodal text analyst + self-anatomist).

4.   The *application phase*, by which time a considerable number of findings will be accumulated and can be fed into theoretical explorations, future performance improvement and materials development such as textbook writing and courseware design (teacher + researcher + designer + developer).

The advantage of re-conceptualising the four components in terms of role development is threefold: (1) it explicitly encourages the trainee teacher to assume new roles; (2) it explicitly invites the trainee teacher to look at the daily task of teaching in fresh and more challenging perspectives; and (3) it provides a design structure for teacher development programmes.

There exists a massive literature concerning each of the roles, except the role as multimodal text analyst. What is being videotaped in a real-life, face-to-face classroom is called *multimodal content*, i.e. human interactions involving multiple modalities. The digitalised video data containing the multimodal content is called *multimodal text*. The multimodal text is materialised in a physical media file that can be copied, downloaded, uploaded, edited, etc. Multimodal text analysis (MTA) refers to analysis of multimodal content on the basis of multimodal text(s). This means a drastic departure from our traditional way of observations, of analysing classroom teaching and learning on the basis of orthographic transcripts, or written texts. What we analyse are chunks of live behaviour captured in video streams.

Armed with digital video annotation tools such as ELAN, I quite enjoy putting my classroom teaching to microscopic scrutiny. It is microscopic in its literary sense, for a piece of behaviour, say, lasting only a second, is captured in 25 or 30 (depending on which standards one adopts) image frames. Oral discourse is sampled at 11–44 kHz. Voice qualities, prosodies, emotions and so on are all made available for reflective scrutiny. The chess-master model proved to be quite appealing to the majority of trainee teachers. The Faculty of Foreign Languages, Tongji University, even established a research laboratory for the purpose.

New challenges: teaching in both real-life and virtual worlds

The chess-master model naturally entrenched me in digital technology. In 2000, Beijing Foreign Studies University set up an online education institute, and I was appointed founding dean. One of the biggest challenges I faced at the time was that I had no campus students. So, I had no face-to-face contact with my students, as I had previously. 'How can I teach students I cannot see, or hear, or feel in direct touch with?' was the thought that haunted me for quite a long while. It also brought me to consider what is called the '3-M learning model', that is, a model for *m*ultimodal, *m*ultimedia and *m*ultiple environment learning.

In the 3-M learning model, the pivot of concern is no longer the teacher, but the student. Everything must be considered and designed from the point of view of absent students scattered around all corners of China. Their needs, concerns, difficulties and learning styles must be foreseen, understood properly and adequately catered for. *Multimodal learning* is learning involving the learner's multiple sense modalities. Face-to-face classroom learning is naturally multimodal. Replication of such learning is a ticklish point for online education. *Multimedia learning* is learning through multimedia presentations. Digital technology has become so advanced that it can enable such modes of learning quite easily. *Multiple environment learning* is learning that can occur wherever, and whenever, with learners staying fixed or on the move. The teacher derives his or her roles from the three modes of learning. Such teaching practice is similar to, but not the same as, what is known as computer-assisted teaching. It is a kind of blended-teaching. Years of personal practice have left me with mixed feelings. It is quite gratifying, for example, that my online teaching can be simultaneously attended by more than 500 students, who can see me, talk to me in turn and text-message me, while I see on the screen icons representing students physically scattered around China. It is, however, quite unsettling that students may approach me from all directions, quite randomly, and by whatever channels of digital communication available to them. I felt morally bound to reply to them all promptly, but found it practically impossible to do so.

The 3-M learning model and its counterpart, blended-teaching, pulled the rug from under my feet: I felt insecure about my hard-earned sense of professionalism, which was founded on the traditional face-to-face classroom. I had now to embark upon another round of self-development, uplifting myself to the level of professionalism in blended-teaching. For this purpose, I launched a platform called AR4TD (action research for teacher development). As of writing, it has gone through its piloting stage and is ready for teachers to use for professional development.

ASD children and Alzheimer's disease patients: back to an amateur again

If blended-teaching made me feel out of my depth – I became an amateur again – the worst was yet to come. One day I was invited to visit a centre for children with ASD. Therapists there faced two groups of 'students': ASD children themselves and their caregivers, normally parents. Therapists on the one hand 'teach' language to ASD children and, on the other, instruct parents how to continue language learning at home. I was cornered, totally at a loss about what to say, when I was approached for advice as a language teaching expert. My former professionalism was based upon an implicit, but fundamental, set of assumptions about students' typical mentality. Once these assumptions were no longer valid, my expertise and professionalism were worthless.

Since the encounter with ASD children, I have often asked myself, 'Speech therapy is a kind of language teaching, isn't it? Is there any difference between the two?' Well, the difference lies in the brain-mind. Speech therapy deals with the abnormal (or atypical) brain-mind, whereas language teaching deals with the normal (or typical) brain-mind. To become a speech therapist, you have to be well-informed about how the brain functions both normally and abnormally. As a language teacher for normal, regular learners, I knew something about learner psychology, but not their brains. I set myself two new tasks. One was to read as much as I could about neuroscience, including brain anatomy, at the same time following some online, open courses on ASD, human physiology and so on. The other was to compile a special corpus of ASD cases. These exercises have had an everlasting impact on me. I started reflecting upon my previous years of teaching experience from a new perspective. Temple Grandin's works (2006; Grandin and Panek, 2013) fully convinced me that ASD children see the world differently from the way we do. Understanding their ways of seeing the world is a precondition of successful speech therapy. The same principle applies to typical children and adults learning foreign languages. A competent language teacher with professionalism must have an understanding of how learners see the world as well as the foreign language they are learning. Why? We all have the experience of so-called 'weak learners'. Some adult learners even label themselves as 'never able to learn any foreign language'. Now I no longer interpret this simply as an issue of self-confidence. These 'non-competent learners' are seriously handicapped by their mindset. They see foreign languages as 'weird', 'bizarre', etc. Once they become aware that foreigners see the world differently from how they see it, and conceptualise it their way, hence speaking accordingly, they are ready to break the constraints imposed by the fixed mindset.

My multimodal, corpus-based study of some Alzheimer's disease (AD) patients has reinforced my position that there is a great deal of common ground between speech/language therapists and language teachers, and that it is of paramount importance that professional help/instruction is built on the understanding of their ways of seeing the world. Based on my limited studies of ASD children and AD patients, I ventured a 3-Welt model for empirical investigation: Umwelt, Innerwelt and Lebenswelt. The first two 'Welts' are insights from Uexkull's (1934/2010) study of animals, and the last from Deely's (2001) philosophy. When a newborn comes into the world, it builds its Umwelt via multimodal interactions – capacities endowed by nature – with the environment, which reinforces the growing Innerwelt with specific experiences. The newborn does not cry until a second or two after the needle injected into its arm is removed. However, on a later occasion, it cries at the first sight of a white-coated nurse, who does not even intend to give any injection. Why so? It has developed its Innerwelt, which affects its Umwelt constructed in the first instance. Lebenswelt is mostly built through language, and is our major concern as language professionals. It takes a year or so before a newborn is able to utter words in its mother tongue. In this 3-Welt model, infant autism cannot construct its Umwelt in the way its normal counterpart does, hence affecting development of its Innerwelt and Lebenswelt. The same reasoning applies to AD patient investigation, only in reverse order.

Future directions

As of writing, I have found myself at a crossroads. Should I retire and quit professional life? Or should I plough ahead to render myself more competent professionally with all sorts of learners, typical and atypical children, normally and abnormally ageing late adults alike? Currently I am sitting on the fence. However, I am determined to do one thing: to mobilise and energise young people in this direction. I have set up the Ageing, Language and Care Research Centre in Tongji University, and the Linguistics and Applied Artificial Intelligence Research Centre in Nanjing Normal University. I have just finished negotiating a blue-print for another research centre for narrative medicine and end-of-life care in still another university.

One of my teams and I have already embarked upon a project known in Chinese as Nanshan Xiyang Waiyu (南山夕阳外语), word-for-word translation being: 'Mountain Nan, Sunset, Foreign Languages'. Mountain Nan is an abbreviation of *shou bi nanshan* (寿比南山), meaning 'one lives a life as long as Mountain Nan'. Xiyang alludes to a famous verse line *xiyang wuxian hao* (夕阳无限好) – 'the beauty of sunset knows no bounds'. *Waiyu*, its semantics quite transparent, signals a foreign language teaching programme specially designed for late adult learners (more than 60 years old). It is designed on the insights drawn from the latest findings in neuroscience. Simply put, to learn foreign languages as a late adult has the therapeutic function of keeping the ageing brain 'young'. Use it or lose it. Appropriate use of the brain is beneficial to its proper maintenance.

Emerging themes and accumulated beliefs, values and practices

Finally, I am particularly grateful for the invitation to write this informal autobiography of professional development. The invitation could not be more timely, for it coincides with another project we are developing, Life-Course Memories: AI-Supported Re-living Initiative. The project will utilise multimedia materials, including old photographs, diaries, good-old-days black and white films, as well as virtual realities.

This present life-course memory of professionalism, regrettably orthographical text only, has helped me sort out verbally and linearly the professional paths I have trodden. Looking back, the greatest challenge the teacher faces – which I feel ever more strongly as I grow older – is grandma's old maxim: individualised teaching. Confucius, revered in China as *wan shi shi biao* (万世师表 – 'the model teacher for thousands of years'), is largely known for his *yin cai shi jiao* (因材施教 – 'teach according to individual learners' potential'). I have always been haunted with the problem of how to. When I first launched the 3-M learning programme at the Institute of Beiwai Online Education, I thought I had found a solution. Now I feel there is still a long way to go. I often feel frustrated with the widespread confusion between online education and online learning, or between education and learning. Education, bound to be provided by a social-political-cultural system, in virtue of this very nature, can only be collective in one way or another. Learning, bound to take place inside the individual's brain-mind, cannot but be individualistic. Learning begins with what has already been constructed up to that point by the individualised experiences, and finishes by successfully bringing what was future to become the present. The 3-Welt model is my attempt at rendering this process researchable and falsifiable. The learner's existing Umwelt–Innerwelt–Lebenswelt frames and enables the present learning activity, which, leading to positive learning if successful, or negative if unsuccessful, no matter which, updates and enriches the existing three Welts. The three Welts can be empirically investigated and assessed: Umwelt in virtue of perception capabilities (or disabilities or impairments); Innerwelt in virtue of life-course development, intelligence, cognitive capacities (or malfunctions), etc.; and Lebenswelt mainly in virtue of linguistic performance (or aphasia).

Since the 3-Welt model accommodates all types of learners, with or without learning difficulties, young or aged, in one framework, I regard my scope of teaching an all-round one. I know that I may never be able to put it completely into practice before I die. But I draw comfort at least in this mental exercise. I gave myself a small trial using this framework of thinking, on 23 January 2019, when I was invited to give a public lecture on translation and artificial intelligence to winter camp university students with mixed academic subjects (science, maths, computers, foreign languages, textile, transportation – you name it) from more than 20 different universities. A real test will come when I teach an elderly class including some mild cognitive impairment (MCI) students.

I also believe in 'non-teaching'. The ideal teaching is what Laozi, the founding father of Chinese Taoist philosophy, would call *wu wei*(无为), that is, taking no action to interfere with the learner's own learning. In practice, what the teacher does is prepare a conducive environment, a swimming pool, as it were, so that learners can jump into it and swim by themselves. This is how I learned to swim myself when, as a kid, I was pushed from behind by a naughty pal into a river. For less capable learners, such as ASD learners, for the teacher/therapist to provide a conducive environment for them and guide construction of their Umwelts–Innerwelts– Lebenswelts towards those of typical children is, though extremely challenging, also recommended by ASD veteran clinicians qua researchers (Siegel, 2010).

We are all familiar with such complaints as 'Kids never learn what is taught, and learn what is not taught.' There is some truth in it. Non-teaching as suggested above is a form of environmental learning, the essence of which is best expounded in Bandura's (1977) theory of social learning.

> In the social learning view, people are neither driven by inner forces nor buffeted by environmental stimuli. Rather ... explained in terms of a continuous reciprocal interaction of personal and environmental determinants ...
>
> By arranging environmental inducements, generating cognitive supports, and producing consequences for their own actions, people are able to exercise some measure of control over their own behavior.
>
> (Bandura, 1977: 11–12)

Bandura's social learning theory is in total harmony with the 3-Welt model I outlined. Am I re-inventing the wheel, since Bandura's is already well established? No! The 3-Welt model has an avowed aim of accommodating all sorts of learners, those with learning difficulties in particular. Whether this aim is achievable or totally unrealistic is another matter!

My support for 'non-teaching' is further motivated by my assessment of current educational practice in China. 'Non-teaching' is actually a kind of oxymoron. Teachers of all ranks at all levels of education tend to regard classroom teaching as their duty proper. Classroom teaching is their concern, and anything else is none of their business, or beyond their control. Mind you, classroom learning via classroom teaching accounts for just a small portion of all the learnings learners are actually engaged in. To me it is extremely disheartening that this kind of learning is often left to the manipulations of non-teaching 'experts' and profit-driven business people, as well as by hi-tech-mongers. Non-teaching is also a form of teaching, the best form of teaching according to Laozi's philosophy! Teachers are equally responsible for it.

The last word. My first teacher had almost nothing, but taught us everything. In comparison, I am far better off, but I lack his tenacity, and his resilience in fighting against all odds. May I not be a bad pupil of my first teacher!

References

Bandura, A (1977) *Social Learning Theory*. New Jersey: Prentice-Hall, Inc.

Deely, J (2001) *Four Ages of Understanding*. Toronto: University of Toronto Press.

Grandin, T (2006) *Thinking in Pictures*. New York: Vintage Books.

Grandin, T and Panek, R (2013) *The Autistic Brain: Thinking Across the Spectrum*. Boston: Houghton Mifflin Harcourt.

Gu, Y (2012) A chess-master model for teaching and teacher/researcher development. *Chinese Journal of Applied Linguistics* 35/1: 5–23.

Siegel, B (2010) 'Reconceptualizing autism spectrum disorders as autism-specific learning disabilities and styles', in Millon, T, Krueger, RF and Simonsen, E (eds) *Contemporary Directions in Psychopathology*. New York: The Guilford Press, 553–564.

Uexkull, J von (1934/2010) A *Foray into the Worlds of Animals and Humans* (translated by JD O'Neil). Minneapolis: University of Minnesota Press.

Wallace, MJ (1991) *Training Foreign Language Teachers: A Reflective Approach*. Cambridge: Cambridge University Press.

Willes, MJ (1998) *A Guide to Success 3: Professionalism*. Beijing: Foreign Language Teaching and Research Press.

For CPD activities, visit e-file link: www.teachingenglish.org.uk/sites/teacheng/files/e-file.pdf

7

My journey from classroom teaching to policymaking

Jennifer Joy Joshua

Introduction

My professional and personal development through a number of significant experiences has reshaped my thinking on many issues pertaining to language acquisition and development, and language teaching and teacher development. The isiZulu saying *umuntu ngumuntu ngabantu* ('a person is who he or she is because of others') rings true for me as I attribute much of my professional growth to interaction with people who have been catalysts for the growth of ideas and have positively influenced my development.

Earliest experiences of language learning and education

Many of my attitudes and values about language learning and education were formed long before I became a teacher. These formative experiences have contributed significantly to my deep interest in, and love for, language learning and teaching. I will cite three of these experiences.

I am the fifth of seven siblings who, for many years, lived in a one-room house. Abject poverty characterised my early childhood years. However, I was fortunate that, while children living in poverty are often culturally deprived and are widely known to have poor language and education exposure, this was not my case. I was raised in a home that valued reading and education. Although small, our home was print-rich. There were stacks of books and magazines my four older siblings acquired each week through the courtesy of the refuse truck driver who threw a few books or magazines onto our stairway when his truck stopped to collect the refuse!

My mother, who had limited schooling, nonetheless would draw my attention to how to prepare family meals and do the household chores; and the stories she made up, paging through the magazines, provided the scaffolding tools for my early learning. Her skilful questioning and creating opportunities for predicting and linking it to prior information (particularly when the staple diet had to be prepared in a different way each day for variety) allowed me to progress step-by-step in my own creation and re-creation of knowledge. These early learning experiences, which took place in a physically under-resourced environment, through the efforts of an intuitive and creative, loving adult, laid a solid foundation for education and language development.

In 1971, at the age of 14, I enrolled at Lakehaven Secondary School, near Durban. The gravel roads leading to the school created clouds of dust on good weather days and made it impossible for the buses to get through the sludge on rainy days. These badly neglected roads posed a threat to the health and safety of learners. My English language teacher used the opportunity to discuss the problem and possible solutions in one of our English language lessons. This was followed by a writing activity in which each of us wrote a letter to the municipality describing the hazardous road conditions and requesting improvements. My teacher used the inputs from our individual letters to craft a letter on behalf of the class to the municipality. Weeks later, the municipality responded positively and upgraded the roads and thereafter provided continued care for the roads. What started off as a mere writing exercise ended up being used to bring positive change to a rural community, without any confrontation or strife.

By my final year at school, English was my best subject. This, I attribute to the many passionate teachers who spurred me on to constantly improve. They encouraged my participation (as a junior secondary school learner) in taking the lead roles in school plays, debates and speech contests with senior secondary learners. Their belief in me gave me confidence and enabled me to compete against the senior students. Each successful contest or debate inspired greater confidence in my public-speaking ability. By the time I left school in 1974, it was clear I was destined to become a teacher myself!

These early experiences served to shape my current views and practices in the following ways:

1. Parent–child talk: making time to talk and creating talk rituals with young children, responding with emotion to their stories and providing a print-rich environment are important for stimulating thinking, creativity and language development.

2. The power of the written word – the pen is mightier than the sword!

3. Having high expectations of learners. Believing in the potential of learners and creating opportunities for their participation inspire confidence and create a desire to succeed.

Influences arising from places/institutions where I have lived and worked

I will trace influences from the five roles I have played over my years in education. These are (1) first teaching appointment; (2) my experiences as a teacher trainer; (3) my experiences as head of department (HoD) in a primary school; (4) my experiences as a subject adviser; and (5) my experiences as a policymaker.

I grew up when South Africa practised the policy of apartheid (separate development) and, being of Indian descent, most of my work was limited to the Indian Education Department in South Africa until 1994, when South Africa became a democracy.

My first teaching appointment (1978–80)

In January 1978, I began my teaching career at a primary school in Chatsworth, a sprawling township for Indians. At the staff meeting on my first day, I was told that I would be teaching a Grade 3 class of 40 learners.

Their academic records showed that the group had diverse language needs. Many were underperforming in language, which also affected their performance in other subjects. Two major realisations dawned on me: more than teaching the subjects that I was qualified to teach, I had to teach *children*, each of them with different needs; and the future of these learners lay in my hands!

I realised that this meant that the normal timetable would not work for this group of learners, it would have to be adapted; and that the approach that I took had to ensure that meaningful learning took place in all subjects.

However, working in a highly bureaucratic system, I had to be careful not to appear to be flouting the expected teaching methods and procedures. Clearly, the methods that the 'underperforming' learners were exposed to in previous years had not worked. After discussion with the HoD, I produced a teaching plan that integrated language learning with music (songs and rhymes) and stories and, in the absence of commercially printed resources, I used the art and crafts lessons to develop resources with learners from waste materials. I chose an eclectic approach to presenting the lessons to ensure that all four language skills received attention. The HoD was concerned that I was on probation as a novice teacher and that my inspection for confirmation should go well. She was, however, supportive throughout the process.

The main problem was that I had to ensure that the rest of the learners were gainfully occupied while I focused on the group that needed extra attention. The fun and laughter that emanated from these lessons were sometimes construed by the management as poor discipline! The positive spin-off was that the learners' attendance remained good throughout the year. The lessons were fun-filled and, in non-threatening ways, the learners' language skills were, very slowly but surely, being developed!

Later, in October 1978, I had a visit from the inspector, who commended me for the music and story programme and confirmed my permanent appointment as a teacher!

What did I learn from my first teaching experience?

1. Children within the same age cohort learn at different paces.

2. For teaching to be effective it has to be learner-based and learner-paced.

3. Songs, rhymes and stories together with the relevant teaching resources can lead to meaningful learning.

4. In limited resource classrooms, teacher improvisation and creativity can be excellent substitutes for commercially produced resources.

5. A less bureaucratic and flexible supervisor can bolster teacher creativity and experimentation with new or less familiar ideas.

6. Improved language learning influences learning in other subjects.

7. Keeping a journal on learner responses to teaching and adjustments to planned activities aids reflection.

Early grades music lecturer (1980–84)

In 1980 I joined Springfield College of Education as an early grades music lecturer. This job took me out of my comfort zone. I had to brush up on my piano and recorder playing; and, more importantly, it gave me the opportunity to read widely on language and numeracy development through songs, rhymes and stories. In compiling language lessons the students and I explored methods to match the selection of themes around which songs and rhymes were grouped. The students used their practical teaching sessions to trial these with learners before we finalised them. This wonderful mutual learning experience between me and the students taught me as much as it did them!

What effects did my lecturing experience have on personal and professional growth?

1. My piano and recorder playing skills were strengthened.

2. I became more conscious of the value of the creative use of stories, songs and rhymes to bolster language and numeracy learning. My repertoire of songs, rhymes and stories increased considerably.

3. A belief that the fun element in teaching makes for easier and sustained learning.

4. Belief in the value of exploring the choice of suitable methods of presenting lessons together with the students.

Middle years 1984–94

From 1985 to 1988 I taught in a local school before becoming Head of Department in 1989 at another rural school. I then had a spell at Springfield College of Education. In 1994 I was appointed HoD of a local school near Durban again. That year, South Africa became a democracy, and there was an influx of learners from poorly resourced schools seeking admission to schools previously closed to them. They came from schools where isiZulu was the language of instruction. Now they sought education at schools where English was the language of instruction.

I was suddenly faced with a group of Grade 3 learners from a different language and cultural background and who did not speak any English. My training had not prepared me for this new situation! Moreover, learners displayed cultural behaviour that troubled me until I understood it – the African learners would not look at my face when I was talking to them! I later learned that in their culture this was a mark of respect!

There were no official policies, coursebooks or guidance on how to manage teaching English to a group of IsiZulu-speaking learners. So, I read extensively around second language learning and teaching issues. The study provided guidelines to teachers on assisting learners for whom English was an additional language. I also did a short course in conversational isiZulu.

The change in the context drew the teachers and me together to strategise our efforts to adjust our plans and approaches to ensure effective learning. Our challenge was that we were expected to teach mathematics and life skills as well as language and literacy.

We proceeded as follows:

1.   Listed our challenges – one of our major challenges was that we could not speak isiZulu and the learners could not speak English.

2.   Drew on literature on theories of language acquisition, and strategies and programmes that had been successful in other countries.

3.   Sifted those ideas that could work in our context that were supported by plans and resources.

4.   Resolved to document weekly how the teaching proceeded, what changes needed to be made and any problems encountered and solutions.

As things developed, what had started out as trial and error was refined with each discussion with teachers. And these school-based development sessions were a source of growth of ideas among the teachers. There was an ethos of trust and honesty, which resulted in confidence building.

We later attended workshops organised by the education department that exposed us to what other teachers, in similar situations, were doing, which further enhanced discussions and learning between teachers.

What did I learn from my post-1994 school experience?

1. Socio-political changes impact on language teaching and learning.

2. Reading on second language learning exposed me to new approaches to teaching English to children of a different language group.

3. A big revelation for me was how things that had worked in other countries did not necessarily work for us. Some ideas worked well and others did not!

4. Familiarisation with socio-cultural behaviour is important for understanding learners of the source culture.

5. In the absence of official policies and guidelines, teacher reflection, sharing of ideas, trying out new ideas and reporting on highlights and challenges become crucial tools in charting new ways of teaching.

6. My limited conversational isiZulu assisted in breaking the ice with my learners and eventually winning their confidence.

Subject adviser and provincial curriculum co-ordinator (1996–2003)

In 1996, I became subject adviser for about 200 schools in the Durban South Region. That year the national Department of Education introduced the Outcomes-Based Curriculum (OBE). In this new approach, the word 'teacher' was replaced by 'facilitator' – teachers began to think that they no longer had to teach in the classroom! The teaching of reading and writing stopped altogether in some classrooms. Teachers became more interested in highly integrated lessons. Walking into a classroom one couldn't tell what lesson was being taught! Excessive record-keeping compromised teaching.

More experienced teachers began to question how the teaching of basic skills fitted into the OBE programme. Together with teachers I began to bring the basic skills back into focus.

Three years later, there was a call to drop the OBE curriculum and re-write it to provide more direction in terms of content and skills that children needed to be taught. Between 2000 and 2003, I joined the national writing team to re-write the literacy curriculum.

What did I learn from this experience?

1. Top-down teacher orientation programmes do not always improve classroom practice.

2. Proper research into the context must precede the design of a new curriculum.

3. Resources and training must be in place before the introduction of the new curriculum.

4. Teachers need to understand reasons for the change, what has to change and how the change will affect what they do in the classroom.

5. Teachers with an active sense of plausibility, who understand their role, will ask the necessary questions, assess the new curriculum, take from it what they need and still keep the basics intact! They will not throw the baby out with the bathwater!

6. A major oversight was that we packaged the curriculum into grade requirements with no term specifications.

My work at the national Department of Education (2003–10) and the Department of Basic Education (2010 to date)
Curriculum Project Manager (2003–06)

In 2003, I was appointed in the Teacher Development unit of the national Department of Education as a chief education specialist – to project-manage the orientation of departmental officials to the revised curriculum. A core team was trained on the orientation materials after which the orientation of provincial officials began. It was my first experience of managing such a large project. Annual evaluations helped improve the training materials for successive years. By the last year (2006) we had reached a stage where our orientation materials were of high quality and so was the training. Provinces replicated this training with teachers. Teachers felt more prepared this time to implement a new curriculum. However, there were rumblings about the lack of direction for each term!

What did I learn from the curriculum project?

1. My greatest learning came from studying the evaluation reports each year and using the recommendations to produce a strengthened version of the materials and training.

2. I learned to work and manage large teams of people.

Director: Foundations for Learning (2008–10)

In 2008, the Department of Education introduced the Foundations for Learning (FFL) campaign, aiming to improve the reading, writing and numeracy abilities of all South African children. This was in response to findings that showed that South African children were unable to read, write and count at expected levels, and were unable to demonstrate key skills associated with literacy and numeracy.

I was appointed to direct the campaign. Although it was a huge undertaking to make a positive impact in a bad situation, I saw it as an opportunity to influence policymaking using the bottom-up approach. I set up groups of teachers from the nine provinces as critical friends who advised on challenges that teachers faced in teaching literacy and numeracy. This exercise revealed that the curriculum was designed in grades with no specific requirements per term, which left teachers without guidance on how to plan teaching and learning per term.

A task team made up of experienced teachers and subject advisers was set up that used the existing curriculum to develop milestones for Grades 1–6 for each term. This was sent out to schools for comment. In general, the documents were agreed to be a useful guide to teachers. The task team then developed lesson plans and resources based on the termly milestones. Distinctive features of the lesson plans were that they provided a teacher development component for teachers struggling with planning lessons, classroom management, resources and assessment; and were flexible enough to allow confident teachers to adapt them.

Two years later, the Minister of Education called for a streamlining and strengthening of the curriculum modelled on the FFL materials.

How did FFL contribute to my personal and professional development?

1. The FFL was introduced because of honest reflection and acknowledgement of non-performance of learners in the country.

2. The FFL succeeded because it was strongly influenced by teacher needs.

3. It gave teachers the direction they needed in their teaching and provided energy and enthusiasm for literacy and numeracy.

4. The voice of the teachers subsequently brought about a revision of the curriculum.

Foundations for Learning campaign (FFLC; 2008–10)
Director, Language and Teaching Support Materials (LTSM; 2011–13)
Curriculum Director (mid-2013 to mid-2016)

As Curriculum Director in the Department of Basic Education (DBE), my first task was to operationalise the Language in Education Policy (LiEP), introduced in 1997. Subsequently, the strategy for the Incremental Introduction of African Languages was developed to ensure that all learners exit the system having learned at least one African language. In the same year, the Minister of Basic Education introduced English as a subject from Grade 1 for all learners who will switch to English as the language of teaching and learning from Grade 4 and beyond. This was done to counteract problems caused by the abrupt transfer to English as a language of instruction in Grade 4.

Recent developments indicate that:

1. Planning for mother-tongue education until Grade 6 is under way (late exit).

2. English as a First Additional Language (EFAL) in the early grades is flourishing through the partnership between the British Council and the DBE. A survey noted that 127,272 teachers were reached through the British Council programme.

3. Almost 1,500 of 3,583 schools that were previously not offering an African language are now offering at least one African language.

What were the influences from my experiences as a Curriculum Director in the DBE?

1. A policy will always remain mere intent if there is no political will, leadership, appropriate resources, professional development of teachers and a costed implementation plan.

2. Understanding the importance of late exit from mother-tongue education to English for stronger conceptual and language development of a second language.

3. To re-skill or upskill language teachers in a huge system requires sustained partnerships because government on its own cannot manage this undertaking.

Director in the Office of the Director-General (2016 to date)

One of my flagship projects is the establishment of the National Association of English Teachers in South Africa (NAETSA). In 2015, I received a Hornby grant for this project. In consultation with provincial officials, we decided to establish the nine provincial associations before launching the national association. Eight provinces have already established provincial associations. NAETSA was launched in March 2019.

What did I learn from this project?

1. Any undertaking of this size and shape requires enlisting the teachers' co-operation, listening to them and following through with agreed decisions. This leads to teachers having confidence in the system.

2. Advocacy and persuasion have helped provinces recognise the value of belonging to an association.

Pivotal ideas that have helped form or change my beliefs and practices

In 2014, I was convinced that I needed to learn more about teaching English to young learners for whom English is an additional language if I was to influence policymaking and teacher education positively. I was awarded a Hornby scholarship and was admitted to a master's programme at the University of Warwick.

My year at Warwick equipped me with a multi-dimensional awareness and ability to apply this awareness in my own context (Mann, 2005: 105). The following three points have radically changed my ideas on teaching English to young learners but also significantly changed my views on the training of teachers.

Structure of the Second Language Acquisition (SLA) module

The module, structured within the Vygotskian socio-cultural theoretical framework, equipped me with the means to analyse language teaching and learning practice through the input (lecture) and experiential, task-based activities (seminar) followed by reflection on the process. The lecture/seminar organisation helped to clarify and consolidate my personal understanding of the topics and the implications for application in my own context. The practical lessons on learning Hungarian and Irish, where students became language learners, and the analysis following the lessons from a socio-cultural theory perspective, are something I valued. Coming from a country where the majority of learners are African language L1 speakers exposed to English for the first time in Grade 1, the methodology used has changed my practice significantly.

The content of the module

While most topics were familiar to me from my master's programme in the 1990s, the major difference was that my previous MA was by distance education so interaction with other students was non-existent and access to the supervisor was very limited. Hence, I truly appreciated the opportunity to attend lectures and participate in activities, listen to other students sharing their experiences and be exposed to different approaches to teaching and learning and cutting-edge developments in research in the field of SLA. I also appreciated the fact that adult learning principles were used in teaching activities that students were requested to participate in. This has refocused my thinking on how to train teachers on SLA.

Autonomy

Reflecting on topics such as motivation and autonomy, I noted that the classes themselves modelled learner autonomy. The provision of reading lists for each topic in the course, space for reflective writing at the end of each lecture, and so on, led me to take responsibility for my own learning. This is another area that I would include in my workshops with teachers.

Key people who have left an enduring mark on my life, beliefs and practices

Some of the beliefs and practices I still hold today I owe to the following.

My mother, who provided me with formative experiences and exposure to language and learning. The beliefs in the importance of talk and reading are so strong that these influenced my early interactions with my own children. Investing early in a love for reading, I believe, is a priceless gift that any parent can give.

My secondary school teachers, who believed in me and gave me opportunities that created a hunger and thirst for reading and writing.

My colleagues, especially the teachers I worked with in 1994 and since then, who participated in planning and reflection activities to give our learners high-quality teaching, ensuring that learning was successful and also growing professionally in the process.

My 2014–15 MA class was truly international. The close relationships among the 11 Hornby scholars made for one-on-one learning about how the English language is taught in different contexts. Challenges were often similar and my colleagues' coping strategies widened my repertoire.

The single most important person at Warwick was my supervisor, personal tutor and academic mentor, in charge of English for Young Learners, Dr Anna-Maria Pinter. Her accomplishments in her own academic journey served to inspire me in mine.

Themes emerging from my chapter

1. Top-down, large-scale, one-size-fits-all staff development programmes versus bottom-up, practically orientated teacher development programmes (Mann, 2005: 105).

2. Teachers' former experiences as learners, in training and other roles they may play in their lives, such as parenting, deeply affect their practice.

3. Teacher education should provide trainees with relevant knowledge, but local context and teachers' critical thinking play a role in their instructional choices.

4. Reflection on practice and trial and error are catalysts for transforming thinking and teaching, and keeping the teacher's sense of plausibility active.

5. Teachers make decisions based on their personal, moral and value judgements before and while teaching; and reflect critically on these decisions (Mann, 2005: 105).

6. Giving adequate tools for exploration will enable practising teachers to produce theories of practice (Kumaravadivelu, 2001: 541).

7. Teacher knowledge is multi-faceted but should also include personal, practical, experiential and local knowledge.

8. Key factors contributing to teacher knowledge are engagement with experience, reflection and collaboration.

9. CPD should:

   a. be based on the needs of teachers (bottom-up)

   b. create space for teacher dialogue

   c. develop learning through collaboration

   d. focus on classroom implementation

   e. allow for reflection.

10. CPD is a lifelong process of becoming with no end-point (Mann, 2005: 105).

Beliefs/values about language and learning languages emerging from my chapter

My beliefs/values about language

1. My experience as learner in the practical learning of Hungarian was pleasurable. Krashen's input hypothesis (1985) was practically demonstrated. My experience is summed up in three keywords: interaction, participation and repetition. The lesson was highly interactive, which ensured active participation, and repetition played a fundamental role in facilitating comprehensible input.

2. Promoting the linguistic rights of all language groups in South Africa is important to counterbalance our recent history of discriminatory language practices.

My beliefs/values about language teaching

3. Talking to a learner in his or her own language (source language) affirms him or her and creates an enabling environment for teaching and learning the target language. 'If you talk to a man in a language he understands, that goes to his head. If you talk to him in his own language, that goes to his heart' (Nelson Mandela).

4. Teachers are professionals and will adapt pedagogy to suit their unique context by applying learning principles that are congruent with their beliefs and practices. This may sometimes run counter to the expectations of school management but the professional judgement of a committed teacher should always prevail.

5. Teacher reflection offers teachers opportunities to think about what works and what doesn't in their classrooms rather than teaching as mere compliance with the curriculum.

6. School-based teacher development where teachers' needs form the basis for customised training allows for continuing support and sustains small, incremental changes in classroom practice and encourages professional growth.

7. Learners learn in different ways and at different paces. As a teacher, my job is to create a learning environment that will stimulate and sustain learning (optimal input) to meet the diverse needs of learners.

8. I need to constantly keep abreast of the latest developments to remain alive in my vocation.

9. My career-long experience convinces me of the power of language acquisition and development through songs, music, rhymes and stories to speed up language learning.

Conclusion

I have traced early influences on my personal language development, experience in teaching languages, beliefs and values derived from my life experiences, and issues relating to teacher development. The common thread running through the chapter is that a teacher with an active sense of plausibility is constantly sharpening his or her skills and reshaping thinking as new knowledge is added to his or her experience.

References

Krashen, S (1985) *The Input Hypothesis*. New York: Longman.

Kumaravadivelu, B (2001) Toward a postmethod perspective on English language. *Teaching World Englishes* 22/4: 539–550.

Mann, S (2005) The language teacher's development. *Language Teaching* 38:103–118.

Suggested further reading

Three categories of publications (among others) that have empowered me with new insights and knowledge in the ELT space and that have resulted in my successful completion of a materials development project are listed below.

Acquisition of second languages

Hatcher, JA and Bringle, RG (1996) Reflection activities for the college classroom. *Evaluation/Reflection* 62. Available online at: https://digitalcommons.unomaha.edu/slceeval/62

Krashen, S (1982) *Principles and Practice in Second Language Acquisition*. Oxford: Pergamon Press.

Pinter, AM (2011) *Children Learning Second Languages*. Hampshire, UK: Palgrave McMillan.

Sloan, D (n.d.) Reflection strategies for classroom activities. Available online at: www.umsl.edu/services/ctl/faculty/instructionalsupport/reflection-strat.html

Materials development in ELT

Tomlinson, B (ed) (1998/2011) *Materials Development in Language Teaching*. Cambridge: Cambridge University Press.

Tomlinson, B (2006) 'Localising the global: Matching materials to the context of learning', in Mukundan, J (ed) *Readings on ELT Materials II*. Petaling Jaya, Malaysia: Pearson Malaysia, 1–16.

Music

Sevik, M (2012) Teaching listening skills to young learners through listen-and-do songs. *English Teaching Forum* 3: 10–12.

Widodo, HP (2005) Teaching children using a Total Physical Response (TPR) Method: *Rethinking. BAHASA DAN SENI* 33/2: 235–247.

For CPD activities, visit e-file link: www.teachingenglish.org.uk/sites/teacheng/files/e-file.pdf

8

From little steps to giant strides: The story of my professional journey

Kuchah Kuchah

Introduction

I shall share the personal story of my professional journey and the experiences, events, publications and people who have shaped my beliefs, practices and vision of the ELT profession. Looking back at the journey so far, my professional identity now appears far more complex than I ever imagined and there might be mismatches between my self-perceptions and the perceptions of me by other members of my professional networks. I have always been presented at conferences or other professional events as a university lecturer and researcher, as a consultant for a number of international organisations and, more recently, as the president of one of the world's largest ELT communities. While these accolades represent how far I have travelled in my professional journey, they often blur the true identity that permeates my being and self-identity.

My story is of an African teacher and teacher educator whose personal and professional identities are rooted in humble beginnings, and complex relationships that have informed my worldview and understanding of my role within the wider ELT family. I use the world 'family' here because the strongest influences on my professional development and identity have been from my own teachers, senior colleagues and managers, whose relationships with me have often transcended professional lines and involved a much more personal dimension. It is these personal relationships that have shaped my current professional identity and approach to teacher education and professional development. My chapter attempts to weave together a representative collection of experiences and encounters to highlight puzzles that might provide insights into how teacher educators like me develop and what might be done, beyond the current traditional approaches to teacher education in Sub-Saharan Africa, to better support developing professionals. I begin by describing important events and experiences as a learner and later as a teacher in my home country, Cameroon. I then show how my studies, research, work and networking in and outside Cameroon have influenced my own professional development over the years. Although this is a personal account, I hope it will raise questions and issues relevant to understanding the complex influences that inform and shape language teacher development and identity formation.

Setting out

I grew up in Cameroon, where 286 local languages are spoken (Ethnologue, 2009) but which, because of its colonial history, is called a bilingual country with English and French as official languages and languages of schooling. In my childhood, I spoke Aghem, my mother tongue, at home and Pidgin English with friends in the playground. Then I went to primary school in a little town in rural Cameroon and was introduced to English-medium education, a language I hardly spoke outside the school environment. Through primary and secondary school, I studied in multilingual classrooms with peers from different local language and cultural backgrounds from across Cameroon. The multilingual nature of our classrooms meant that our teachers were often justified in promoting English-only practices because just too many local languages were involved. However, for my peers and me, Pidgin English remained the preferred means of communication outside the classroom, despite the risk of punishment for speaking any other language than English.

Primary school classrooms were generally less crowded than my secondary classrooms, with sometimes as few as 60 children. I barely remember how our teachers taught us, but much of my learning consisted of rote-memorisation and reciting concepts and definitions. I learned, for example, that democracy was 'government of the people, by the people and for the people' but how this related to our country, where we had only one political party and one president who always ran for elections uncontested, was never discussed. In English language and geography, I learned about the four seasons of winter, summer, autumn and spring, and about Mr and Mrs Smith at the train station talking about the weather, in a country with only two seasons and where a train station was a faraway reality. The teacher was the main source of knowledge and remembering what he told us was the key to passing exams. There was little opportunity to engage in developing learning content through interaction as our teachers often resorted to 'safe-talk'; that is, co-ordinated chorusing prompts to which we responded with a phrase or single words to show knowledge rather than understanding and analytical depth (Chick, 1996; Ngwaru and Opoku-Amankwa, 2010). Only in my final year at primary school did my teacher, Pa Wachong, introduce us to more creative ways of using language to talk about things that mattered to us. He noticed that I was 'good in words, but not good in figures'. This is where my love for the English language actually started and I will return to this later.

Secondary school was more challenging and exciting and introduced me to French, English and maths as the most important and heavily weighted subjects. Having struggled through maths in primary school, it was clear that to achieve a good average score in end-of-year promotion exams, I had to rely more on scoring high grades in languages to compensate for the low scores in maths. My father was keen on my learning French because it was the dominant language in the country. I went on to pass in French at the GCE Ordinary levels and was determined to pursue French in high school.

In high school, I had a passionate French teacher, Mr Tobias Ayuk (aka Prof), who made French fun. While the study of complex grammatical rules was still central to French classes, our teacher drew from the different literary genres we were studying to help us see the relationships between French language, literature and culture and, more importantly, to use French as a medium for talking about our own cultural values and personal interests. Prof gave us as much time as we needed, even offering to organise classes over weekends to help us get the best learning experience possible. Weekend lessons were often organised around an event; for example, when Nelson Mandela was released from prison in 1990, we organised a simulated 'national freedom event' in which we invited 'diplomats' from other countries and held a round-table conference on the necessity for peace and reconciliation in the country. Because the distance to school was 7km, he gave us the freedom to agree on where best we could organise weekend classes and that meant negotiating for classroom space or even open playgrounds with local primary schools nearer to the town centre. So, we participated in organising our own learning activities and deciding on venue and timing of our out-of-school learning.

In 1991, I went on to the University of Yaounde, the country's only university at the time. For a teenager who had spent his entire life in a remote town, life in the capital city was intimidating. In my first year, there were 900 students in the same lecture hall scrambling for a seat and listening to lecturers over loudspeakers! In my second year, there were more than 600 students studying English modern letters crammed into halls meant for 300 to 500 students. For early morning, 8 a.m. lectures we had to be up at 4 a.m. to get to university by 6 a.m., if we hoped to get a seat. Latecomers scrambled for space outside below loudspeakers to be able to hear the lecturer. Rumours of 'sexually transmitted' exam results and other forms of unethical conduct by both staff and students were rife. Class representatives were often 'elected' by students who had repeated the class and such repeaters, whom we referred to pejoratively as 'Les ancients' (oldies), did what they could to make sure we newbies experienced failure. Over the three years of my studies, education was a battle for survival.

Though my experience was challenging, it was also where I learned the value of collaborative learning, peer collaboration and autonomous learning. Eight of us formed a study group that we called the 'Cactus transcendentalists academics' because we saw ourselves as cactus plants resisting tough educational conditions, transcending our challenges through self- and group study. Our group had a committee made up of a chairperson, a social affairs officer and a dean of studies. As dean of studies, I was responsible for finding reading resources and assigning different group members to lead discussions around specific topics. This group helped my self-confidence and I was able to muster the courage to approach some of our lecturers for advice about readings and ask for photocopying resources not readily available to us. In the process, I discovered that among the apparently scary lecturers were people who genuinely cared for their students and were happy to support our learning where possible and despite the demographic challenges.

After graduation, I applied to Yaounde University College of Education and enrolled in the Department of Sciences of Education, specialising in English didactics. I trained as an English language teacher trainer for primary teachers just when bilingual education (i.e. French in English-medium schools and English in French-medium schools) was being introduced into primary schools. In Cameroon, teacher trainers for primary schools do not necessarily emerge from a successful and lengthy teaching career as they do in places like the UK. Rather, some are trained for two years as an elite group with or without any prior teaching experience and sent to train primary-level teachers in state teacher training colleges (TTCs). My training consisted of a full year and a half of theoretical input on different aspects of education, as well as an ELT component that reviewed different language teaching methods, insisting on the strengths of the communicative approach and promoting an eclectic method of teaching English language. There was no reference to the specific issues, ideas and practices of teaching English to young learners. Only two months of the two years were allocated for teaching practice. The practicum consisted of teaching academic subject content to trainees in a regional TTC for primary school teachers in Bamenda supervised by a co-operating trainer. Exceptionally (and uniquely too), local authorities in Bamenda included an additional component – to spend our first month teaching primary school children (supervised by the class teacher) to give us some hands-on experience. The two months practice teaching exposed me to another reality: while the co-operating teachers we worked closely with offered us as much support as they could, they did not assess our practicum. By contrast, the regional pedagogic inspectors and school administrators assigned to assess our training made us realise how little trained we were, and referred to us openly as theoreticians. They lost no opportunity to ridicule any of us having problems with our teaching. In all of my practicum experience, I did not have the opportunity to teach English language or language teaching methodology. So it was that I graduated from the College of Education as an English language teacher trainer with neither an understanding of young learner ELT materials and methods, nor any experience of teaching English to young learners.

Learning-in-action to become a teacher

After graduating from the College of Education in 1996, I was sent to teach English language and ELT methodology in a French-medium TTC in Kaele, a town in the far-north region of Cameroon. Coming from the southern part of the country with a Christian upbringing, living in a predominantly Muslim community was a new experience for me. Moreover, not only were all my students older than me but their cultural and religious values were largely different from those in my home area. For example, a strong awareness of age differences influenced classroom interaction and power relationships. It was therefore impossible for me to apply certain forms of discipline that I would have used in a classroom in Bamenda. The low proficiency of my trainees, together with the challenges of classroom management imposed upon me by their age and culture, forced me to reconsider my teaching strategies. There was no clear curriculum for English language in TTCs, and the primary English curriculum for French-medium schools was still being developed when I arrived. However, there was an English language component in the final examination for graduating teachers that was purely language based, and an expectation that teachers' performance would be observed and assessed during the practicum. As a result, I had to develop my own curriculum, to meet both requirements. Drawing on my previous experiences of learning French and the practices of my high school teacher, I encouraged a dialogic approach to developing the language content with my trainees. My students had collections of past official exam questions, which they brought to me and together we identified specific language areas that they found useful for their exams. On my part, I tried to introduce more contextualised use of grammar and vocabulary, encouraging my students to use the language items they learned to talk about themselves, their families and their cultures. Exploring the cultural differences among them and between them and myself became an important part of my course and this helped them build confidence and a willingness to communicate, at least in class.

Instead of offering them theories of language teaching and learning, I focused on classroom observation and analysis. Sometimes we observed teachers in the practice primary schools attached to the TTC; sometimes I volunteered to teach English in a primary or nursery classroom for them to observe, encouraging my trainees to both observe and critique my practice. This helped stimulate them to risk presenting their own English lessons to their classmates. If their trainer could accept criticism then they too should not fear criticism. On my part, volunteering to teach English in both primary and nursery schools enabled me gain more experience and insights about the real issues involved at this level and helped enrich my approach to pre-service teacher training. I cannot claim that the same thing happened in other schools, especially as I never had the opportunity to observe or be observed by another teacher trainer or even a regional inspector during the seven years I spent in the TTC. So, my own development as a language teacher and teacher trainer was mainly through feedback on my practice from my students.

In 2001, two other English language teacher trainers arrived in the TTC. With reduced workload, I decided to teach English part-time to teenagers in a neighbouring secondary school in the regional capital town, Maroua. I taught four different classes/levels ranging between 147 and 235 students per class. Teaching more than 200 teenagers in a classroom built to accommodate fewer than 80 students was challenging, enriching and fulfilling. With fewer than 20 textbooks in class, students standing outside the window eager to learn English and a packed classroom in temperatures above 40 degrees Celsius, I had to rely on my students to generate both the materials and processes of our English lessons. Drawing on my own experience of navigating university education through collaboration with peers, I managed to negotiate learning processes with my students using group work under trees outside the classroom as the main way of organising learning. (See Kuchah and Smith (2011) for a detailed account of my experiences and the development of my ideas about the value of autonomous learning.)

While in Maroua, I joined the Cameroon English Language and Literature Teachers' Association (CAMELTA) and quickly became involved in the teacher community in the region. Through CAMELTA I had the first opportunity to share stories of my practices with colleagues and to learn about their ideas and practices. Through CAMELTA, I was able to find colleagues who could speak to my students about different aspects of their cultures, so that they learned not only English, but also about the cultures of the different peoples of the Anglophone parts of Cameroon. My experiences teaching these younger students, the experiences with my trainees and my affiliation to CAMELTA helped to shape my vision of my professional role as teacher and teacher trainer, but also of my eventual role as National Pedagogic Inspector (NPI) for Bilingual Education in the Ministry of Basic Education.

As NPI, I was jointly responsible for defining and disseminating language policy relating to curriculum content, pedagogic orientations and assessment of learning. This was the time that bilingual education was fully implemented in primary schools nationwide and first assessed at the end through primary certificate examinations.

My role included contact with regional pedagogic inspectors and teachers, some of whom were my seniors. Negotiating power relationships with them constituted a challenge for me. More importantly, my work as a policymaker was influenced by the realities of the contexts in which I had worked, so my ideas were often at odds with colleagues whose experiences of teaching had been in the more privileged metropolitan cities in the country (Kuchah, 2008).

In 2006–07 I studied for an MA in EYL at the University of Warwick. This allowed me to reflect back on my practice as a teacher and teacher trainer. For the first time in my professional career, I encountered socio-cultural theory and the discourse of learner autonomy, which made me realise there were theoretical connections to my practice that I knew nothing of. My practice with my teenage students in the far-north of Cameroon has since May 2007 gained recognition within the learner autonomy community, although I was unaware of the concept at the time of my teaching. Kuchah and Smith (2011) refer to my early practice as a pedagogy of autonomy as distinct from a pedagogy for autonomy, which is a more conscious and deliberately autonomy-oriented pedagogy. Conceptualising my early practice as a pedagogy of autonomy highlights the fact that a teacher's pragmatic response to the particular challenges of their working context might not be explicitly aimed at promoting a theoretical orientation but might be more effective than the practice of teachers whose aim is to promote the same theoretical ideal. It may therefore sometimes be more useful to encourage teachers to theorise from their practice (Kumaravadivelu, 2001; Ramani, 1987) than to expect them to implement some learned theory.

Working with teachers over the years, I have come to realise that my story is not unique. Cameroonian teachers work in very difficult circumstances, some of which are inconceivable to teachers elsewhere. With inadequate initial training, classes of more than 100 pupils from many first language backgrounds, the near absence of prescribed coursebooks, pupils learning in very high temperatures and with only blackboard and chalk, many Cameroonian teachers manage to achieve success through creative solutions that respond to the realities of their working contexts. Working with these teachers, I came to learn that there are many teachers like them, rarely represented in mainstream ELT literature, whose practices are the outcome, not of their training, but of their own interpretations of their previous experiences as learners as well as their pragmatic responses to particular contexts and classroom cultures. Though sometimes pedagogic authorities may not approve of their practices, there is no doubt that their learners are benefiting. My own professional development has been characterised by an interplay of experiential knowledge and theoretical knowledge, lived knowledge and learned knowledge, received wisdom and informed wisdom – with the latter directing the former and the former correcting and reconstructing the latter in significant ways. This professional experience has developed my sense of empathy and respect for teachers in under-resourced contexts and influenced my role as teacher educator and researcher.

Becoming a member of the ELT family

I have already mentioned some people who influenced my professional development. My primary school teacher, Mr Wachong (aka Pa Wachong), sowed in me the first seeds of English language and later the motivation to become an English teacher. His creative approach to language teaching departed significantly from the rote-learning and safe-talk I had been used to and helped me explore language to talk about the things that mattered to me. Pa Wachong was more than a father. He was the only primary school teacher I knew who did not flog his students: he often found time to talk discipline problems through with children. Pa Wachong first made me aware I was good at English and encouraged me to write stories, poems and songs in English. He even bought me a notebook and nicknamed me jotter-boy, a name that stuck for years after I left primary school.

Mr Ayuk (Prof), my high school French teacher, was the strongest influence on my approach to pedagogy. He made me feel valued and empowered, seeing myself not just as a learner but, more importantly, as co-participant in decisions about my own learning. He helped me see how much I was capable of achieving if I worked collaboratively with my peers. It was his inspiration that led us to start an autonomous study group in the university, a group that helped me survive the hostile university environment. Furthermore, it was this experience of being his student that taught me to negotiate learning content and activities with my own students later. My current practice as a university teacher is still heavily focused on developing students' agency and I elicit feedback on my teaching quite regularly from students and discuss openly how I plan to respond to their suggestions.

There are other important significant people who have acted as my mentors, helping forge my professional development through their personal relationships with me. The most important was my late boss in the Ministry of Basic Education, Mr Michael D Nama. In 2001, I travelled to Yaounde from the far-north to seek advice on my challenges and practices from a National Pedagogic Inspector, as I had never had the opportunity to be observed and advised by a pedagogic authority. He was overjoyed that a young man had come from the far-north to talk about how to improve his teaching. This was strange to him because most people from the north would come to lobby to be transferred back to the south. As we talked, he invited me to attend the first annual conference of CAMELTA the following week in Yaounde. After the conference, he invited me to dinner in his home with his regional pedagogic inspectors and welcomed me into the family of what he called 'change makers'. The next academic year, there was a nationwide study of ways to improve bilingual education in primary schools and I was appointed as a 'key teacher' to work with regional inspectors in my region to make suggestions. There followed an invitation to be plenary speaker at the next CAMELTA annual conference. Two years later I was appointed National Pedagogic Inspector at the Ministry of Basic Education to work under him. He continued to encourage me to further my education and was instrumental in my decision to apply for a Hornby scholarship to study in the UK. On my return to Cameroon in 2007, he challenged me to work towards obtaining a PhD. More than being a boss, he was like a father and I always referred to him as Pa. He came to know every member of my family and was instrumental in my marriage. When I moved to the UK for my PhD, we spoke on the phone at least once every fortnight. Each time, he encouraged me to expand my horizons and not to return to Cameroon as he felt I would have a bigger impact on language education in Africa as a researcher in the UK or the US. I was devastated when he died in 2015.

Through him, I learned that being a policymaker granted administrative power but not knowledge of the reality on the ground. It was in helping to empower teachers bring out the best in them that we could identify potential sources of knowledge of the realities of teaching in a country as diverse culturally and in resources as Cameroon. His leadership model was based on teamwork – inspectors and teachers working together to develop ideas to respond to the real needs of our teachers. He dismantled the power differentials characteristic of the hierarchical structures and made our team of inspectors the envy of the Ministry. He contributed massively to my self-image as a competent professional capable of expressing my thoughts and ideas.

Learning from experts

The experiences I have shared here indicate clearly that my contexts of learning and teaching in Cameroon are significantly different from those represented in most mainstream ELT literature – and my professional development has been shaped by the challenges I encountered as teacher and teacher educator. A major interest is how teachers in such contexts navigate their challenges and how teacher education and research might help them deal with these challenges. Two authors have been instrumental in framing my thinking about the importance of understanding the teaching of English in difficult circumstances, what might constitute good practice in such circumstances and how this can be shaped by the contexts and participants in the teaching-learning encounter. Michael West's book *Teaching English in Difficult Circumstance*s (1960) was the first book I read that explicitly focused on contexts like mine and highlighted the inappropriateness of teacher education provision that still characterises it. West argues that:

> Teacher-training colleges tend naturally to advocate and demonstrate the best possible methods … But in training their students to use such methods, they naturally assume the favourable conditions in which such methods are practicable … they should also teach their students what can best be done under unfavourable conditions, in case they find themselves in them or are called upon to inspect or train teachers who work in them.

(West, 1960: 2)

The training described by West here is very reminiscent of my own training, which never referred to the specific contexts we were going to be working in. West's ideas about how language teaching in such contexts can best focus on developing learning and learning-to-learn confirmed my perspectives on teaching in difficult circumstances and has continued into my research and approach to teacher education (Shamim and Kuchah, 2016; Kuchah and Shamim, 2018).

Adrian Holliday's *Appropriate Methodology and Social Context* (1994) also influenced my research focus. He argues that there is an unequal and unfair transfer of ELT 'technology' from BANA institutional contexts to mainstream educational systems in the world without understanding and consideration of the socio-cultural factors affecting learning in these contexts. Holliday suggests that the dominance of BANA integrationist ELT discourses in the training of Teacher Earth Science Education Programme (TESEP) professionals poses a grave danger:

> ... of teachers and curriculum developers, from both the BANA and TESEP groups, naively accepting BANA practice as superior and boldly carrying out what are in fact the ethnocentric norms of particular professional-academic cultures in English language education from one context to another, without proper research into the effect of their actions.

(Holliday, 1994: 102)

My PhD research into context-appropriate pedagogy in primary ELT in Cameroon built on Holliday's ideas and developed a research procedure that took into account teachers' and learners' practices, experiences and perspectives of good and appropriate pedagogic practices in two distinct contexts in Cameroon. My current research mainly focuses on the teaching of English in challenging contexts and aims at replacing the predominantly deficit paradigm that characterises the top-down approach to teacher education and policy dissemination with an enhancement paradigm that draws on teachers' and learners' appraisals of current teaching practices to develop a framework for contextually appropriate pedagogic innovation. I see my responsibility as empowering and supporting the development of these teachers struggling with their day-to-day constraints in creative and innovative ways, which are unfortunately under-represented in mainstream ELT literature.

Key moments of self-discovery and learning

These two key incidents not only have helped me learn, but have resulted in significant developments in my life. Earlier, I mentioned my first CAMELTA conference in 2001. At the conference, I was overwhelmed by the many experienced professionals participating from around the country. One person caught my attention: the Secretary-General of CAMELTA, Dorothy Forbin, had been busy ensuring that this first annual conference was a success. She looked tired so I offered to help, an offer she accepted with much relief. So, I became involved in the organisation, carrying stationery from one room to the other, time-keeping and helping with photocopying and other chores. At the closing ceremony, she asked me to present a participant's impression of the conference and asked a group of colleagues to help me write it. That is how I found myself on stage at a conference I barely knew anything about. On return to the far-north, I was nominated as president of the regional chapter, a position I held for two years, until I replaced Dorothy as Secretary-General in 2005. I eventually became vice president for international outreach in 2009 for four years. During this time, CAMELTA became an International Association of Teachers of English as a Foreign Language (IATEFL) Associate.

My first IATEFL conference was in 2007 in Aberdeen. I participated in the Young Learners and Teenagers (YLT) Special Interest Group (SIG) showcase event. There, I listened to a teacher from Uganda talk about a British Council toolkit produced in West Africa but resisted by teachers in Uganda. In discussing why an apparently rich document was not being used by teachers, I described how the document was conceived and pointed to problems with contributions in the toolkit about teaching large classes written by British Council teachers with no experience of teaching large classes themselves, so the document was not a good investment of British Council money. The SIG co-ordinator Wendy Arnold later invited me to join the YLT SIG committee as events co-ordinator. This was the start of my leadership path in IATEFL. Four years later I became outreach co-ordinator and later co-editor for the Research SIG and member of the Associates Committee, and was nominated for and voted into the role of IATEFL vice president!

Pulling my story together

The experiences and incidents I have presented seem to confirm that traditional approaches to teacher education that focus on theories of language and language learning, and provide limited practicum experiences for trainees to apply these theories, do not take into account the complex network of relationships necessary to support teachers through their profession. It might be worth drawing more from teachers' own experiences of learning to see which teachers impacted their lives positively and what they may learn from their own teachers. Learning-to-learn how to teach should be as important for teacher education as learning-to-learn is for language learning. Clearly, the art of teaching continues to be learned long after trainees have completed their training, so helping teachers respond creatively to contextual factors by working in partnership with their learners and taking risks together is a possible way of transforming classrooms into learning communities where the responsibility for teaching and learning is shared. 'Technical' knowledge of the profession is not enough; attention needs to be paid to relationship-building and creativity in teacher education programmes so that teachers are supported not only to be professionals but also to be humans conscious of their role in building other human beings – their students. Professional communities are also vital in helping teachers grow, and studying how these work could be part of the curriculum for initial teacher education. I have recently been exploring how teacher associations (TA) could play a vital role in generating, refining and disseminating good practice from the bottom up. I became a teacher trainer with very little experience of teaching, and later became a National Pedagogic Inspector without ever having been observed by an inspector myself. Throughout my career as a teacher educator in Cameroon, my only source of professional development was through the TA. That is why I have become interested in how TAs can both provide the enabling environment for teachers' personal and professional development and engage in collaborative research projects that generate local knowledge of contextually appropriate practice. I believe that, while professional development remains a personal matter, the driving force behind it is often a collective endeavour with people who share the same experiences and can motivate each other to grow to their individual full potential.

References

Chick, K (1996) 'Safe-talk: Collusion in apartheid education', in Coleman, H (ed) *Society and the Language Classroom*. Cambridge: Cambridge University Press, 21–39.

Ethnologue (2009) *Ethnologue: Languages of the world*. SIL: Dallas: Texas.

Holliday, A (1994) *Appropriate Methodology and Social Context*. Cambridge: Cambridge University Press.

Kuchah, K (2008) 'Developing as a professional in Cameroon: challenges and visions', in Garton, S and Richards, K (eds) *Professional Encounters in TESOL: Discourses of Teachers in Teaching*. New York: Palgrave Macmillan, 203–217.

Kuchah, K and Shamim, F (eds) (2018) *International Perspectives on Teaching English in Difficult Circumstances: Contexts, Challenges and Possibilities*. Basingstoke: Palgrave Macmillan.

Kuchah, K and Smith, RC (2011) Pedagogy of autonomy for difficult circumstances: From practice to principles. *Innovation in Language Learning and Teaching* 5(2): 119–140.

Ngwaru, JM and Opoku-Amankwa, K (2010) Home and school literacy practices in Africa: listening to inner voices. *Language and Education* 24/4: 295–307.

Ramani, E (1987) Theorizing from the classroom. *ELT Journal* 41/1: 3–11.

Shamim, F and Kuchah, K (2016) 'Teaching large classes in difficult circumstances', in Hall, G (ed) *The Routledge Handbook of English Language Teaching*. New York/London: Routledge, 527–541.

West, M (1960) *Teaching English in Difficult Circumstances: Teaching English as a Foreign Language with Notes in the Technique of Textbook Construction*. London: Longmans, Green.

For CPD activities, visit e-file link: www.teachingenglish.org.uk/sites/teacheng/files/e-file.pdf

9

Growing up

Péter Medgyes

Introduction

I was born on 6 August 1945, the day when the nuclear bomb was dropped on Hiroshima, Japan. Year after year, my birthday is made miserable by some grim reference in the morning papers to the calamity. 'How will I be able to compensate for my unlucky date of birth when I grow up?' I asked myself as a child.

By the time I reached nursery school age, communists had seized power in Hungary, nationalised 'bourgeois' property and banned all foreign languages other than Russian. Nevertheless, I was fortunate enough to attend a private kindergarten run by Aunt Ida, where the language of instruction was half-Hungarian, half-English. It boggles the mind how she managed to stay private and, on top of that, to teach English, the language of 'imperialists'. Be that as it may, it was there that I made my first acquaintance with Humpty Dumpty and others in the treasure trove of English nursery rhymes.

I never learned English at school. Instead, my parents hired private English teachers for their two sons. The one I recall most distinctly was Privatdozent Dr Koncz, who had lost his university job by being stigmatised as a relic of the old regime. He was a tall, bespectacled man in his fifties. He had a very low opinion of English, regarding it as an *ersatz* language, a primitive variety of German. When I rang the doorbell, his wife would come and open the door. As I sat down, I heard Dr Koncz cleaning his teeth and then gargling in the adjacent bathroom. A minute later he would join me, always wearing the same old tie and grey cardigan. He would greet me with a firm handshake and a stern 'How do you do?' Learning English with him was not much fun; his facial muscles would tighten whenever he caught me not knowing something I was supposed to have learned. The coursebook we used was in sharp contrast to his gloomy character: Eckersley's four-volume *Essential English for Foreign Students* (Eckersley, 1938–42) was full of jokes and light-hearted anecdotes. With hindsight, I owe Dr Koncz a great deal of gratitude for the rigour and consistency with which he would inflict the grammar-translation method on me.

Why English? I often wondered. After all, we were a family rooted in and surrounded by German language and culture. My grandmother's mother tongue was German and she never learned to speak proper Hungarian. (Ironically, I could not learn German *von Haus aus* as she was stone-deaf.) My father, too, spent many an hour improving his broken command of German. I found a German vocabulary book even by his deathbed, as if this were his umbilical cord to life. And yet, my parents insisted that their two sons learn English before German, as England was their ideal of liberty and prosperity, and they were convinced that English was to become the language of the future. Hence, I took my English lessons for granted. I must have been around ten years old when my elder brother decided to give up his piano lessons. I immediately wanted to follow suit whereupon my mother said, 'All right, but only if you promise never to quit English.' That was a deal.

Up to the regime change in 1989, learning Russian was compulsory for everyone between the ages of 10 and 18, and yet a mere 1.2 per cent of the Hungarian population claimed to speak it to any level. By the time I had reached secondary school, 'Western' languages were gradually allowed back into the curriculum, so I could have chosen German, French or Italian as a second foreign language, but my parents sent me to a class that specialised in Latin and Russian. Latin, because my father belonged to a generation capable of reeling off the long list of Latin prepositions backwards and forwards, and Russian because as a realist he knew that a good command of Russian was an asset in communist Hungary. Personally, I loved Russian, thanks to our young teacher, Mrs Ganczer, who taught us to communicate in Russian at a time when communicative language teaching was still waiting to be invented.

University years

Upon graduation from secondary school, I decided to study English and Russian at Eötvös Loránd University in Budapest. This made my mother cry, 'You don't want to become the slave of the nation, do you?', implying that teaching was (and still is) one of the worst-paid professions in Hungary. I tried in vain to assure her that teaching was the last thing on my mind; my lofty goal was to become a 'man of letters' – whatever that meant.

It was at university that I met my first native English speaker in the flesh. An elderly language instructor recruited by the British Council, Miss Galton began her first tutorial by asking us which English-language newspapers we were in the habit of reading. When our group replied in chorus that it was the *Morning Star*, the daily of the British Communist Party (and the only English-language paper available on the news-stands), she was flabbergasted – and left Hungary after the first term. Her successors were far more open-minded and enjoyed the privilege of being pampered by the affection and, quite often, adulation that Hungarians felt was due to samples of the rare species of native-speakers.

Meanwhile, I had a pen-pal from Ireland, who kindly invited me to Dublin. Waving the official translation of the invitation letter, I went to the district military headquarters, as one had to in those days, to apply for permission to make the trip. Taking a quick glance at the letter, the officer said, 'You wanna go to Dublin, eh? And you know where you gonna go? F***ing nowhere.' So I stayed at home.

Foreign-language majors were obliged to do their school practice in the final year of their studies. Internship included a one-month practice period in a provincial town. I had to teach two groups of secondary school students, the vast majority of whom were girls, under the supervision of their regular teacher, Aunt Aliz. While the students' eyes were glued on me, a strapping young man, Aunt Aliz would doze off in the back of the classroom as soon as I started the lesson, only to wake up for the bell. 'Splendid!' she said. 'You're a born teacher, Péter.' Since the second part of my teaching practice at Radnóti School in Budapest turned out to be just as exhilarating, my fate was sealed. After graduation I was offered as many as seven jobs. This had much less to do with my excellence than with the fact that I happened to be a male in an overwhelmingly female profession, and that English from the late 1960s was more and more in demand. I accepted the job offer at Radnóti School.

Being a school teacher

Initially, I was teaching from the one and only mandatory coursebook, written by Hungarian authors – and I found it deadly boring. A couple of years later, I supplemented the Hungarian book with all kinds of British material written by Candlin, Broughton, Alexander, O'Neill, Abbs and Freebairn, and many others. My pupils thoroughly enjoyed these books, thanks to the multiple pirate copies run off on their parents' office photocopiers.

One day I was summoned by my school principal, Sándor Lukács. He said that my illegal use of foreign books had been brought to the attention of authorities in the Ministry of Education. My heart sank. Then he asked, 'Do you find those British books any better than the Hungarian ones?' I stammered that I did. 'Well, you're the professional, Péter,' Lukács said. 'It's *your* responsibility to decide what's best for your students.' 'But ... but what about the Ministry?' I asked. 'That's *my* responsibility. I'll deal with it if necessary,' he answered. Thus, unruffled under his protective wings, I chucked out the Hungarian books altogether and used the British materials only. From then on, I appreciated every minute of my professional freedom – and simultaneously carried the burden of responsibility this freedom entailed.

By the time I began my teaching career, the grammar-translation method had fallen from favour in methodology books, even though it was widely adopted by classroom teachers (and still is, by the way). Jumping on the bandwagon, I mixed elements from both the direct method and the audio-lingual method. Thus, I would never open my mouth in Hungarian and would go to great lengths to explain the meaning of even the most abstract words through demonstration. Needless to say, this often led to misunderstanding. For example, as I was introducing the word 'light', I pointed to the ceiling light, which many students got wrong, thinking that what I actually meant was the ceiling itself.

At the same time, I was hooked on the four-step drill: stimulus → response → reinforcement → second response. I even persuaded the principal to get a cutting-edge language lab installed in our school. It was a love–hate relationship: I loved the lab, while my students hated it because they were forced to sit in solitary cubicles and 'drill and kill' on the open-reel tape recorder for hours on end. And yet, they passed their exams with flying colours and, as an added value, I personally managed to automatise even the most difficult grammar structures through doing the drills together with the group. It was much later that I realised that every method has its pros and cons, but what really matters is not the method being applied but the teacher's enthusiasm and professionalism.

I had been a teacher for four years before I visited an English-speaking country for the first time in my life. That British Council summer course for teachers of English in Newcastle was an unforgettable experience. I was suddenly faced with the harsh reality that my listening skills left a lot to be desired; no wonder, since radio broadcasts in English were jammed in Hungary until the 1980s. It was especially hard for me to understand an accent as thick as Geordie, spoken in the north-east of England. On my first day, I went for a walk in the city centre and lost my way. When I asked a local to show me the way back to the university campus, I could not make head or tail of his explanation. After a couple of unsuccessful attempts, the guy just shrugged his shoulders and went on his way. A deadly experience!

I was in my late twenties when I was commissioned to write my first English coursebook, which was followed by several others designed for both primary and secondary students. To be fair, my work was not hindered by political dictates. However, although I was never forced to include 'politically correct' content, I instinctively knew what *not* to include. The most serious objection of a political nature was raised by an editor who insisted that I delete the word 'godfather' from a text because of its 'religious connotations'. More devastating was a comment that came from a native English-speaking reader: 'The manuscript is perfect as it is, apart from the fact that it smacks of foreign authorship from the first letter to the last.' So much for my writing skills ...

My most successful book, *Linda and the Greenies* (Medgyes, 1984), was written for eight- to ten-year-olds. The story is about a teenage girl who is kidnapped by cute little monsters living in the London sewage system to teach them English. I drew the inspiration from a book series, *Kaleidoscope*, written by Andrew Wright (1976). In fact, it was more than inspiration – I borrowed a lot of nursery rhymes, songs, tongue-twisters and riddles from Andrew's brilliant work. When *Linda and the Greenies* came out with an accompanying set of six cassettes, a colleague I had never met before phoned to ask me whether I would be kind enough to copy the cassettes for him. I was about to slam down the receiver, but then I realised that I was no better than him when it came to illegal copying. So I reluctantly agreed to do it.

A master pirate himself, György Horlai was the most generous colleague I had ever met. In possession of a rich collection of English audio-materials that were unavailable in Hungary, he would copy anything for any colleague on his most up-to-date, open-reel tape recorders. However, personally I am far more grateful to him for his sense of judgement and justice. When I showed him the first draft of an article in which I dressed down the communicative approach, he just said: 'It's easier to destroy than to build something, huh?' In shame, I went home and set about pointing out the positive aspects of the communicative approach, too. Balance redressed.

Even though Hungary became the 'happiest barracks' in the Soviet bloc in the 1980s, English teachers were still considered a suspicious lot. Typically, when I applied to the Ministry of Education with the idea of establishing an English teachers' association, I was rejected out of hand. It took me a while to realise that my case was considerably weakened by the unfortunate choice of the acronym ATAK, which was the Hungarian acronym of English Teachers' Association. It was only after the regime change in 1989 that we were given the green light to found IATEFL-Hungary. In our effort to establish the Hungarian branch of the British-based association, we were given tremendous encouragement and support from Alan Maley, who at the time was president of the mother institution.

Being a university lecturer

To return to the early 1980s. After having taught at Radnóti School for 15 years as a teacher, I could not resist the invitation to join the English department of my *alma mater* as a teacher trainer. I soon discovered, however, that the department was as conservative professionally as it was liberal politically. In the eyes of my colleagues, the phrase 'teacher education' was anathema. I shall never forget when a highly respected professor of literature came up to me after a frustrating staff meeting and said: 'You're right, Péter. There's no point in teaching methodology in just one course.' As I beamed, he added, 'So I'd bring down the number of courses to zero.' The mantra in the English department was that good teachers are born and not trained, and greenhorns pick up the tricks of trade as they go along in the classroom. Sadly, many scholars query the justification for teacher education even in our day.

Nevertheless, the years I spent in the English department were rewarding in the sense that I had far more time to engage in research activities than when I was a school teacher. The only snag was that, whereas our library was quite well stocked with novels, poetry anthologies and theoretical books on literature and linguistics, not a single book on methodology or applied linguistics could be found on the shelves. The first book I bought at my own expense was Corder's *Introducing Applied Linguistics* (1973) and indeed it was a fine introduction to what applied linguistics was all about. I assiduously typed out more than two hundred extracts from the book on index cards, and I resorted to the same painstaking procedure with all the books I could lay my hands on in subsequent years. I still cherish these cards even though many of the ideas put forward may since have lost their freshness. In addition to Corder, the authors from whom I learned most were Krashen (1982), Stern (1983), Stevick (1990) and Widdowson (1978).

However, even the best failed to show me the bridge that would connect theoretical arguments to what was going on at the chalk-face. Although they succeeded in sparking my research interests and helped me absorb the academic jargon expected of someone planning to write a doctoral dissertation, I could not see the relevance of theory for the classroom teacher. Frankly, I still can't. In my daily work as a teacher trainer, I found the ideas and techniques generated by Maley and Duff (1978), Mortimer (1980), Rinvolucri (1984) and Wright (1976) far more relevant and stimulating.

Even though I kept complaining about the glaring deficiencies in my English-language competence (and in those of my fellow non-natives), I began to realise that this did not mean we were inferior as teachers. 'How come? What gives us a competitive edge to offset our linguistic handicap?' I asked myself. 'Surely, this is only possible if we have certain attributes that native colleagues are lacking. OK, but what exactly are they?' Seeking the answers to my questions, I browsed the shelves of our growing library but was unable to find a single reference to this issue.

'If not in Budapest, then in Los Angeles,' I thought to myself after receiving a Fulbright research grant for an academic year. To my astonishment, however, nor did the huge library of the University of Southern California (USC) contain anything worthwhile on the topic. 'Wow, but then this must be *terra incognita!*' I rejoiced. 'It cries out for exploring!' With the generous support of the renowned applied linguist, Robert B Kaplan, the director of the American Language Institute at USC, I designed a questionnaire and, in collaboration with Thea Reves from Israel, circulated it among teachers, both natives and non-natives. I am proud to say that the questionnaire was filled in by a total of 325 respondents, which was quite a feat at a time when only snail-mail was available! I decided to process the data and write a book on the native/non-native conundrum as soon as I was back home again.

Easier said than done! By the time I returned to Hungary in 1989, communism was all but dead, and the Russian language ceased to be the mandatory foreign language in school education, whereupon thousands of parents demanded that their children study English or German instead of Russian. As there was an acute shortage of qualified teachers to teach these languages, a quick fix had to be found. One day, I was called by the Minister of Education to conceive and implement a retraining programme for Russian teachers and, simultaneously, launch a new fast-track pre-service training programme at colleges and universities. With this job completed, I was appointed as the founding director of the Centre for English Teacher Training (CETT) at Eötvös Loránd University. Our programme differed from traditional pre-service programmes not only in duration (three years instead of five), but also in that methodology and teaching practice were granted a much larger place in the curriculum. But all of this left me no time to write that book!

Once the pioneering period was over, I carved out some time from my daily schedule to continue my investigation into the native/non-native issue. A ten-week-long scholarship at Lancaster University enabled me to complete a book-length manuscript, which I boldly submitted to one of the largest British publishing houses – and was turned down point-blank. I was devastated. Hearing about my aborted attempt, Susan Holden, who was the general editor and publisher at Macmillan, encouraged me to send her the manuscript. And, amazingly, the book was published a few months later and won the Duke of Edinburgh Book Prize the year after! If it had not been for Susan's support, *The Non-Native Teacher* (1994) might never have seen the light of day. (Incidentally, she helped bring out the second as well as the third edition of the book by two different publishers.) I am glad to say that since the first edition of the book, hundreds of papers and around a dozen books have been published on the subject.

Detours

In the 1990s, my professional routine was interrupted by two consecutive job offers that I could not reasonably refuse. First, I was appointed vice-president of my university and subsequently deputy-state secretary in the Ministry of Education; on both occasions I was mainly responsible for international affairs. Upon returning to CETT a few years later, I was saddened to see that, despite the remarkable achievements and international recognition the fast-track programme had achieved, it was being brought to an end. Once the problem of teacher shortage had eased, it was no longer thought to be vital to keep the programme alive.

Around the turn of the millennium, I was increasingly haunted by reminiscences of the years I had spent as a school teacher. With a gap of nearly 20 years, what if I asked to teach a group of 15-year-olds in the same school where I started my career? I wondered. With all the experience I have accumulated over the years, would I be able to cope with teenagers better than when I was a fledgling teacher? To cut a long story short, I did a stint of two years in the classroom, and although I occasionally had a hard time (especially when it came to maintaining discipline), it was a most rewarding experience. Once a teacher, forever a teacher.

I then had another chance to work in the Ministry of Education. In addition to my previous functions, my second term included implementing projects with the aim of rendering foreign language education more effective in Hungary. I successfully put on track a large-scale programme called World – Language, whose most essential component was the introduction of the Year of Intensive Language Learning (YILL). This programme made it possible for 15-year-olds to spend a full school year focusing exclusively on foreign language study; needless to say, the overwhelming majority opted for English. I am glad to say that YILL is still up and running, and in fact has since widened its scope.

After a couple of years in the Ministry, I had the opportunity to try my hand at diplomacy, too. As Ambassador of Hungary in Damascus, on one occasion I volunteered to give a talk on teacher education to Syrian language teachers at their annual national conference. Although the audience politely applauded at the end of my presentation, I could not help feeling that I did not fit in: one cannot wear two hats at the same time.

When my term of office in Syria was over, I sneaked back to the university, where I felt comfortably on home turf again. A few years later, since age caught up with me, I retired. But I cannot stop teaching. For my own pleasure – and hopefully, for my students' pleasure too.

Yes, I love teaching, but I am also fond of doing research and presenting at conferences at home and abroad. In addition, I am a grapho-maniac with a crop of 40 books and some 200 papers to my name. But what I love first and foremost is the English language. Whenever I decide to brush up my Russian, French or German, by default I reach out for an English newspaper, turn on an English television channel or look up a new word in the dictionary. For me, English is far more than a means of earning a living or a tool of communication – it is my most loyal companion. For better or for worse, I am desperately in love with it.

The lessons I have learned

As I was thinking about how to conclude this brief *tour de force*, a number of things came to my mind. Let me single out a few, which encapsulate the lessons I have drawn from my lengthy career as a teacher and teacher trainer, however unorthodox some of the ideas may appear to be. I suggest you give some thought to each of them, and then choose the ones you agree with. Should you disagree with any of them, all the better.

- In many countries, teachers are as poorly paid as we in Hungary are – or perhaps even worse. Decide to become a teacher only if you are aware that becoming a millionaire is just wishful thinking.

- Trust yourself! How else can you expect your students to put their faith in you?

- Enjoy every (other) minute of what you are doing in the classroom! Bored teachers generate bored students.

- Your own needs come first; your students' needs come second! This may sound like an egocentric, teacher-centred attitude, but it is not. Your wellbeing is a necessary, albeit not sufficient, condition for your students to feel contented, too.

- There is no such thing as the best method. It all depends on whatever suits you and your students.

- Every teacher needs to have a rest. The summer break being too short to replenish, go and find a non-teaching job after X number of years. If possible, go on (paid) sabbatical.

- Should you feel completely burnt out, quit teaching. Better for you, better for your students. Hopefully, you will find your way back to the classroom one day.

- Do not believe that academics are worth more than you are. Do not listen to the 'professional' advice of those who have never worked at the chalk-face full-time.

- A high level of language competence is more important than anything else; it is a make-or-break requirement. Therefore, non-native English teachers should go out of their way to improve their command of English.

References

Corder, SP (1973) *Introducing Applied Linguistics*. Harmondsworth: Penguin Education.

Eckersley, CE (1938–42) *Essential English, Books 1–4*. London: Longman.

Krashen, SD (1982) *Principles and Practice in Second Language Acquisition*. Oxford: Pergamon Press.

Maley, A and Duff, A (1978) *Variations on a Theme*. Cambridge: Cambridge University Press.

Medgyes, P (1984) *Linda and the Greenies*. Budapest: Tankönyvkiadó [Textbook Publishing].

Medgyes, P (1994) *The Non-Native Teacher*. Basingstoke: Macmillan Publishers.

Mortimer, C (1980) *Dramatic Monologues for Listening Comprehension*. Cambridge: Cambridge University Press.

Rinvolucri, M (1984) *Grammar Games*. Cambridge: Cambridge University Press.

Stern, HH (1983) *Fundamental Concepts of Language Teaching*. Oxford: Oxford University Press.

Stevick, EW (1990) *Humanism in Language Teaching*. Oxford: Oxford University Press.

Widdowson, HG (1978) *Teaching Language as Communication*. Oxford: Oxford University Press.

Wright, A (1976) *Kaleidoscope*. London and Basingstoke: University of York/ Macmillan Education.

For CPD activities, visit e-file link: www.teachingenglish.org.uk/sites/teacheng/files/e-file.pdf

10

Learning from teaching: A life in ELT

Freda Mishan

Earliest experiences of language learning and education that have affected my current views and practices

When I was aged around eight, a French *assistante* came to our primary school and taught us some children's songs. I can still sing *Il était un petit navire* to this day. I went on to read French at university and became fluent in the language during my undergraduate year abroad. Early experiences of second language learning like this extend our conceptual awareness at the initial stages of our cognitive development, opening us up to further language learning.

When we were children, my mother (whose first language was Yiddish) always referred to our backside as our *tushi* (the diminutive of the Yiddish *tokhes*), when our baby sister whinged she was referred to as a *kvetch* (a person who always complains) and when we sneezed my mother would say *gesundheit* (good health). I never questioned the use of these and other Yiddish words, they were just part of my 'family lexicon' and, most importantly, I understood that there were other, English words for them too.

Exposure to multiple languages early on is also fundamental to our lifelong attitude to languages and to language learning. There are proficiency implications too: learners who start learning an L2 in childhood in 'naturalistic' (as distinct from instructed) settings tend to become more proficient than those commencing learning later (Ellis, 2008; Singleton, 1989).

Influences arising from places/institutions in which I have lived and worked

I followed the well-trodden trajectory of many English as a foreign language (EFL) teachers in the 1980s and 1990s: teaching EFL first in Italy, then in the UK for a short time, followed by some years in Israel and, once I had satisfied my wanderlust, finally settling in Ireland.

In my first experience teaching English in Italy, I would say I learned far more about language learning than about teaching. Teaching via the notorious Inlingua method was mindless at best, but the classroom proved the starting point for my own acquisition of Italian, as I scribbled down the students' whispered translations ('table – *tavola*', etc.). I followed this up by quickly eschewing the company of fellow ex-pats, making friends in the small Italian town in which I had landed, and discovering my ability as a cultural 'chameleon' that has been a characteristic ever since. Years later, reading about Dörnyei and Ushioda's concept of the L2 self (2009), I was to realise that the experience of 'metamorphising' into a speaker of the L2 is quite a normal part of language learning. My self-imposed, 'total immersion' experience meant that at the end of my four years there, I had become almost 'more Italian than the Italians' linguistically and culturally.

Neither did I learn much, directly, about teaching English in Israel, where teaching English for academic purposes at Ben Gurion University was basically providing grinds for students to pass their English examinations (at the time, English was mandatory in order to gain an undergraduate degree). To say that the motivation for these students was 'extrinsic' is an understatement; their sole focus was to pass the English examinations by any means possible. It gave me, however, my first opportunity for materials writing, which was to prove the direction I would take in my research and teaching some years later. Intermediate Experimental Readings in English for Science and Technology (INTEREST) was a compilation of practice examinations – comprehension questions on texts that were, furthermore, authentic and also prefigured my passion for authenticity in my later research and teaching.

What I learned about teaching from my experience in Israel was, as in Italy, less from my actual teaching experience than from my learning of the language. Prior to getting the teaching job, I had taken an *ulpan*, a Hebrew language course, which took place on a kibbutz, where students worked a half-day as payment for the course. It was not until some years later, when I studied English teaching formally, that I realised our *ulpan* teacher had been very in touch with teaching approaches, using a communicative approach that had us working in groups and creating projects, with a 'focus on form' only for the absolute fundamentals of the language, such as learning the alphabet, as Hebrew uses a different writing system. Shoshana's use of realia has remained the practice I offer to students to this day. One morning, she brought in a selection of spices that we named (and tasted!) – particularly memorable as the class started at 7 a.m., hardly a time one's palate is ready for turmeric, pepper or cumin.

My first two teaching situations abroad were therefore lessons in, on the downside, how not to teach language, but more positively, how to learn it. An interesting feature of my 'total immersion' language learning was experiencing what Barber (1980) and later Krashen called 'the din in the head' (1983), and as with communicativeness, experienced long before I was able to put a name to it. 'The din in the head' describes the 'involuntary mental rehearsal' of a language being learned, which occurs after we have had extensive comprehensible input in it. Dins of Italian, and later Hebrew, in my head, became a normal, if sometimes disconcerting, part of my language learning, in particular when these were internal 'conversations' that I didn't fully understand!

Taken together, these experiences helped me realise that the experience of living and working in a different culture, learning and speaking a different language from one's L1, is essential to become an effective and empathetic language teacher; it is one that needs to be lived and cannot be formally 'taught'.

Key people who have left an enduring mark on my life, beliefs and practices

The first language practitioner/writer to really grab my attention was NS Prabhu, via his seminal work, *Second Language Pedagogy* (1987). This book charted the piloting of a prototype for task-based learning (TBL), later task-based language teaching (TBLT). The methodology was intrinsically communicative at a time when communicative language teaching was in its infancy and still hidebound by dogma and a fixed repertoire of techniques. Prabhu's approach was broader and more far-sighted: 'The development of competence in a second language requires [...] the creation of conditions in which learners engage in an effort to cope with communication' (1987: 1) and further, 'language ability develops in direct relation to communicational effort' (*ibid.*: 5). The approach was innovative and rooted in 'real life', in stark contrast to the wooden characters and contrived situations found in ELT books of the time. This attraction to the 'authentic' set me on the route towards 'authenticity', which was to become a *leitmotif* of my subsequent research and teaching.

My second 'key influence' was a result of attending my first Materials Development Association (MATSDA) workshop in Dublin in the early 1990s: my introduction to Brian Tomlinson. It would be true to say that his has been the greatest influence on the last 25 years of my professional life. Tomlinson's work helped me crystallise my intuitions about language learning and teaching: that language learning is about affective and intellectual engagement, creativity and fun, that it is one of the most natural, 'authentic' activities human beings can engage in.

Key ideas I have encountered that have helped form or change my beliefs and practices

I quickly realised from my earliest experience of teaching, that teaching and learning do not constitute a 'cause and effect' process. Learners might acquire a language item taught in class; they might learn it partially, incorrectly, temporarily or not at all. Pienemann's teachability hypothesis (1984), was the first 'key idea' I encountered after some years of teaching, and crystallised these intuitions and rationalised why this was so. Learning, it transpired, was to do with learner readiness. As I learned theories about motivation (see below), to these I added willingness and openness, and thanks to the likes of Tomlinson, 'perceived need'.

Another key idea that was the springboard for my teaching and research derives from a quote from Pit Corder, also focusing on motivation just referenced above: 'Given motivation, it is inevitable that a human being will learn a second language if he is exposed to the language data' (Corder, 1974: 22). This quote encapsulates the two vital elements of language learning, *motivation* and *input*. How to marry the two proved the catalyst for my research into language learning and teaching. Exploration of motivation, 'one of the most elusive concepts in the whole of the social sciences' (Dörnyei, 2001: 2), reveals its complex, multi-faceted nature. In motivation, there is a complementary interplay between the affective and cognitive domains that translates as principles for language teaching and teaching materials – the importance of engaging both affect and cognition in language-learning activities and materials. But most crucially perhaps, motivation is identified as individual and internal. Dörnyei (1998) characterises it as a factor of such elements as personality, behaviour, thoughts, beliefs and emotions, inner-force/power and mental energy. Relating this to language *learning*, this suggests that, as it is an internal process, teachers cannot directly 'motivate' their students – as I tell my students, 'motivate is not a transitive verb'! – they can only offer *opportunities* for motivation, in the form of experiences and interactions in the L2, as well, of course, as *materials*, inputted 'language data' (the second part of Pit Corder's quote), designed to best attract, interest, intrigue and engage.

Input, in fact, may have another role, however: 'input does not only input language, it releases it' (Tomalin, 2000). One issue with the comprehensible-input hypothesis (more of which below) is that it conceives input narrowly as potential 'intake' (i.e. for acquisition), ignoring its potential for stimulating output – which is actually far greater. Minimal language input – a cartoon, a headline, a 'meme', a tweet, a chance remark from a famous personality – can promote enormous discussion (as we know from incessant social media storms). Transferred to the language classroom, we can see that input carefully selected for its impact will stimulate response, manifested as language output, i.e. it will 'release language', and is thus potentially far more powerful for language learning.

The importance of capturing *response* to language input was another influence of Tomlinson's; response has long been central to his frameworks for language learning tasks. Garnering the learner's instantaneous response to (oral, written or visual) input is a one-off opportunity for the teacher to exploit the affective and/or intellectual punch of input, pushing him or her to express it via language (Prabhu's 'communicational effort'). The importance Tomlinson and others attached to response as a stimulus for language learning has been vindicated in the digital age, as response has become a key signifier in social media, often expressed via emoticons representing a range of emotions from love to anger, laughter to sorrow. The importance of response in language learning loops back to motivation, which, as discussed earlier, is a factor of interlinked affective and cognitive domains, so it would seem critical to stimulate response in order to ignite this motivational spark as early as possible in any given language learning situation. Once engaged thus, there is a higher disposition to learning (resisting the temptation to refer to one of the clichés of ELT – 'the affective filter' – more of which below).

As noted above, encounters with the work of the likes of Prabhu and Tomlinson convinced me that the human, authentic act of learning a language needed to be matched with authenticity in teaching it. Exploring this in my doctoral research, I found many allies, most unexpectedly perhaps, a 19th-century phonetician named Henry Sweet. Reading Sweet's *The Practical Study of Languages*, first published in 1900, was like recognising a long-lost friend: 'the great advantage of natural idiomatic texts [...] is that they do justice to every feature of the language' (Sweet, 1900: 178) and 'it is only in the connected texts that the language itself can be given with each word a natural and adequate context' (*ibid.*: 164).

Establishing the credentials for authentic texts for language learning was not enough, of course, without a pedagogical framework for using them; namely, authenticity of *task* to endorse authenticity of *text*. Again, for this I was able to look at inspiring theoretical precedents, most notably, perhaps, in the work of Henry Widdowson (1998) and Leo van Lier (1996), which helped me towards an understanding of authenticity as acts of 'authentication' by the task enactors.

Other inspiration came from the work of Swales, in genre analysis, providing the concept of 'communicative purpose', which proved the spark for my 'principles for task authenticity', central to which is: 'In order for tasks to be authentic, they should be designed to reflect the original communicative purpose of the text on which they are based'. Although I have tweaked them recently (Mishan, 2017), I stand by these principles nearly 20 years on and have been gratified to see students adopting them in their own materials design to this day.

Taking into account that there are so many variables influencing learning (of which the above are just a few) has led me to a belief (or perhaps agnosticism) that has influenced my work as teacher trainer as well as language teacher: I don't believe in teaching – only learning.

Important publications in my personal and professional development

I have described above how NS Prabhu's *Second Language Pedagogy* (1987) alerted me to the importance of authenticity in language learning and of task as a pedagogical paradigm.

Another book that 'spoke to me', in its unorthodox and down-to-earth approach to language learning, was Guy Cook's *Language Play, Language Learning* (2000). How could play, songs and games *not* be important for L2 learning when they were so intrinsic a part of L1 learning?

Reading Henry Sweet's *The Practical Study of Languages* (1900) just mentioned above, as well as confirming my intuitions about authentic language and learning, was also humbling. It helped me recognise the cyclical nature of approaches to language teaching; we are only ever reinventing the wheel when it comes to language teaching methodologies – as reading Michel de Montaigne's description of his father's communicative approach to teaching him Latin in 16th-century France brings home to us.

The influence of Tomlinson's work on my professional development has been such that it is hard to single out one of his many publications. Nevertheless, I think that his *Materials Development in Language Teaching* (1998) is seminal, as the book that in many ways 'launched' materials development as a field in its own right, and included much-cited chapters by some of the field's key actors including Rod Bolitho, Andrew Littlewood, Roger Gower, Rod Ellis and Alan Maley.

My personal 'go to' list would not be complete without reference to the work of David Crystal. The linguist who made linguistics palatable is one of the most prolific writers in the field; he has remained up to date and relevant and his positive disposition towards language change is refreshing. His *Cambridge Encyclopaedia of the English Language* (2019, third edition) is never far from hand when I am researching, but I have also enjoyed his more 'lay' publications, his autobiography *Just a Phrase I am Going Through* (2009a) and ones exploring technological impacts on language change such as *Language and the Internet* (2002, 2006) and *Txting the gr8 db8* (2009b).

Critical incidents/epiphanies in life and work that have given me new insights

As mentioned earlier, my first language teaching experience came in Italy, where I taught at an Inlingua school using the Inlingua method in which I had received training. This method used a distinctly linear approach: tenses were taught in sequence – the present tense, the future, the past, the present perfect and so on – with a sprinkling of other grammar items thrown in (such as 'some' and 'any'). Fairly early on, I remember coming into a class on a Monday morning and, as is quite natural, asking the students 'did you have a nice weekend?' As I said this, I realised, too late, that *we had not studied the past tense!* I think I expected, at the very least, for smoke to come out of their ears as they went into overdrive trying to comprehend this as-yet unencountered language. But instead, of course, they just replied variously with 'Yes, I went to the cinema' or 'Yes, I go to the house of my grandmother' and the like. A lucky escape indeed! It was my first inkling that language learners are not a tabula rasa, and that 'teaching' and 'learning' are not a cause-and-effect process (probably just as well given my early inexperience!).

Themes emerging from my chapter

The overarching theme that best captures the ideas around teaching in this chapter is *a critical approach to ELT orthodoxy*.

One characteristic of our profession is its addiction to acronyms – from TEFL to TESOL, ESOL to ELF, not to mention those spawned by technology, CALL, TELL, MALL and so on, in an endless proliferation. As an aside, I wonder what this says about our profession – perhaps, that, as purveyors of language, we are permitted to 'invent' it? On top of this, we have the irresistible siren call of the ELT jargon soundbite – affective filter, comprehensible input, i+1, teachable moment, communicative – which (novice) teachers latch onto like lifelines, while the research underpinning them gets progressively oversimplified/misinterpreted in a sort of Chinese whispers effect.

Then we have the tyranny of 'the four skills'. The question 'why four?' has often been asked and indeed, as far back as the 1990s, Claire Kramsch argued for the addition of a fifth – 'culture' (Kramsch, 1993). The skills, particularly listening and reading, overlap with the senses of course, which begs the question, so what about other senses, such as smell, taste … ? Once again, this question has already been asked, and neurolinguistic programming (NLP, developed by Bandler and Grinder, 1979) brought these into play in language learning, although NLP has remained sidelined as a quirky 'alternative' approach. Teacher education, meanwhile, adheres to the concept of the original four skills that teachers are instructed to focus on in turn and feature equally in their lessons. In my opinion this perception acts as a constraint, a delimiting factor that belies how people 'use' skills in real-world communication.

A third area of language teaching orthodoxy I would like to challenge is the obsession with 'input'. The importance of 'language data', i.e. input, for language learning is unquestionable (the phenomena of so-called 'wolf children' brought up in isolation from other humans, described throughout history, are proof of that). But while language learning requires *exposure to* language, it does not require *protection from* it. Yet it could be said that with its populist appeal, Krashen's comprehensible input hypothesis ('i +1') (1985) implies doing just that – and has consequently been single-handedly responsible for stultifying learner input for a generation. In more recent times, the concept has been rationalised in the shape of taxonomies, such as word lists at different *Common European Framework of Reference* (CEFR) levels, intended to buffer learners from language beyond their level. In an era in which the internet – a digital environment inhabited by the majority of our learners – gives unfettered access to information and thus to language, it seems almost ludicrous to have the equivalent of a 'parental lock' on the language material they are presented with in the classroom. Today's learners have a high tolerance for non-comprehension; faced with swathes of information online, they do what we all do (whether working in our first or other languages), they develop strategies for dealing with this information-overload by skimming, scanning for desired information and, most importantly, getting used to ignoring a high percentage of it. If we must resort to theorising level of input suitable for our learners, then it should be notated as (i+1, i+2, i+3, i+4 → i + infinity ...). The final 'nail in the coffin' of 'comprehensible input' for me is Gilmore's challenging of the 'causal link' between comprehension and language acquisition (Gilmore, 2007). For all these years, then, the comprehensible input concept may have been sending us down the wrong track; striving for comprehension at all costs has us diverted from, and obscured, its underlying rationale – language acquisition.

A brief statement of my beliefs/values about language and about learning languages that have emerged from the experiential pathway I have described

Learning

- As with any learning, motivation and/or incentive are crucial: 'you can take a horse to water', etc.
- Openness: language and culture are inseparably intertwined – learning the language means absorbing something of the culture of the place(s) in which it is spoken – so an openness to new concepts, values and behaviours is essential.
- Good language learners are good mimics – learning a language is a form of 'acting', so a 'good ear' is important.
- Good language learners are chameleons, morphing into 'L2 selves' in the L2 environment.
- Good language learners are confident – getting one's tongue around another language can be difficult and even embarrassing at times, so it's important to be prepared to make a fool of ourselves sometimes.
- Language cannot be taught: it can only be *learned*.

Teaching

- Effective language teaching is rooted in the experience of language learning.
- ELT orthodoxy has to be approached critically, by resisting established teaching formats and thinking outside the box.
- Language learning is the most natural, authentic act for human beings – classroom activities should reflect this.
- Response, both affective and cognitive, is a key trigger for the language-learning process.

References

Bandler, R and Grinder, J (1979) *Frogs into Princes*. Moab: Real People Press.

Barber, E (1980) Language acquisition and applied linguistics. *ADFL Bulletin* 12/1: 26–32.

Cook, G (2000) *Language Play, Language Learning*. Oxford: Oxford University Press.

Corder, SP (1974) 'Error analysis', in Allen, JPB and Corder, SP (eds) *The Edinburgh Course in Applied Linguistics Volume 3*. Oxford: Oxford University Press, 122–131.

Crystal, D (2006) *Language and the Internet*. Cambridge: Cambridge University Press.

Crystal, D (2009a) *Just a Phrase I am Going Through*. Abingdon: Routledge.

Crystal, D (2009b) *Txting the gr8 db8*. Oxford: Oxford University Press.

Crystal, D (2019) *Cambridge Encyclopaedia of the English Language*. Third edition. Cambridge: Cambridge University Press.

Dörnyei, Z (1998) Motivation in second and foreign language learning. *Language Teaching* 31/3: 117–135.

Dörnyei, Z (2001) *Teaching and researching motivation*. Harlow: Longman, 2.

Dörnyei, Z and Ushioda, E (eds) (2009) *Motivation, Language Identity and the L2 Self*. Bristol: Multilingual Matters.

Ellis, R (2008) *The Study of Second Language Acquisition.* Second edition. Oxford: Oxford University Press.

Gilmore, A (2007) Authentic materials and authenticity in foreign language learning. *Language Teaching* 40/2: 97–118.

Kramsch, C (1993) *Context and Culture in Language Teaching*. Oxford: Oxford University Press.

Krashen, S (1983) The din in the head, input, and the language acquisition device. *Foreign Language Annals* 16: 41–44.

Krashen, S (1985) *The Input Hypothesis: Issues and implications*. Addison-Wesley Longman Ltd.

Mishan, F (2017) 'Authenticity 2.0: Reconceptualising authenticity in the digital era', in Maley, A and Tomlinson, B (eds) *Authenticity in Materials Development for Language Learning*. Newcastle: Cambridge Scholars, 10–24.

Prabhu, NS (1987) *Second Language Pedagogy.* Oxford: Oxford University Press.

Pienemann, M (1984). The psychological constraints on the teachability of languages. *Studies in Second Language Acquisition* 6/2: 186–214.

Singleton, D (1989) *Language Acquisition: The Age Factor.* Clevedon: Multilingual Matters.

Sweet, H (1900) *The Practical Study of Languages.* New York: Henry Holt and Co.

Tomalin, B (2000) Using films in ELT. Paper presented at IATEFL conference, Dublin, Ireland.

Tomlinson, B (ed) (1998) *Materials Development in Language Teaching.* Cambridge: Cambridge University Press.

van Lier, L (1996) *Interaction in the Language Curriculum: Awareness, Autonomy and Authenticity.* Harlow, Essex: Longman.

Widdowson, HG (1998) Context, community and authentic language. *TESOL Quarterly* 32/4: 705–716.

For CPD activities, visit e-file link: www.teachingenglish.org.uk/sites/teacheng/files/e-file.pdf

11

Some teachers tell stories, some sing – the world of teaching can do with more of both!

Jayakaran Mukundan

Being different

As a little sickly child (someone the Rubber Estate dispenser teased as 'pale-faced monkey') and being challenged, mentally and physically, it was always the case of differentiating between good and evil. Survival seemed everything. All the time. Sensing bad situations and bad people quickly was a mechanism for me to keep away from danger. And as a child I learned to quickly figure out the good and the evil and define them within the complexities of my unique operating system. Very few people knew about or bothered to find out about it. But some understood the differences between normal kids and myself and chose to either understand or tolerate – and these were the first people who I defined as good. All others – some uncles and aunts and cousins, and a lot of teachers – I classified as evil.

The first person who figured out something was wrong with me was my mother, who was married off at 14, brought into Malaya from India to become wife and mother (to 11 children). Despite the challenges she faced, she found time to lead me through the *Oxford English Textbook for Primary One* and her first instincts were to make me understand words (of course nothing made sense to me). But there were other things she was better at. She consistently showed patience when faced with the bed-wetting that I had no control over. And despite having to look after my three younger siblings (numbers nine, ten and 11) her desperation to find me when I frequently went missing seemed a more pressing task. I would often retreat to the back of the house, among the rubber trees, where I sat almost all day (if I wasn't caught) sucking my thumb until it bled. Even pacifiers do bleed.

I am dyslexic. And wired differently.

Lessons from primary school

Primary One was a new test of my survival instincts – I was finally away from the comfort of home. The most unlikely of things happened. An angel appeared in the form of Ong Siok Lay, the Primary One teacher assigned to my class. She played the piano. The school piano was in my classroom (when the sliding walls dividing the classrooms were open, it was used as a hall for special functions).

There was a textbook for English but Ms Ong never used it. She knew something intuitively about methodologies and materials. One C, the bottom class after A and B, was a class of kids who never had pre-schooling, kids like me from the Rubber

Estates. She used Big Books to tell us stories, my favourite being the *Three Little Pigs*, and sang songs together with us, my favourite being 'The Grand Old Duke of York'. Her songs were special. She sang well and played the piano with an enthusiasm that makes me feel sometimes that some of the greatest teachers have a particular DNA, and are not mere followers of the SOP (standard operating procedure) that teacher training institutions instil in them.

The wonderful input, the stories she told, the songs sung together, never exposed errors of the learners in One C. Instead, the correct forms of usage were reinforced through repetition, and errors were drowned in the collective sounds of 43 young and eager learners. Ms Ong's greatest challenge, however, would come soon after lavatory break. We were led two-by-two and in a long row, girls in front, boys behind them, to visit the lavatories. This was never easy. I took a long while to get used to standing in a row to urinate against the tall walls of the urinals – I kept particularly looking at the words 'Jackson Stoke-on-Trent', trying to figure out if that was the word used to call this big beautiful white porcelain thing. Lavatory break was approximately three minutes and most kids never managed to finish in time. One particular girl would sit on her chair ten minutes after lavatory break and release a river of urine across the floor. It proves one thing – you can get kids to a lavatory but they can never be forced to pee. Teaching agendas and timescales and a child's own may differ.

The post-lavatory class was writing. A dyslexic's nightmare. The lines in the exercise book for writing were blue with a set of red ones at the top and bottom of the page. The blue lines in the middle were for writing, the reds at the top and bottom were for art. The person who invented this must have been a genius. 'If you can't write, draw!' Or, like football, you do your stretching and warm up by the sides before you get into the real game. Brilliant! So I usually started by the sides and then made my way to the blue lines. The teacher had written the target letter on the board and the other kids were seriously copying it. I would look around and there was nobody to write with, unlike with the singing. I was alone. So I attempted a B and this was the B with my personality. It looked the other way. A shy B. The Ds were the same, both capital and small letters. My S was a tired snake finding a new route, going the other way round.

Help would not be long in arriving, and Ms Ong would come by to crouch next to me, hold my hand and work on doing the conventional B. This she did after cleaning the page using the eraser at the tip of the pencil. Another discovery! As soon as Ms Ong left to another student's desk I would pick up courage and write on my own, now aware of the antidote for errors that was attached to the pencil tip. My new-found enthusiasm had led me to continue writing not only `backwards but outside the blue lines as well. The letters seemed to want to fall off. The eraser sorted many out, but some were stubborn and I had to resort to a trick I learned at home when at the end of the month Papa had to do the check roll to sort out the salaries of the rubber tappers. For the stubborn errors he spat on the eraser and somehow when he erased it cleared. Obviously the paper was different. Mine started developing black holes. I soon started using coloured pencils and drawing patterns at the top and bottom of the page, inspired mostly by the embroidery of Mum's saris. Ms Ong would return. Looking at my page her face never showed a trace of despair. She would pick up my book, cover the centre with her palm, revealing just the top and bottom, and delightfully declare that mine were the best patterns she had seen.

My Standard One adventures in Ms Ong's class still linger in my head. Some shaped my personal philosophies about teaching and learning. There are many things that also influenced me as a teacher in the early years of my teaching. I started resisting the textbook, especially in the weaker classes, obviously taking the cue from my early immersion into the school of fantasy as envisioned by Ms Ong. Most other good teachers also scarcely used textbooks. Mr Koe (my science teacher), who rarely used the textbook, told us stories about Archimedes and how he discovered the theory of water displacement while having his bath, how he ran through the streets naked yelling 'Eureka!' This teacher inspired us through stories – and King Hiero, the Second King of Syracuse, also featured alongside Archimedes in our science lessons! This same teacher taught us English in Form Three and some of his unorthodox ways included encouraging us to create our own comic books. While no other English language teacher featured in my Top Five list, having just two was a miracle – I always felt the rest were there to make us hate the language. I, like Ms Ong and Mr Koe, have a fascination for using the performing arts in my teaching. This is how my early exposure to these two teachers helped shape my views on best practices in teaching.

Goodbye textbooks

Abandoning textbooks was not always an easy thing. First textbooks are artefacts as powerful as religious texts. They are untouchable and immutable. Also, schools are embodiments of government and bureaucracy: the levels of scrutiny and checks were so high that English language teachers, already heavily suffocated by numerous non-academic duties, had to find ways to stifle their own intuitions and follow the script provided by the Ministry. The Ministry of course had their own Gestapo unit (affectionately called the Inspectorate) and inspectors were despatched to schools frequently to check on teachers and teaching. I was later visited by one, who within the course of the 40 minutes of my teaching that he observed sought to advise me on how important it was to use the textbook and why my deviations from the weekly syllabus would derail the examination preparations of the students. I rarely rebutted the comments of the inspectors. They were impossible to argue with.

Sometimes, as a teacher, logic precedes everything, especially if you believe in doing the best for your students. I disliked most textbooks – they could not engage my learners – and I slowly began to be influenced by the Dogme movement (Meddings and Thornbury: Thornbury, 2009), which seemed like a hippie movement in education and which advocated the discarding of textbooks. Personally, I was also convinced that textbooks were simply unsuitable most times because:

1. Malaysian students were never streamed based on the proficiency levels in the English Language, so using the textbook was ridiculously silly as the weaker students (who were automatically promoted from level to level) could not cope with textbooks (which followed the structural syllabus) that taught too much and too soon.

2. School textbooks were boring and the topics were not meant for young adults (my teaching was in secondary schools). The book was filled with grammar exercises, pages and pages of them, and the natural instincts of teachers led them into drills.

So, I decided to create unique environments in my classrooms. No class was the same. I used a lot of songs, role play and drama in classrooms and the introduction of the reading programmes allowed me more opportunity to do unconventional teaching. It was at this time (in the 1970s and 1980s) when new methodologies were also surfacing and I spent a lot of time reading about them. Then USIS (United States Information Services, through the US Embassy) began sending out the teaching tapes on methodology (featuring Dianne Larsen-Freeman), which changed the way I taught English. It was neither structural nor communicative but eclectic.

There are two major things I would like to focus on that have emerged from my analysis of Ms Ong's classes: songs and stories.

Songs

While songs are natural to humans (they sing to celebrate), the use of songs in learning-teaching had other amazing effects:

1. Most humans love songs but teachers who know about jazz chants and Carolyn Graham, the creator of *Jazz Chants* (1978), know that language and songs have rhythms that are similar so it's natural to complement language learning with songs. Obviously, they are better than mundane repetitive drills.

2. In Ms Ong's class, none of whom had pre-schooling, choral singing of songs was an opportunity to be involved – kids who didn't know the whole song sang the parts they could and those who made mistakes with the lyrics had no fear (the voices of the others made up for those who couldn't contribute and Ms Ong made sure choral singing drowned those errors!). Obviously, this was one wonderful way to raise awareness of errors and, of course, positive reinforcement. Those who committed errors were never threatened and this contributed to what is described in the literature as a 'non-threatening learning environment'.

3. Songs are strange in so many ways, so strange that the scientific basis of their impact on learners' lives, which should come from research, has been either ignored or not considered serious enough for documentation in academic journals. Some ideas on involuntary playback and 'dinning', as proposed by Stevick (1996), began to influence me. Stevick spoke about learning new languages and how intense learning activity in a language can lead to a 'din in the head'. This suggests the activation of the so-called language acquisition device (LAD). The dinning usually leads to 'involuntary playback'. Krashen (1983) explains verbal dinning by saying that it happens when we are experiencing something new and attempting to integrate it into the 'networks of the files'. Stevick and Krashen suggest that most people working on drills (especially basic-level learners in a foreign language class) experience dinning and involuntary playback. I believe that songs learned by young learners (non-native speakers) probably have similar effects. They sing (and there's a lot of interesting auditory input) and the words swim in the head, sometimes leading to involuntary recall. This partly explains, I believe, the experiences I went through – the LAD must have activated the song in my head, which led me into singing it out even on the school bus!

4. In my later years as teacher, I can remember how I incorporated songs in my class while teaching adverbs. I used the 'Ly song' from Electric Company (that was meant to teach adverbs; of course this was not made known to my learners). But this came after I had done some total physical response (TPR) routines with my students. I selected a theme (cleaning the house) and I acted out some cleaning routines in the house, verbalising my actions. The focus was on introducing the verbs first. I got the students to physically respond to my commands (sweep the floor, dust the curtains, etc.). From this we moved to adverbs (sweep the floor carefully, quickly, etc.). I remember this one class where they had just got back from physical education and were sweating in the humid afternoon and so were very restless. Getting up to do physical actions seemed to be the best strategy. The students were engaged throughout. After we finished the TPR activity we went on to watch (notice how it has moved from non-teacher-dominated teaching to even more of the same) the 'Ly song'. I did not even have to tell them to focus on anything – they were singing their hearts out. This Electric Company cartoon worked so well because there was a huge element of humour in it! When it was time to check on lesson outcomes I gave them a worksheet that had all the adverbs within the lyrics removed. Everyone scored full marks. I gave them the exercise 60 days after that lesson and they still scored full marks. I was convinced that the balance of right- and left-brain activity had helped with recall. It was magic.

What made me so happy was that last part of the lesson which led to 'noticing' (Schmidt, 1990). Tomlinson (2011) claims that, while direct approaches to grammar may not lead to anything fruitful (because they are not meaningful), an eventual, gradual focus on grammar would still be necessary. This is precisely what happened for me, without the bullying intrusion of grammar.

Stories

Stories are just as amazing as songs. And the magic of Ms Ong lay in the way her intuitions led her into telling stories rather than asking her students to read. Some other classes had a set of storybooks laid out at the back of the class and the other teachers got the students to read silently. The teacher then read the book aloud. Questions on the story followed. Nothing like that in Ms Ong's class.

Ms Ong would ask the entire class to huddle up around her. She would sit on her chair and we'd all sit on the floor, encircling her. Ms Ong's stories were really good, engaging tales. There were no exercises during or after the stories. She was always animated and we were drawn into her stories. Sometimes she would sit at her piano and retell the stories with musical accompaniment! Stories depend very much on the storytelling skills of the teacher, so it would be very useful for teachers to immerse themselves in the techniques of storytelling. A storyteller teacher is such an asset, especially in second language and foreign language classrooms, where it is so difficult to engage students. Stories and music combined are like natural steroids! But that gift (the power of stories and music) that helped teachers like Ms Ong so effectively does not come on a platter. In Ms Ong's case she studied the piano, then songs led to stories and vice versa. My induction to storytelling was somewhat different from hers.

My storytelling baptism of fire

My introduction to storytelling (performance storytelling) started in a strange way. I was forcefully kicked into it. The official storyteller for Penguin Books fell ill. The general manager of Penguin Books called to say that he'd lost a storyteller and he was depending on me. I immediately tried to get out of it. He assured me I was an experienced professor who could do this with my eyes closed, hands tied and a mouth wide open for the story to flow, profusely (these were his exact words!). I finally said yes (the gun pointed at my head). I was to tell Roald Dahl stories at MPH bookstore in Mid-Valley Megamall (I thought this would be the Valley of Death, like the ones in cowboy movies of the past!). It was September and Roald Dahl month. I loved his stories – but telling them live (and to kids!) would be the equivalent of self-immolation. I spent the three weeks before the event stressed and preparing. I called Penguin's marketing manager and asked about audience type and numbers and all she could say was that it was open to the public! No hope there! I finally shortlisted just two stories – *James and the Giant Peach* and *The Enormous Crocodile*.

On the day, I arrived one hour early. The kidzone in MPH bookstore looked like a mini-amphitheatre (I sometimes have little mind games of my own and I comforted myself saying maybe it would be a lion that I saved in a previous life!). The kids were not there yet so I went for a coffee and rehearsed mentally the target story – *James and the Giant Peach*. Nothing could go wrong with that story, I reassured myself. I was wrong. I greeted the Penguin marketing crew who introduced me to the store manager and briefed me on the logistics. The amphitheatre was full. I got a rundown on the kids (they told me that many were from an orphanage nearby, with hardly any English, all aged three and four). Then I saw about ten Caucasian kids (around the age of four to five years) and my heart sank. Trouble! Well, eventually the event went well but there are lessons I learned from this first venture into storytelling that had a huge impact on my own re-education:

1. First, individual differences really matter. The little boys from the orphanage were behind in more ways than one. Their proficiency levels in English were low. The Caucasian kids were not just native speakers of English; I presume they were read to or did a lot of reading on their own. I thought I could pick one of the eight or nine Roald Dahl books I was familiar with and these Caucasian kids would know it already. *James and the Giant Peach* had to be dropped. The three- to four-year-olds would not cope with that. I had to go to Plan B. *The Enormous Crocodile* – I felt I could be extra-animated with this nice little story – and hopefully we'd all laugh along, until this 60 minutes of my life was over!

2. There were rewards from Penguin Books for the kids but not enough to go around! There were close to 25 kids and only about ten gifts (this I pointed out to the people in Penguin Books, who had no idea of realistic charity – in kids' terms). I paused in the middle of the story several times for a prediction activity (this was a disaster – poor strategy) and all the questions were clinically and correctly responded to by the Caucasian kids. The younger kids from the orphanage stared in bewilderment and so I started activating that part of the brain that you don't access until in deep trouble. I changed questioning strategies and this time I pointed to individuals to respond to me. One of the nicest was this one: As soon as the kids saw the enormous crocodile what did

they do? The orphanage kids responded wonderfully with a scream befitting a celebration. That non-Caucasian sector of my audience finally started living. And the gifts flowed to the less able, less fortunate.

3. I keep telling my undergraduate students that when they grow older and feel they have taken on all challenges and overcome them, they should turn to storytelling to kids. It's definitely an ego-buster! Soon after realising that we needed an army of storytellers for ELT, I worked on getting a reserve team of storytellers (a younger group). I enlisted two more storytellers, both teachers and former students of mine. The following September they were despatched to malls to tell stories. Their stories were well liked but they confirmed that it was one of the most challenging things they had done as teachers!

The thing about teachers who are good storytellers is that their classrooms are always exciting. Even if they are not formally telling stories, they are picking even the smallest of incidents in class (like someone coming late to class) as an opportunity to develop a story. I am convinced that storytelling workshops should be part of every teachers' professional development.

There are constantly emerging stories in the lives of educators. Some of these teachers have untold stories; little stories that add up and eventually sum up things, like the joining of dots – and sometimes these patterned joined dots gel within them and create personal philosophies that transcend space and time and create new selves, new teachers. My very first engagement with Ms Ong led me into believing all things are possible. That 'no child left behind' statement, which politicians often unashamedly use for their own convenience, is there in some teachers. In these honest teachers it grows within and they respond spontaneously to the call to do good, all the time.

Conferences with a difference

From 1996 I started a series of bi-annual, international conferences called Malaysia International Conferences on ELT (MICELT). After my 2008 MICELT conference I realised that a deep fatigue for ELT was gathering within me. I was bored. I was surrounded by linguists and applied linguists (most of whom don't need to try very hard to put a conference of teachers into a coma). I was aware that teachers were staying away from conferences organised by university academics (who by this time had infiltrated teacher organisations as well). These people were dumping data from their research on teachers, all of whom were much more interested in 'best practices' in teaching.

In 2009, I decided on an alternative conference, the sibling to MICELT. I called it ICELT and this would be my attempt at finally giving teachers what they deserved. I needed a conference full of teachers to be inspired by storytellers, musicians, poets, comedians, artists ... you name it. I constantly asked myself whether this was going to work. Then the website and the first call went out and the hate mail started pouring in. The academics called this my Waterloo. The rivals to MICELT were celebrating, thinking this would be the Pepsi moment (when they forced Coke to derail the Classic and follow Pepsi into sweetness). Someone even said, look, the war is over, he finally blinked. He has now moved into the circus business!

I never looked back. At the second ICELT conference (just to spite the detractors) there was a clown who featured alongside all the other performing arts people. Teachers registered in droves. The first ICELT had close to 1,500 teachers. In order to appease the academics, I sponsored up to 100 of them as a way of telling the larger population of academics that if I couldn't convince them immediately, I was still going to try. Along the way (from 2009 to 2015) I'd managed to even convince the newspapers, including the biggest English daily *The Star* (which of course had a huge interest in ELT), that ICELT was what teachers wanted. *The Star* gave us the coverage we needed.

Throughout those years of ICELT, I saw the 'circus' grow to include more entertainers, people from the streets (those who even performed in pubs and piano bars, and the list is huge). We had Jan Blake, and many other storytellers, musicians (including Carolyn Graham), clowns (including Vivien Gladwell), the Two Steves (who entertain kids), poets, Valerie Bloom the performance poet, and so many others, people who wrote children's story books, such as Janeen Brian and so many others – entire casts of fun-loving people who advocated enjoyment in learning! Then I moved ICELT from being just a conference to something resembling a festival! I started having 'performances' – plays, stories, etc. – within the ICELT conferences. I wanted teachers to just enjoy these performances by professionals (who were not teachers) and perhaps take a pointer or two from these people and diversify their own teaching strategies accordingly.

Looking back, I recall that two personalities supported my unconventional ways of thinking – Brian Tomlinson and Alan Maley. Brian was a materials person who knew I was working on alternatives in materials evaluation – he made me Visiting Research Fellow at Leeds Metropolitan University in the UK. This widened my horizons in the field as I was also contributing to the MATSDA conferences. Brian himself has views on methodology that offer alternatives to textbook-based teaching. Working with him inspired me to work on teacher-friendly alternatives to materials evaluation instruments, some of which won gold medals at the British Invention Show and at IENA, Nuremberg, Germany.

Alan Maley and I had worked on the creative writing workshops for Asian teacher-writers. I offered to start a big one in Melaka in 2004, immediately after his Bangkok event. About 25 teachers were writing in the presidential suite (the size of 20 regular hotel rooms put together) of the Riviera Bay Hotel in Melaka. All these creative writers then went on to present at an international conference, immediately after their writing workshops. We anticipated a 200-odd teacher participation. More than 600 teachers attended and we made a huge profit, which of course went into getting more internationally renowned speakers for my other conferences. The biggest contribution to this was of course in teacher professional development. All these teacher participants also developed personally – their work was later published by publishers such as Pearson Longman. The earliest of these was *Asian Stories for Young Readers* (Volume 1) (Maley and Mukundan, 2005).

We had developed teachers capable of making their writing classrooms non-threatening environments. Some even confessed that they had moved their students away from exam-based essays into creative writing. Some of these teachers (mainly from the MRSM (MARA) schools, who participated in another series of workshops on creative writing) even published their students' work!

On looking back, I feel that it was my instincts rather than most learning in formal education that have moved me to do things. I took in the schooling aspects of it all and, when it was performance time, the other things that floated outside the thoughts about schooling took over. I was like a singer inspired by audience needs and fitting the script accordingly, reacting spontaneously, sometimes even recklessly. But it was the memories of Ms Ong's loving care in my primary school days that gave me my direction and my impetus.

References

Graham, C (1978) *Jazz Chants*. New York: Oxford University Press.

Krashen, S (1983) The din in the head, input and the second language acquisition device. *Foreign Language Annals* 16: 41–44.

Maley, A and Mukundan, J (eds) (2005) *Asian Stories for Young Readers, Volume 1*. Petaling Jaya: Pearson Longman.

Meddings, L and Thornbury, S (2009) *Teaching Unplugged: Dogme in English Language Teaching*. Peaslake, UK: Delta.

Schmidt, RW (1990) The role of consciousness in second language learning. *Applied Linguistics* 11: 129–158.

Stevick, E (1996) *Memory, Meaning and Method*. Boston: Heinle & Heinle Publishers.

Thornbury, S (2005) Dogme: dancing in the dark? *Folio* 20.

Tomlinson, B (ed) (2011) *Materials Development in Language Teaching*. Cambridge: Cambridge University Press.

For CPD activities, visit e-file link: www.teachingenglish.org.uk/sites/teacheng/files/e-file.pdf

12

The art of growing

Chrysa Papalazarou

Early experiences

The silence of ABC

I grew up in Greece in the 1970s. The country was going through a difficult but forward-looking transition period of re-establishing a stable and democratic political scene, after years of devastation and turmoil. I started primary school just as the military junta was collapsing in 1974. My first primary school teacher, with a group of some 40 students under her responsibility, was very strict. I remember her looking at us from behind her huge spectacles, inspiring a mixture of awe and fear. She would demand absolute silence in the classroom, often resorting to her cane to maintain order. I felt bad when that happened and have had a distrust of authoritarian teacher behaviour ever since. I liked school nevertheless.

Arthur's adventures and *The Secret Garden*

In the late 1970s, at the age of ten, I started learning English. There was no provision for foreign language teaching in the primary state sector at that time so my parents enrolled me in a private language school. The owner of the school had made two curricular choices that for me triggered a good initial rapport with the English language: a captivating coursebook and the use of videos. The coursebook *Starting Out* dealt with the adventures of Arthur, a shy young librarian. The story was funny, the texts and dialogues humorous, and the brilliant illustrations pop up in my mind's eye even today. I liked the combination of engaging texts and intriguing visuals, which offset the boredom of class translation. Until it was my turn to read and translate, I drew speech bubbles and wrote my own dialogues for the heroes.

Once a week, for a designated time, we watched video. At a time when most of our own homes did not have a video player, let alone our state school, that was really special. My most vivid memories are from the *Follow Me* BBC television course and *The Secret Garden*, a dramatised version of Frances Hodgson Burnett's novel. The latter also triggered my desire to read literature in English. As I moved onwards to exam goals, books became dull and exposure to videos was minimal. We had to study a lot of grammar, memorise vocabulary lists, and undergo drilling. I missed my first years of learning English.

Language and culture

In the late 1980s, I found myself at university, in the Department of English Language and Literature. The department was characterised by poor resources and facilities, lectures for large groups of students, a teacher-led approach and minimal contact with the faculty. From dealing with reading extracts and multiple-choice questions I moved on to productive work on essays about culture, literature, theatre and history. The amount of reading I did at that time boosted my language proficiency and my fascination with other cultures. I realised how learning a foreign language opened up a whole new world of understanding and how language and culture could not exist without each other.

The pedagogue and the flow
In my last year at university I met John Chioles. His classes introduced us to literature as a cultural phenomenon. We did a performance of Shakespeare's *A Midsummer Night's Dream*. Pushed by a friend, and against my reserved nature, I auditioned for the role of Puck, Oberon's naughty messenger. I got accepted in the group and spent the next few months being part of day-long rehearsals. Chioles designed and created an experience into which we were immersed, first unconsciously and then, as time went by, more and more consciously. He pushed us to higher levels of performance and got us absorbed in speaking Shakespearean language in the most fascinating hands-on way. In retrospect I think Chioles was a brilliant pedagogue. It was the first time I had experienced an alternative to the teacher-led approach I had been exposed to until then. He created the conditions for a flow, an optimal experience that helped us push our boundaries forward, feel more skilled and invest our energy in meaningful and enjoyable learning. A lifelong love for theatre was instilled in me.

Influences from workplaces
Testing: master of the game
In the early 1990s I started working full-time. My first job was in a private language school. I got a decent salary, but did not have all the insurance benefits I was entitled to. I had had no training so the coursebook was a life jacket at that time. The book was focused on skill-based activities, bits and pieces of artificial language and extensive reliance on grammar through the presentation, practice and production (PPP) method. After my first year there, I was assigned exam classes. This necessitated endless drilling, gap-filling, doing multiple-choice tests and memorising vocabulary on the part of the students. Testing was the master of the game of teaching. I thought this was the norm. I had obtained my certificates through a similar mode and had internalised this process as the only one available. As time passed, I began to feel frustrated that students could not learn what I wished to teach. I also noticed how students, although they had a very clear and visible goal, failed to remain motivated. It seemed as though the goal of taking examinations and acquiring a language certificate was not convincing enough for them. These were mechanised working conditions. I felt stress and anxiety weighing on me. I left after four years.

Teaching the outcasts
My university degree entitled me to start looking for work within the state sector. My first job was on an hourly basis in a vocational training school in a deprived area of Athens. My first day there was a bit of a shock. I had to teach 200 young men. The school operated in the late afternoon and evening, and students got there after finishing their working day. Classes had more than 20 students. Most of them came from lower-income backgrounds. They thought of themselves as the outcasts of the education system; their self-esteem and motivation were low. Their level of English was basic or worse. I started using the set coursebooks, but soon this proved to be totally fruitless. After flirting with the initial thought of quitting, I started searching for a solution. I asked students to bring any useful material they

came across. We ended up with a materials bank comprising safety precautions, instruction manuals, machine diagrams and packaging instructions. We would go through these together and I helped them with terminology. Progress was slow, but there were signs of appreciation and motivation on the part of the students. We also talked a lot about their worries and problems. I then felt that learning could occur beyond coursebooks and that teaching is a deeply human endeavour.

Teaching in difficult circumstances

In 1994 I was temporarily appointed to a primary school in a suburb of Athens. I knew nothing about teaching primary school children and nothing in my university classes or previous experience had prepared me for this. My classes were mixed-ability, multi-level and multi-ethnic, since the school was in an area with a large Roma population. A number of their children were attending our school. I came to learn how difficult school was for them because their Romani language was not written, but only spoken. They were often absent from classes and some of them literally disappeared for parts of the year, travelling to other areas in the country for seasonal work. Sustained progress was extremely difficult. They were bright children, but mostly low achievers or below average at best. They were a minority in the classroom and relationships with other students varied from marginalisation to passive acceptance. Coursebooks were totally irrelevant to their culture and life, and this might have been one cause of their disruptive behaviour. Although I mainly adhered to direct instruction through the PPP method following the coursebook syllabus, I integrated more communicative tasks: simple dialogues, miming, role plays and songs. These were small changes of an impromptu kind, but they improved the classroom atmosphere. The Roma students felt more motivated and responded better. I came to believe that coursebooks could be totally irrelevant for some students and that small changes could have noticeably positive effects in the classroom.

A second chance

In 2007 I returned to work after a few years off for family reasons and an educational leave where I completed an MA in comparative education and human rights. I then came across an announcement by the Ministry of Education asking for teachers interested in being seconded in second chance schools (SCSs). I applied and got the post of English tutor in an SCS in the Athens area. SCSs aim at integrating adults at risk of social exclusion, through an innovative programme involving a coursebook-free syllabus, and no testing and marking. The initial training I received was generic and transmissive, touching briefly upon topics such as student-centred pedagogy, multi-literacies, multimodality, critical literacy and group work. It was the first time I heard about these theoretical and methodological concepts.

One main difficulty I encountered was how to accommodate in the same classroom the needs of adults from such diverse backgrounds in terms of ethnic origin, age, and social and educational needs, as well as language needs. There were beginners, false-beginners and very few cases of pre-intermediate students. After consulting colleagues, I started designing a communicative syllabus based on collaboration with the students. We also worked extensively with projects and held class assemblies to discuss outcomes, and students were encouraged to keep portfolios. It was a lifetime achievement for these people that they began to feel literate in a social and media environment where English dominated. The timetable also offered the opportunity to conduct weekly workshops. In one of these I used art for the first time and came in contact with the visible thinking approach (Perkins, 2003). My period at the SCS whetted my appetite for further experimentation and discovery. It was a second chance for me as well as for them. The autonomy I enjoyed facilitated curricular initiatives and risk-taking. I felt more confident. I came to see how art could be used in the language class. This whole experience also confirmed my belief that learning could occur beyond coursebooks.

Following the thread

My return to mainstream primary education in 2011 in a district of Athens coincided with the introduction of the Integrated Foreign Language Curriculum. The syllabus was still a coursebook-based one. However, elements such as the communicative dimension of foreign language teaching and the promotion of student thinking and socialisation were emphasised. Other emerging curricular innovations were multi-literacies and multimodality. This felt like a continuation from my SCS experience. At the time my school adviser set up a special interest group for art in teaching as part of her development programme. I joined and started exchanging ideas with colleagues. In 2013, I started the Art in the English Class project with my upper-primary, 11-year-old students. I wanted to do something about the problem of low motivation related to coursebooks. The project aimed at creating a more affective and effective learning experience.

In this continuing approach students are exposed to paintings and other forms of visual media that are linked to a topic. Student thinking is encouraged through relevant activities. Other activities hone the ability to find meaning in imagery. We share our thinking and ideas and take notes. Student writing involves describing and reflecting on lesson experience. The topics bring real-world issues in the classroom. It is rewarding to see how well these topics resonate with students' needs. Sharing their thoughts dissolves students' fear and anxiety of expressing themselves in English. I intervene at the point of need to give feedback and information about the language they need. Thus, new language and language they already know are used in a meaningful context of communication. This approach has boosted my belief that alternatives to coursebook work are possible and fruitful even in mainstream education.

At the same time I started blogging. Sharing classroom ideas and insights with other colleagues all over the world has been a mind-blowing experience. I felt strongly I could learn so much from others, and that there was a vast terrain of online possibilities for continuous professional development. I became curious about the global ELT discourse. I attended online webinars and was invited to give them. I joined associations and presented at conferences. I also contributed to publications. Overall, I have pursued new ways for my professional growth as a teacher.

Key people

Some of the people who have contributed to my continuing sense of plausibility are mentioned here in the order our paths first crossed.

John Chioles, my BA university professor. A brilliant pedagogue who unleashed creative and expressive potential I had no idea was in me. His influence has had a lifelong impact and proved to me that teachers can be agents of transformation.

My school adviser, Eleni Manolopoulou, is the person who set up an art special interest group that sparked my systematic work with art and visuals. Through her support, I had the chance to share my work with colleagues, conduct workshops, give presentations and grow professionally.

I would not have started my own blog had it not been for Kieran Donaghy's Film English website. He is a pioneer in using video in language teaching to embrace values and empathy. Kieran has been a source of inspiration. Being a member of the Visual Arts Circle that he and Anna Whitcher founded (www.visiblethinkingpz. org/VisibleThinking_html_files/VisibleThinking1.html) got me in touch with a group of like-minded people.

The first online course I attended was Contrasting Conversations by John Fanselow at the International Teacher Development Institute (iTDi). I learned the importance of recording and transcribing lessons and was surprised to see how much I talk during class time. I also had my first encounter with reflective practice, which led me to observe and analyse my classes more systematically.

My precious friend and mentor Arnold Mühren, a truly reflective thinker, made me realise how important a teacher's personal voice of experience is and he encouraged me to express my own. Engaging with him in many conversations has enriched my ideas on teaching and learning. He has helped me appreciate clarity in written expression.

I have also been influenced by Alan Maley's impactful work on an aesthetic approach in ELT and on the theory and practice of creativity. Being a member of the C Group (Creativity for Change in Language Education) (www.thecreativitygroup.weebly.com) that he initiated has brought me in contact with various facets and practices of creativity in ELT around the world. His support of colleagues has been a constant source of motivation for me.

Key ideas

These are some key ideas that have contributed to my current beliefs and practice.

Art

I am interested in the role of paintings in language teaching and learning. Working with art is an emotional experience that helps students direct their attention inward to what they believe or feel, engage their imagination and open a dialogue to share their thoughts and build on the thoughts of others (Eisner, 2002). Paintings also weave values about our world into an aesthetic visual representation. By exposing students to this fabric, we give them the chance to understand better the world they live in.

Creativity in thinking

Over time, I have come to pay more attention to developing students' thinking skills. These involve observing, describing, reasoning with evidence, looking for more than one possible answer, sharing thinking with others, connecting and capturing the heart (Ritchhart et al., 2011). These activities stem from the visible and artful thinking approach developed within Project Zero, an educational research group at the Harvard Graduate School of Education. They nurture a creative mindset (Perkins, 2003; Tishman and Palmer, 2007). I view creativity as a process promoting a more open and questioning relationship with others and the world.

Aesthetic experience

Paintings help students generate their own discourse in the language class. Using them starts a process of making meaning whereby students build understanding individually, but also through their classmates' points of view (Vygotsky, 1978). This merging of the personal and collective also stimulates aesthetic experience (Housen, 1999). My role is to create and manage the learning environment. As the process unfolds, students teach each other and they become the source of their own learning in terms of language, observations and views (Housen, 2007). They are more willing to take risks with language because they are engaged.

Visual literacy

I have also drawn on the visual thinking strategies framework (Housen, 1999, 2007; Yenawine, 2003). This is an approach towards developing visual literacy where viewing and representing are key processes. Both comprehending complexity and finding meaning in imagery are involved, as well as communicating visually through drawing and creating diagrams or graphs (Begoray, 2001). I am fascinated by the way students' notes and writing are highly individualised when working with paintings and visuals. They involve diverse modes of expression where language and drawings, diagrams, colours and symbols happily co-exist.

Social issues

We live in a highly turbulent world. In this world, especially in Western societies, children are increasingly regarded as economic units. They are targeted by multi-million ad campaigns and grow up with contradictory messages and mass-media imagery that often create an exploitative attitude towards each other and the environment. Their coursebooks also often depict a consumerist lifestyle. The antidote is selecting imagery of a different kind when introducing relevant social issues.

Influential reading

Some important publications in my professional life include:

- *Arts and the Creation of the Mind* (Eisner, 2002). A compelling book on the value of arts education. Among other things it has influenced my belief that standardisation of learning should not be the goal of schools.

- *Making Thinking Visible* (Ritchhart, et al., 2011). This book gives the theoretical and research background to the visible thinking approach. I have been greatly helped and motivated by its practical advice on how to foster thinking by encouraging imaginative and creative learning.

- *The Image in ELT* (Donaghy and Xerri, 2017). A seminal publication on the use of imagery in language teaching and learning.

- *Creativity in the English Language Classroom* (Maley and Peachey, 2015). An inspirational publication with a plethora of practical ideas on the diverse aspects of creativity.

- *Integrating Global Issues in the Creative English Language Classroom* (Maley and Peachey, 2017). An innovative book in marrying creative teaching ideas and the UN's Sustainable Development Goals.

- *Breaking Rules* (Fanselow, 1987). A groundbreaking work that introduced me to exploring the effects on teaching of greater diversity in content, process and roles.

- *Tuiavii's Way: A South Sea Chief's Comments on Western Society* (Tuiavii, translated by Cavelti, 1997). An intriguing mixture of anthropology and fiction that has given me a new perspective on our way of life in Western societies. It has also alerted me to the 'civilised' vs 'uncivilised' discourse.

Insightful moments

Into powerful language

While working on the topic of war and peace through Picasso's *Guernica*, I had used a see, think, wonder routine and had asked students to observe carefully and answer the questions: What do you see? What do you think about it? What does it make you wonder? As I walked around the class to check whether they needed help with the language to express their ideas, a student asked for two words: *drown* and *chaos*. When they had finished writing, they started speaking and sharing ideas. This particular student, when reaching the 'I think' part, said: 'I think people are drowning in chaos.' I was taken aback at how powerful, metaphoric and poetic this was. An 11-year-old had captured in one sentence all the complexity of the painting and its symbolism with such economy of words and without knowing anything about the artwork. And all this had happened in the English class. Up until that moment I had been applying the approach intuitively. This was the first time I started thinking consciously about the importance of powerful visual input for producing meaningful language and about the deep student engagement the approach could create. I reminded myself that I should stay on this track.

Creative chaos

Students were working in groups on the war and peace topic mentioned before. We used a colour, symbol, image routine where students chose colours, symbols and images that they felt represented the ideas they had discussed. Things got quite noisy as each group talked about their choices. They also made use of their first language. My first thought was to stop this chaotic situation and encourage them to use only the target language. My second thought was to step back – which is what I finally did. By doing so, I saw more clearly that ideas began to emerge. Each group was exploring what they needed to do for this task. Roles were defined to establish who would draw, colour, take notes and write on the final poster. Ideas worth further exploration were put forward, while others were discarded. I stepped in whenever students asked for help with language they needed and then stepped back again. Final selections of colours, symbols and images showed how the students had developed their understanding of war and peace by making connections and thinking metaphorically. They used images and thought in terms of images. Meanings were the outcome of the negotiation that took place. I was convinced that from this kind of 'chaos' there could be collaborative creativity.

A moment of silence

In a recent class we used *What After*, a powerful painting by the Syrian artist Louay Kayyali. It shows 11 characters (eight women, a young man and two children, one of them holding a white dove, all in a standing position). Misery is shown on all faces. The characters are all barefoot, illustrating hurried eviction. The students first described what the painting showed and reached the conclusion that these are refugees. Then I asked each student to identify with one of the figures. From their chosen perspective, they reflected on the questions: 'What do you perceive? What do you believe? What do you care about?' The students were absorbed in this activity because the painting had such an emotional impact on them. Once they had written their ideas, I asked them to dramatise their lines in class. 'I perceive that I will die and have nothing, no food, no home and I feel so empty like I have no blood in me.' 'I perceive that all the good memories have suddenly disappeared and in their turn there are only bad memories.' 'I perceive that my country will be in ruins after this war.' 'I believe that all the countries should help us to find shelter.' 'I believe that we don't have hope to survive and I'm scared.' 'I care about my family and I'm angry because I can't do anything to save us.' 'I care about my relatives and I want them to be safe.' 'I care about my white dove because it's my only hope.' These words fell like bombs in the classroom. The whole refugee narrative was there. A narrative of war, ruins, death, emptiness, hopelessness, impotence, survival. But also one of love, hope and solidarity. When that part finished there was a remarkable moment of unexpected, absolute silence. This is something not common in primary classes. To me that silence signified awareness, understanding and empathy. Then some children asked if they could work out an extra perspective, different from the one they had initially chosen.

I think how important it is to deal with such issues and how art can enable us to step into the shoes of others. This is a capacity closely linked with cross-cultural development. It is what makes us human, how we discern values, make choices and express our moral commitment.

Suggestions for teacher training

If I were to be trained now, I would like the programme to include more attention to roles that in general are minimally dealt with at present.

Teacher as materials designer

Having more control over materials design, we can be more responsive to classroom diversity. It also gives us more control over topics and skills. When choosing appropriate material, we make a series of choices and decisions that are informed by our students' needs. We should strive for materials that are interesting and relevant, materials that can enable students to respond both personally and intellectually.

Teacher as writer

Blogging about practice improves a teacher's writing and communication skills. It also hones their reflective skills in what, how and why they do certain things in the classroom. I believe that a blog gives voice to our profession and communicates it with the wider community. Writing interacts with reading and with each post the author is pushed to do some relevant reading, which adds to their learning. In my case, writing for the blog motivates me to pursue other genres such as articles and book chapters, each contributing to my professional knowledge and development.

Teacher as critical pedagogue

In coursebooks visuals do play a role, but their full potential is rarely exploited. Social issues are virtually non-existent. Student needs should be dealt with not only in terms of their cognitive and linguistic development, but also their emotional, aesthetic and social growth. Issues such as bullying, intolerance, racism, disability, poverty and refugees are worth bringing into the classroom. It is not a matter of telling students what to think, but of giving them the opportunity to do their own thinking.

My beliefs

Beliefs about the student experience:

- Knowing learners' needs is important.
- Lack of motivation is often the outcome of low self-esteem.
- Exam goals do not guarantee students' motivation.
- Students can always surprise me.
- Interesting and motivating content stimulates the imagination of students.

Beliefs about language learning:

- Visuals have a powerful impact on language learning.
- Affective aspects of content matter interact positively with language learning.
- Learning a foreign language can nurture open-mindedness.
- Language learning is effective when it takes place in a meaningful context.
- Language learning is severely affected by testing goals.
- The linear way of presentation in coursebooks does not guarantee progress in learning.

Beliefs about growing as a teacher:

- Experimentation and curiosity help me grow professionally.
- Being inventive is an important asset for a language teacher.
- Small changes in teaching can have a disproportionately great impact.
- Autonomy is important for teacher confidence.
- Writing materials relevant to my students' needs is a powerful form of professional development.
- Colleagues are a valuable source of learning.
- Teachers can and should be agents of transformation.

References

Begoray, D (2001) Through a class darkly: visual literacy in the classroom. *Canada Journal of Education* 26/2: 201–217.

Donaghy, K and Xerri, D (eds) (2017) *The Image in English Language Teaching.* Malta: ELT Council. Available online at: https://visualmanifesto.files.wordpress.com/2017/09/the-image-in-english-language-teaching-2017.pdf

Eisner, EW (2002) *The Arts and the Creation of the Mind.* New Haven & London: Yale University Press.

Fanselow, JF (1987) *Breaking Rules: Generating and Exploring Alternatives in Language Teaching.* New York: Longman.

Housen, A (1999) *Eye of the beholder: Research, theory and practice.* Paper presented at Aesthetic and Art Education: A Transdisciplinary Approach, Lisbon, Portugal. Available online at: https://vtshome.org/wp-content/uploads/2016/08/5Eye-of-the-Beholder.pdf

Housen, A (2007) Art Viewing and Aesthetic Development: Designing for the Viewer. Available online at: https://vtshome.org/wp-content/.../08/2Housen-Art-Viewing-.pdf

Maley, A and Peachey, N (eds) (2015) *Creativity in the English Language Classroom.* London: British Council. Available online at: https://englishagenda.britishcouncil.org/sites/default/files/attachments/pub_f004_elt_creativity_final_v2_web-1.pdf

Maley, A and Peachey, N (eds) (2017) *Integrating Global Issues in the Creative English Language Classroom: With Reference to the United Nations Sustainable Development Goals.* London: British Council. Available online at: https://www.teachingenglish.org.uk/.../PUB_29200_Creativity_UN_SDG_v4S_WEB.pdf

Perkins, D (2003) *Making Thinking Visible.* Harvard Graduate School of Education. Available online at: www.visiblethinkingpz.org/VisibleThinking_html_files/06_AdditionalResources/MakingThinkingVisible_DP.pdf

Project Zero (n.d.a) Artful Thinking Website. Available online at: http://pzartfulthinking.org

Project Zero (n.d.b) Visible Thinking Website. Available online at: www.visiblethinkingpz.org/VisibleThinking_html_files/VisibleThinking1.html

Ritchhart, R, Church, M and Morrison, K (2011) *Making Thinking Visible: How to Promote Engagement, Understanding, and Independence for All Learners.* San Francisco: Jossey-Bass.

The C Group (n.d.). Available online at: www.thecreativitygroup.weebly.com

Tishman, S and Palmer, P (2007). *Works of art are good things to think about.* Paper presented at Evaluating the Impact of Arts and Cultural Education Conference, Paris, France. Available online at: https://goo.gl/xl40sh

Tuiavii, ES (1997) *Tuiavii's Way: A South Sea Chief's Comments on Western Society* (translated by PC Cavelti). Legacy Editions.

Visual Thinking Strategies (n.d.) Website. Available online at: https://vtshome.org/

Vygotsky, LS (1978) *Mind in Society: The Development of Higher Psychological Processes.* Cambridge, Massachusetts: Harvard University Press.

Yenawine, P (2003) Jump starting visual literacy: thoughts on image selection. *Art Education* 56/1: 6–12.

For CPD activities, visit e-file link: www.teachingenglish.org.uk/sites/teacheng/files/e-file.pdf

Suggested further reading

Maley, A (2010) Towards an Aesthetics of ELT. *Advances in Language and Literary Studies*. Available online at: www.journals.aiac.org.au/index.php/alls/article/view/26

Maley, A (2013) 'Creative approaches to writing materials', in Tomlinson, B (ed) *Developing Materials for Language Teaching*. London: Bloomsbury Academic, 167–188.

Papalazarou, C (2015) 'Making thinking visible in the English classroom: Nurturing a creative mind-set', in Maley, A and Peachey, N (eds) *Creativity in the English language classroom*. London: British Council, 37–43. Available online at: https://englishagenda.britishcouncil.org/sites/default/files/attachments/pub_f004_elt_creativity_final_v2_web-1.pdf

Papalazarou, C (2017a) 'Images on canvas: art, thinking and creativity', in Donaghy, K and Xerri, D (eds) The Image in English Language Teaching. Malta: ELT Council, 89–104. Available online at: https://visualmanifesto.files.wordpress.com/2017/09/the-image-in-english-language-teaching-2017.pdf

Papalazarou, C (2017b) 'Protect, restore and promote sustainable use of terrestrial ecosystems, sustainably manage forests, combat desertification, and halt and reverse land degradation and halt biodiversity loss', in Maley, A and Peachey, N (eds) *Integrating Global Issues in the Creative English Language Classroom: With Reference to the United Nations Sustainable Development Goals*. London: British Council, 145–155. Available online at: https://www.teachingenglish.org.uk/.../PUB_29200_Creativity_UN_SDG_v4S_WEB.pdf

Prabhu, NS (1987) *Second Language Pedagogy*. Oxford: Oxford University Press.

Tomlinson, B (ed) (2013) *Developing Materials for Language Teaching*. London: Bloomsbury Academic.

13

My road unfolds as I walk

Phuong thi Anh Le

Earliest experiences of language learning and education that have affected my current views and practices

School education

I passed the entrance exam to enter a prestigious secondary school in my town with flying colours. There I had a solid education foundation that many students would envy.

In English lessons from Grades 6 to 9, we learned mainly about reading comprehension, grammar and vocabulary. My teachers were very good at providing us with a sound basis of grammar, vocabulary and pronunciation. Also, I did a lot of grammar and vocabulary tests independently.

At the end of Grade 7, I took an English course for about nine months at an American culture centre where I learned listening and speaking skills. This centre had a fantastic self-access centre with lots of great English books that varied from picture books, short stories and science books to dictionaries, with an audio-visual room with language videos and recordings. This was where I spent a lot of time browsing books and watching videos of all kinds, about animals, inventions, films and music, etc. I did not completely understand these materials, but I found the activities fascinating.

From this centre, I also bought a lot of graded readers from 1,000 to 3,000 words about famous people and abridged stories, both fiction and non-fiction, to form my own library of English books. My home library was big enough for me to read until I was in Grade 10 when it was destroyed during the war. I was highly attracted to the contents of the books even when I did not understand them completely. During my reading, I often jotted down interesting sentences I found to learn by heart. These experiences made my exposure to English a joy, rather than a chore.

When I was in Grade 10, I became a co-founder and member of an English club that consisted of about ten high school students who loved English. We met once a week to practise speaking English and we also took turns giving presentations about topics that we chose ourselves. To improve my speaking skill in English, I often talked to myself in English, trying to express what I wanted on my daily 20-minute walk to school or back home.

I was also influenced by my teachers of Vietnamese literature who inspired us with their lessons of literary works and activities in storytelling or debates. One of our teachers sometimes even shared his own poems with us. This made me love literature.

In this way, my school education not only provided me with a general knowledge of various subjects but also developed my analytical and critical-thinking skills.

College education

I entered college right after the war, which ended in 1975. The whole country experienced serious economic difficulties. I went to a prestigious college of education and majored in English education. Like many of my classmates, I appreciated the opportunity to go to university and classes were actually a happy time for us because in class we temporarily forgot daily challenges, like the lack of food, clothes, electricity and water in our lives.

In those years, basic facilities such as books, videos, photocopiers and cassette players were not available at my college. Very often, our teachers brought their own books and cassette players to class to teach us. I did not even have notebooks to write in and one day, when I passed by a photocopy shop, I saw many strips of unused A4 paper of about 7cm wide lying on the floor and I had a good idea. I was very happy when they gave me this waste paper for free because the quality of the paper was relatively good. I made my own notebooks by just binding the sheets together with a rubber band.

Our college lecturers often lent us their books to be photocopied at shops and these copies were of the worst quality paper that I have ever known. It was yellowish paper dotted with sand and straw and the words were practically illegible in the poor light of rainy days. However, it was my lecturers' dedication and my friends' enthusiasm that compensated for the lack of facilities in my studies during those years. I still remember in our second and third years at university, whenever there was a power-cut at the college, our lecturer of listening skills sometimes had to take us to his home to teach. We then had listening lessons from his family's cassette recorder. Such classes were a big treat to us because we were able to learn in an informal setting, on the floor of our teacher's tiny living room.

I enjoyed college classes, particularly dramatisation tasks and musical and drama performances in English in the English department. These events left a strong impression on me.

My college education likewise provided me with favourable learning environments where I had dedicated and competent lecturers in addition to supportive and motivated classmates. All this helped me tremendously in becoming a passionate and responsible learner who loved the English language – its music and beauty. Four years at college passed happily. Learning was always a pleasure for me because I loved the English language and its cultures, and I had great teachers and classmates.

Overseas education

After working for 15 years, I won a scholarship for a one-year postgraduate diploma in TESOL at an Australian university. After that, I had several trips overseas to do further training in various countries, including the UK (British life and literature), Australia (MA in applied linguistics) and the US (as a Fulbright research scholar). I also did my Doctor of Education (EdD) at an Australian university. These opportunities marked a great development in my professional awareness. The experiences I gained from these opportunities have exerted a huge influence on my teaching, enabling me to become an independent researcher, to apply what I had learned to my teaching and to share my experiences in national and international conferences and journals.

Influences arising from places/institutions in which I have lived and worked

Hometown

I was born and grew up in a town that was a former capital of my country. It was renowned not only for its beauty but also for the strong appreciation for education. It was common for parents to make sacrifices to give their children a good schooling, and my family was no exception.

Because of the war and its aftermath, sending me to school was a big burden for big families like mine. My father, a shoe-maker, and my mother, a small shop owner, had to work from dawn to dusk to raise nine children. Therefore, together with other siblings, I shared the housework and helped my mother with her shop from being a teenager. I also worked as a tutor during school and college years.

Teachers' college

My official teaching post was in a teachers' college in a seaside city 650km from my hometown. This was where I worked for more than 30 years as a TESOL teacher and teacher educator.

During those years, it was hard to find a desirable teaching post. University graduates were often sent to remote mountainous areas hundreds of kilometres from home. Therefore, with some classmates, I ventured to look for work myself in this town because we learned that it was beautiful with a nice climate. Another major reason was that it had various means of transportation for me to travel home twice a year.

I was happy to be accepted into a teachers' college, which was in the town centre by the beach. Like many other colleagues, I lived upstairs in the college dormitory while our students lived downstairs. This made us teachers who lived there dedicate nearly all of our time to English teaching and learning.

Our students had to complete a three-year course to become secondary school teachers. Many years later, we co-operated with other universities to train students of English for high schools and the hospitality industry and upgraded their qualification to degree level. This required us, teacher educators of English, to improve our knowledge and skills to meet the new requirements of our society.

Even though the college was small (about 200 to 400 students of English) and had very basic facilities, with no English books in the college library, the management boards at college and department levels believed in the competence and dedication of the English staff so we had a fair amount of freedom in our work to choose suitable textbooks, ways of teaching and forms of assessment. This gave me favourable conditions to frequently integrate new things into my teaching and improve it.

During my first ten years at the college I taught language skills for students, but later I taught communicative language teaching methodology, American/British life, American/British literature and intercultural communication. In a small college, we had to be a teacher of many things, so even though I was not an expert in any specific fields, I had the chance to learn and teach a range of various subjects.

Apart from teaching at the college, I also taught English to adult learners in private English language centres and worked as a translator/interpreter for many organisations, including UNICEF, UNDP and Medecins Sans Frontieres, for many years.

Project work
For about eight years, I also worked for Australian projects, team-teaching with Australian counterparts to prepare local students for Australian universities and to train local teacher educators in communicative language teaching. These projects not only gave me experience in working with native-speaker counterparts but also gave me access to TESOL materials, which were a valuable resource for English teachers in those days. These experiences also equipped me to work as a trainer for similar national and regional workshops on various occasions.

Over the years, I have played various roles (learner, teacher, teacher educator, assessor, researcher, presenter, thesis supervisor and journal reviewer) and these experiences have all helped to shape my professional life.

Key people who have left an enduring mark on my life, beliefs and practices.

My high school teachers, university lecturers, colleagues and students have all been important influences on my professional path.

School teachers
My Grade 4 teacher was the first to inspire me to become a teacher. She was so caring and gentle to her pupils that I really idolised her. One day, she asked me to help her carry a pile of her pupils' copy books to her home and we had a friendly conversation on the way. She gave me some encouragements in my studies and that incident made me like her even more. From then on, I truly wanted to become a teacher like her. My choice of this profession started just like that.

In high school, my teachers were all highly devoted and competent. They gave me a solid, comprehensive high school education. They also impressed me with their care and devotion to teaching and this consolidated my passion for becoming a teacher.

University lecturers
Most of my lecturers were highly experienced and some had trained in English-speaking countries. They had successfully produced many generations of English teachers for my country. Like my classmates, I enjoyed their classes. For example, the translation lessons were full of laughter because our lecturer, who possessed a very good sense of humour, often made witty remarks and made us pay close attention to the ways language was used. Our teacher of listening and speaking skills attracted us with popular folk songs and stories of US culture, in addition to dramatisation tasks in our conversation classes. Our teacher of writing skills gave us a fair amount of freedom in his classes and encouraged us to do peer-editing.

We had a very friendly relationship with our lecturers and felt comfortable with them both in and outside classrooms. These teachers loved teaching and truly cared for us so we always tried to study hard to make them happy.

The subject that made a strong impression on me was teaching methodology. At that time the war in our country was only just over and life was extremely hard. Our college did not have a library of English books so our lecturer of teaching methodology lent us a book called *Language Teaching: A Scientific Approach* by Robert Lado (1964). Each group in our class was allowed to keep the book for one week to copy one chapter before we shared these chapters among ourselves. Our course lasted for about four months with a weekly class of 150 minutes. During these lessons, our lecturer talked about an issue in language teaching and we noted down key ideas. By the end of the course, I had managed to copy just a few chapters before we had to participate in our three-week practicum. During this practicum, each student teacher had to give a lesson of 50 minutes. Actually, I do not remember what and how I taught this lesson, but I still remember that when I looked at my wristwatch to check the time some time before the lesson ended, I was so nervous that I could not see the hands on the watch screen!

It is true that before I became a teacher of English, I did not learn from books. My methods of teaching were formed and shaped mainly from the people I met in my studies and work. Certainly, my school teachers and university lecturers played an essential role in my teaching career.

Australian trainers/lecturers
In my early years as a teacher, I participated in various workshops on language teaching methodology organised by the Overseas Service Bureau (an Australian organisation), and later became one of the trainers myself. These workshops provided me with practical skills and techniques in how to teach English more effectively.

During my postgraduate education, it was the Australian lecturers who inspired, motivated and guided me towards my work as a researcher. They not only taught me the theoretical foundations, but also gave me constant support and practical advice in my research work, guiding me towards my independence. Besides, my EdD supervisor was an excellent mentor in providing me with valuable professional advice in my research projects.

Local colleagues
I became more aware of teaching skills when I observed my colleagues' lessons in the college where I worked. These colleagues – about ten of them in their twenties – were all graduates from our National College of Teacher Education. From these people, I learned practical and useful lessons in language teaching.

I spent every day of my first six months at the college observing their classes and I was impressed with the teaching of two teachers in particular. One was a teacher of translation and writing, who was a gifted teacher with not only a broad knowledge of different fields but also an exceptional sense of humour. Every lesson he taught was integrated with interesting stories that he told in a humorous voice, which generated a lot of laughter in his class. The other one taught reading comprehension and mesmerised his students with his knowledge of literature. Their classes were highly lively and relaxing, with plenty of student participation. They showed me how to establish a strong bond between teacher and students.

What I also learned from these teachers was the close relationship with the students not only in class but also in life, where the teacher acted as a guide for academic issues but also as a friend in everyday life.

At that time, in my college, there was no fixed curriculum that teachers were obliged to follow so teachers were responsible for what they taught, with only some general guidelines for them to follow. This gave the teachers enough freedom to find suitable ways and materials to teach their students. I was also accustomed to using my own way of teaching, which was a combination of what I learned from people and my education. In a way, my colleagues were also my trainers – always very willing to answer my questions regarding teaching.

Foreign colleagues

I also had opportunities to team-teach with native-speaker trainers in various projects in my country. From them, I learned about the Western working styles and ways of thinking. When I was studying overseas, I also had innumerable class observations of different disciplines at various school levels, language centres and university environments. These sessions helped broaden my experience about how to teach creatively and effectively.

In addition, conferences have always been valuable events for me to exchange my knowledge about teaching with my international colleagues. Over the years, I have made full use of these opportunities to accumulate innovative ideas and practices from different countries to update my teaching.

My participation in the Asian Teacher-Writer Creative Writing Group with many other Asian teachers of English had a profound influence on my teaching. Thanks to this group, I learned how to write poems and how to develop the learners' creative writing skills. As a result, I have been able to have poems published and to show my students' poems and stories at various international conferences.

Students

It is impossible not to mention the roles that my students have played in my professional development because it is their learning difficulties and successes that have challenged and motivated me to improve my teaching.

I have been lucky in having had many students who loved learning English. As students, they have been willing to try new things that I have asked them to do. For example, they were ready to spend many evenings rehearsing a performance for a dramatisation or to write poems as part of their work. They also went out of their way to write scripts for a dramatisation and to make their own props for their performance for a literature course. They seemed to willingly accept the challenges in their learning. It is because of these hard-working students that I continued to seek out effective methods and introduce them in my teaching.

In my career, all these people have accompanied me and helped to make me develop as a professional in the field.

Key ideas I have encountered that have helped form my beliefs and practices

As an English learner and a professional, I have picked up numerous principles, approaches, techniques and lessons from various experts and materials. The approach that I find most effective is the eclectic approach. This is:

> ... a method of language education that combines various approaches and methodologies to teach language depending on the aims of the lesson and the abilities of the learners.

> Wikipedia (n.d.)

Furthermore, I find the following principles in language teaching by Michael Lewis and Jimmie Hill (1985) particularly useful and they have significantly influenced my teaching:

- Learning is more important than teaching.
- Teach the students, not the book.
- Involve students in the learning process.
- Don't tell students what they can tell you.
- Students need practice, not you.
- Vary what you do, and how you do it.
- Students need to learn how to learn.
- Useful and fun is better than either alone.

Critical incidents in life and work that have given me new insights

First workshop in communicative language teaching (CLT)

My first participation in a CLT workshop organised by native-speaker trainers took place ten years after I started my teaching career at a small college. At that time, very few teachers in my country had the opportunity to access modern ways of English teaching so this was a unique chance for me. There, I first learned about how to conduct pre–while–post stages in a language lesson, how to use songs as listening texts and how to conduct top-down and bottom-up approaches in teaching reading. This workshop marked a great change in my practical teaching techniques and my choice of teaching materials.

Class observation

During my years overseas, I had more chances to observe numerous classes at various language centres and schools where teachers were highly creative in their teaching. My most interesting and useful class observations were in a famous high school in Melbourne, Australia, where I saw sessions on book reports in Grade 8. Students illustrated the books they read with dramatisation and designed their own booklets with the story summaries. In this school, I also observed literature lessons where students watched excerpts from films and shared their analysis. From this, I understood further the significance of promoting students' critical thinking skills and creativity.

Shakespeare's plays

I attended a one-week workshop on teaching Shakespeare plays given by an American lecturer for university lecturers in my country. In this course, participants were introduced to simplified forms of Shakespeare's plays, which we learned to dramatise and justify our attitudes and actions to the audience. This showed me a new way of introducing Shakespeare's plays, completely different from what I had learned in traditional university lessons on Shakespeare.

A further chance to learn more about Shakespeare works occurred during a summer course in Oxford. The organisers invited a local theatre group to come and perform an excerpt of Hamlet to the course participants. After that, these performers answered our questions about their roles in the play. This experience helped me understand more about the characters and inspired me to watch other Shakespeare plays performed by various theatre groups in Oxford. These experiences triggered new ideas about how literature can be introduced into classrooms with different activities, such as storytelling, dramatisation, story writing and poem writing, which can motivate learners and tap into their creativity in learning literature.

Doing research

My research skills started informally by observing numerous lessons of various disciplines in different educational contexts. However, I formally learned research skills from my MA and EdD thesis supervisors.

My first attempt at doing research actually began with a contrastive study of fillers such as 'well', 'uhm' and 'er' between native speakers and non-native speakers. My supervisor asked me to transcribe several conversation recordings that I had collected during a week. I worked very hard to transcribe these and proudly showed her several pages of my work. It took her only 30 seconds to glance at these pages before she said, 'This is meaningless.' I was shocked. I learned later that I had to note the raising and lowering tones of these words, as well as the pauses before and after them. I also learned that I had to pay attention to the context, the participants' relationships and the aims of the conversation, etc. to interpret the meanings and the functions of those fillers. That was a memorable lesson to me in doing linguistic research.

I learned a lot more about conducting research and writing research reports from my EdD supervisor with his frequent questions of How? and Why? He also taught me to look closely and critically at what I did as a teacher and action researcher. This helped me to ask the right questions and find ways to deal with them appropriately.

Asian Teacher-Writer Creative Writing group

In 2010, I joined a group of teachers from various countries, mainly in Asia, headed by Alan Maley. The aim of this group was to assist ESL teachers in Asia to write creatively and to promote learners' abilities to write creatively in English. Participation in this group actually marked a radical turning point in my teaching and research career when I began to focus increasingly on creativity in teaching and learning.

Themes emerging from my chapter

My current teaching has undeniably been developed and influenced by various factors and people over the years. This impact comes from a combination of the environments I have lived, learned and worked in, as well as the people I have met and worked with. They all have played their roles in shaping my teaching.

I believe that no single training course can provide all the skills and knowledge that a teacher needs. Professional development should be a long process of being exposed to, accumulating and selecting the most appropriate techniques for one's own teaching. During this time, it is the teachers who should regularly update their knowledge and skills by observing, reading and selecting and trying out what they learn in the classrooms. This process develops with time.

Regarding teacher education, it might be a good idea for teacher training courses to focus more on trainees' understanding and practice of the following themes.

In language teaching and learning

- Learners' passion and motivation are key factors for their successful learning.
- Learners' formal and informal exposure to language should be strongly encouraged.
- Learners need to be trained in how-to-learn skills.
- An eclectic approach can accommodate diverse types of learners, learning styles and learning environments.
- Teaching is both a science and an art.
- Successful teaching is a lifelong process that should start from learning to teaching, researching, improving, sharing and further learning.

In teacher training and development

- Each teacher needs to learn to shape their own way of teaching from various sources (materials, teachers and students, etc.).
- Informal and formal reflection on one's own and others' teaching is highly recommended.
- Adaptation and flexibility are essential to make methods of teaching, syllabuses and materials appropriate to the learners.
- Teachers need proper training on how to do action research on their teaching.

A brief statement of my beliefs/values about language and about learning languages

- Language and culture cannot be separated.

- Knowing another language can change a person's viewpoints and lifestyles.

- Learning a language can be done both formally and informally.

- The more fun learners have in learning, the more success they have as learners.

- Successful learning requires various thinking skills, such as those elaborated first by Bloom in 1956 and subsequently revised in 2001 (Krathwohl, 2010).

- Skills in learning how to learn play a critical role in learning languages.

References

Krathwohl, DR (2010) A revision of Bloom's taxonomy: an overview. *Theory into Practice* 41/4: 212–218. Available online at: https://doi.org/10.1207/s15430421tip4104_2

Lado, R (1964) *Language Teaching: A Scientific Approach*. New York: McGraw-Hill, Inc.

Lewis, M and Hill, J (1985) *Practical Techniques in Language Teaching*. London: Language Teaching Publications.

Wikipedia (n.d.) Eclectic approach. Available online at: https://en.wikipedia.org/wiki/Eclectic_approach#cite_note-1

Suggested further reading

Cross, D (1995) *A Practical Handbook of Language Teaching*. New York: Prentice Hall/Phoenix ELT.

Hedge, T (2000) *Teaching and Learning in the Language Classroom*. Oxford: Oxford University Press.

Scrivener, J (1994) *Learning Teaching: A Guidebook for English Language Teachers*. Oxford: Heinemann.

Ur, P (1996) *A Course in Language Teaching: Practice and Theory*. Cambridge: Cambridge University Press.

For CPD activities, visit e-file link: www.teachingenglish.org.uk/sites/teacheng/files/e-file.pdf

14

Lurching into discovery
Shelagh Rixon

Introduction

My take on Prabhu's notion of plausibility in teaching is that it is a form of authenticity – truth to one's deeper convictions, professional knowledge and (possibly) perceived talents – but essentially underpinned by a due and honest attention to the requirements of the context in which one is trying to act.

As teacher and teacher educator, I have worked with children and adults in many different contexts. For the past 30 years, I have worked as a teacher educator and student research supervisor in academia, specialising in the teaching of English at primary school level.

Here are my definitions of the main terms in the book title:

Expertise – a blend of knowing and capacity for doing. It is typically hard-won and when well achieved it is seamless in its performance. An example in language teaching terms might be the ability in real time to spot a learner's difficulty and show the way to work on it without missing a beat in class and while not humiliating the recipient of our wisdom. That requires a sense of flow and a sensitivity to appropriate correction techniques but is often crucially underpinned by a solid understanding of how the English language works.

Experience – what you perceive and learn from operating in the world: We start life with potential and dispositions that nurture and the environment can shape or chip away at. I have been affected by what I noticed in my teachers and what I learned from working alongside my colleagues and from trying to fathom what students in my classes were making of what I was trying to do.

This chapter is largely an exercise in memory and questions might be asked about the accuracy of what I claim to recall. As Gardner (2001: 193) puts it:

> ... remembering is more akin to a state of mind than a mechanical trawl through an archive by an independently conscious 'I' ... Accordingly, memory cannot be thought of as providing anything like complete and accurate accounts of events and processes.

I do not think that I am retrofitting my claimed memories to match current stances, but even if this is inescapable, I would say that the state of mind that underpins them is valid.

Earliest experiences of language learning and education

Although while growing up I had no thought of becoming a teacher, aspects of my own learning experiences caught my attention from very early on and remained as latent queries until the time came, much later, for a revelation or an investigation in my teaching life. The approach in this part of the chapter will therefore be chronological, signalling the key people and events that played a part in my development but also referring to information and issues that became salient again only many years later.

Early learning out of school

I had no formal language learning experience before secondary school. I was, however, fortunate in having parents who fostered linguistic curiosity, experimentation and bounce at both pre-school and primary school ages. Significant non-school linguistic encounters were singing French songs ('*Frère Jacques*', '*Sur le Pont d'Avignon*'), relishing the Hindi names in the Jungle Books (Shere Khan, Bandar Log, etc.), intoning the Latin scientific names in my animal books and dinosaur names, of course. The family enthusiasm for Gilbert and Sullivan meant singing along with the macaronic chorus from *Iolanthe*:

> *Your lordly style we'll quickly quench with base canaille! (That word is French.)*
> *Distinction ebbs before a herd of vulgar plebs! (A Latin word.)*
> *'Twill fill with joy and madness stark the hoi polloi! (A Greek remark.)*

with its roared punch line:

> *One Latin word, one Greek remark, and one that's French.*

Our dachshund dog was also involved. Though I later found out that the word in German for 'Dachshund' is apparently not 'Dachshund', I was proud at the age of seven to be announcing to the world that Bambi was a 'badger dog'.

So, by then, I had learned about breaking words down into their meaning-components and I knew that other languages could contain different sounds from English and might allow even familiar sounds to come out in a different order. I think that by these means I was being helped unconsciously to forge *language awareness* (Hawkins, 1999; Svalberg, 2012). My conviction today is that even very young children can benefit from encouragement to be curious about language and languages and can arrive at their own insights.

Life as a language learner

One of the most widely cited accounts of how teachers get to where they are in their professional practice is Lortie's (1975) discussion of 'the apprenticeship of observation', which holds that teachers tend to teach as they themselves were taught. Yet over-application of the imitation aspect of apprenticeship of observation as an explanation of later practice offers a depressing prospect. Therefore, key questions to ask are what triggers change and departure from practices that developing teachers have undergone as learners and what consolidates new ones. Indignation may be a key, which I think my story will confirm, but is clearly not enough in itself. While attempting to eradicate those things that I hated as a learner, I have looked for new practices to emulate or adapt but by nature have always wanted additionally to investigate and find a rationale.

I did not enjoy learning my only school-learned modern foreign language, French. Having arrived at secondary school buoyed up by the curiosity and prior knowledge outlined above, my launch into French was not the expected adventure in a new domain. Instead, I underwent gloom, tension, frustration and some humiliation. This left me from the start of my language teaching career on the alert for ways of preventing similar things happening to other learners, particularly young ones who often have little chance to complain. It has made me a strong supporter of the principle of *pupil voice*, which I have seen in action in UK primary schools in the last ten years.

Here are some of the gloom-producing factors I recall.

French was presented to us as a glisteningly slippery, sacred mountain whose summit few would reach and whose enormity and wonder no one could ever encompass. This may be a fine way for a teacher to express love for the subject but it is not an encouraging start for an 11-year-old new learner. It was perhaps also an early manifestation of native speaker-ism in that this vision implicitly excluded non-Francophones from the shrine, except for a small future elect. This experience helped me, when I became a teacher of English for specific purposes, to appreciate how vital and liberating it is for learners to know that their course designers and teachers have considered their needs (and wants) concerning their future uses of the language that they are learning (Munby, 1978; Hutchinson and Waters, 1987) and have made appropriate selections of subsets of aspects such as grammar, vocabulary and genres of text to suit them.

Principled recycling of language was not part of the plan. Material was presented piecemeal as separate facts or items to be internalised once and for all. Most items were set as homework so that they could be put into immediate operation from the next lesson onwards. The idea of gradual accretion and deepening, especially with regard to nuances of vocabulary knowledge (Carter, 1987; Nation, 2015), was not in play. Yet my experience, especially when I started to read French for myself, was that this was exactly how it worked for me. My inability/refusal to learn items by heart on my own became an enduring battle of wills between my teacher and me. I was always behind. This may well explain why I have spent much of my energy as a teacher, a materials writer and eventually as a trainer of materials writers trying to ensure two things:

- ample encounters with the language in terms of both quantity and frequency
- depth of processing/engagement with the meaning as well as the form.

My later comments on integrating educational content with language learning and the use of communication tasks in class also resonate here.

A horror of risk was instilled in us. In spoken work, mistakes resulted in an instant 'no' and a brusque reformulation from the teacher. I recognised, years later, that there may have been a somewhat diluted version of audio-lingual theory lying behind the attempts to head off mistakes. However, lowering the affective filter was clearly not on anyone's agenda! Correction was all the more crushing since interaction was only with adults and in the hearing of the whole class. This took place in short self-contained bursts, strictly following the initiate–respond–feedback (IRF) pattern of Sinclair and Coulthard (1975). In written work, there was an easily detected belief that mistakes were caused by perverse failure to apply what had been taught. The school nomenclature ('carelessness'), however, did not reflect the hours of toil it took to produce my largely non-standard offerings.

A major related misdemeanour was 'trying to do what you haven't been taught to do yet'. Attempts to go 'beyond what you know' were not welcomed, scaffolded or shaped but abruptly cut off. This felt wrong, as well as frustrating, at the time and shaped my own teaching behaviour (in the opposite direction). When communicative tasks came into language teaching, they made very plausible sense as engaging but challenging activities requiring cognitive engagement and also deliberately stretching learners' linguistic resources to the limits. In this way, they were then ready to seek and receive sympathetic support to take the next step.

A principal figure for me in making sense of all this later was Pit Corder, especially for his analysis of learners' risk-taking and risk-avoiding strategies and the ways in which fostering and engaging sympathetically with the former could lead to learners expanding their language repertoire (Corder, 1967). This in turn led me to investigate scaffolding (Bruner, 1966).

It should be recognised that the French teachers probably meant me no harm and that things improved immensely once we arrived at what for me was 'proper' French, which meant engaging with the authentic written word and reading literature. It was French itself that saved my French. I have always since then had a copy of Voltaire's *Candide* on my shelves. I may not have got far up the slopes under the guidance of my teachers but I found some more interesting paths of my own.

Meanwhile, out-of-school learning continued but was not seen really to count either by me or by the school. Because I studied singing, I had to understand and render words in German, Italian and French, learning most of them by heart, pleasurably – with an ease of recall that would have probably perplexed my French teacher. Of course, music and rhythm help recall – another focus that I can detect in my later life as a teacher and trainer. Mozart is on a rather higher plane than 'If you're happy and you know it' but I still know just where in *The Marriage of Figaro* those second conditionals can be found. A belief that learned 'chunks' of language can be returned to at a later date as a matrix for language resource expansion is another legacy of personal experience that later reading (Myles et al., 2008; Wray, 2013) has consolidated.

At school, I went on to study Latin, and later Ancient Greek, with which I thrived. The difference for me was that I had chosen to be there, no one forced me to simulate conversations in public and we started reading real and worthwhile texts very soon. St Luke was first, within months, and Homer soon after and that is exactly how I wanted to spend my time. I went on to study classics at university and left intent on a career in archaeology.

This took me to Italy and caused my out-of-school Italian learning to catch up with my current needs. When I started working on excavations, I needed, and thus learned, Italian in quite another register from the Countess's laments in Figaro: 'Does that dog bite?' and 'Bucket please'. I also became proficient at measurements, numbers and spatial language since it was my job to record the location of finds. This was the first time my utterances in any language had gained a real response from another human being. I asked for a bucket and I got one. Communication games, anybody?

From learner to apprentice teacher

In 1970, high and dry in Italy and in need of a job to fund my studies, I thought for the first time of teaching, but still as a necessity rather than a choice. I was very fortunate to be taken on as a teacher of English at the British Institute in Rome, on the basis only of an Oxbridge degree and general presentability. The Institute was by then a private language school, having been cast off by the British Council in the 1950s before, some 20 years later, they rediscovered the revenue-earning potential of ELT. It was under the flamboyant direction of Patrick Clare, a charismatic and honourable man who was reputedly the only language school owner in Italy at that time operating within the law. None of the staff was professionally qualified in language teaching (there were very few qualifications available at that time anyway) and, like me, they tended to identify themselves as something other than an English teacher – ballet critic, poet, resting actor, art historian. Working there taught me much more than just about language teaching – principally the importance of employees being treated decently (we were) and the value of collegiality. Untrained as we were, we discussed our work and generally constructed if not a full professional identity at least a sense of the worth of what we were doing. This chimes strongly with my later life belief in the value of finding ways of supporting teachers in their collective work, expressed at its most formalised in teachers' associations. It is good to think of the work that IATEFL has done, not only in building an international network of professionals, but over the past 20 years in promoting a more local sense of belonging together through regional and national associations.

But what did I take from my first experiences as an untrained newcomer to the classroom?

First was my (continuing) conviction of the value of a good textbook, especially if it can make innovatory ideas concrete to teachers (Hutchinson and Torres, 1994). A copy of LG Alexander's *Practice and Progress* (1967) was provided for my first assignment – off-site lessons with workers in a pharmaceutical company just outside Rome. I became intrigued by how skilfully it was crafted. Methodology was not at an elaborated stage in the early 1970s; rather, the ingenuity lay in the syllabus choices and the ways in which opportunities for recycling both the vocabulary and the grammar were built in. A piece from the incomplete puzzle of my school learning fell into place with a very loud click. It seemed glaringly obvious, now that I saw it on the page, that learning should be supported by multiple, deliberately planned encounters with a language item or a grammar pattern during several lessons extending over a period of time rather than relying on the 'Learn that tonight for homework' or the 'You should know that. We did it last year' climate of my former schooling. Another book of the time in which this was achieved, and with great literary skill, was Donn Byrne's *Intermediate Comprehension Passages* (1970) in which recycling and careful grading of the passages intended for building reading comprehension skills both increased the challenge as time went by and supported retention of language. I loved teaching with this book as I could trace its outcomes week by week in my classes.

In the recent controversy and discussion about Dogme and teaching without textbooks, mine may seem an outdated view. However, although I can by now create my own lesson materials, I remain a happy user of an appropriate and well-crafted textbook. My view is that, especially in cases where teachers lack the planning time and the facility for real-time decision-making in class to replicate the essential 'adequate engagement and encounters' aspect of language learning discussed above, a suitable set of course materials can do much to help. Equally, an unsuitable set of course materials may do much harm, as a later episode in my story perhaps illustrates.

My second area of learning was how to develop an independent classroom presence, flow and stamina. When I acquitted myself well enough with the off-site lessons, I was 'promoted' to classroom teaching in the Institute itself. The most daunting form of in-house teaching was the first month of the beginners' course, which was conducted entirely orally with only an outline script for the teacher. I am grateful that this stage in my development came after my off-site experiences in which I had relied very heavily on the textbook. To support my first steps with no book to guide me, I shadowed a colleague who was able to keep up the patter and drills for a whole teaching hour with few perceptible breaths. I found emulating this challenging but needed the work and persevered. Things improved greatly after I gained enough fluency to dare to let go a little and be myself. The first time I got a laugh from camping it up was perhaps the first time the learners saw me as an authentic teacher. Another side of plausibility.

Being trained

After three years, I was identifying as a teacher of English rather than as a would-be archaeologist and felt it was time to consolidate my experience with some study. I joined the University College of North Wales, Bangor (now Bangor University) for a postgraduate certificate in education (PGCE), specialising in TESOL with L1 English and drama as subsidiaries. This course would qualify me as a teacher of children in mainstream education, which was the path that at the time I wanted to take. The course was strong both on education and on teaching us description and analysis of the English language. English phonology, taught enthrallingly by Kenneth Allbrow, captured me instantly and set me on a path that would colour much of the rest of my career as a teacher and later a trainer. As I recall, there was little direct discussion of the classroom uses of what we were learning but it was obvious to me after my years of teaching that expertise in the sound system and articulation of English would have answered many teaching puzzles of the past and was going to serve me well in the future. Of course, not everybody responded as I did. Some found the subject matter rebarbative and others doubted that they could use it. I must confess that this was my own response to transformational grammar, also rigorously and thoroughly taught on the Bangor course.

During this time, I realised that, whereas I might by now have the classroom moves and the patter well sorted for the purposes of the private language schools of the day, what I was offering was a rather meagre diet centred around little more than the language itself. It was time to consider different types of learners and see what they needed in addition to the English language. One of our teaching practice attachments took place in Birmingham in an institution called an 'immigrant centre', which in those days catered to the needs of newly arrived children who were seen as needing separate preparation for entry to mainstream schooling. I was looking forward to this first taste of what I saw as my future career and specifically to learning to work further with the *Scope* materials (Schools Council, 1969, 1972a, 1972b) on which some of our university-based training had focused. These were a multi-resource and culturally attuned kit of materials, justly renowned in their time, produced to facilitate English support for children for whom English was to be an additional language.

Yet I found myself in an institution in contradiction with its stated aims and indeed with the reputation that Birmingham had for high-quality support of newly arrived children. My teaching-practice journal of 45 years ago is an angry documentation of what was a critical period of my career. I was clearly seeking a plausible response in a tricky situation in the best interests of the children, as I saw them.

I was working, under the mentorship of an experienced teacher, with a class of 16 boys, mostly from rural backgrounds, not yet literate in their own languages and trying to settle with their far from affluent families in the inner city. Supporting them clearly demanded more than merely providing the English they needed in order to 'access the curriculum' (as modern jargon would have it). The tricky situation came from the fact that someone who had recently moved into a management role had astonishingly sidelined *Scope*. Instead, multiple copies of book one of a current ELT adult textbook, *Success with English* (Broughton, 1968), had been ordered on the grounds that it was 'more structured' and had drill tapes. I had used this book, with its elegant minimalist line drawings by Quentin Blake and comedic middle-class social situations, with sophisticated adults in Rome. Seeing the bemused looks of my class of boys, faced not only with language and situations but with exercise formats and illustrations incomprehensible to them, removed all doubt of its inappropriacy. I was angry, not least because I recognised that, as a bottom-of-the-heap trainee in a host institution, I was unlikely to influence matters for the better in the wider organisation. Fortunately, the situation was improved for my class by empathy and subterfuge. The teacher who acted as my mentor was excluded from the institutional in-group for reasons that did him credit. He was an older man, whose long experience had included time in India and whose beliefs and practice were firmly rooted in a concern to ensure that the boys were getting an education and some social support alongside their English. He was as horrified as I at the imposition of the white middle-class soap opera on lads of 11 and 12 but we worked out how to play the institutional game. Since I knew the book, I took on the sacrificial moments with its language contents, converting them as neatly as I could towards relevance to school life, while he led on integrating education with language, with which I colluded with gusto. His practices of the time would have stood examination in many a modern version of content and language integrated learning (CLIL). As an example, the boys learned about shapes while we talked them step-by-step through handling a ruler and compass accurately to measure up the paper for the colourful cut-outs that they took such pleasure in making. (Teachers in other classes taught role plays of ordering meals in restaurants.)

Mr G, my mentor, will be long gone by now, but he is high on my roll of honour not only because he showed me so much about integrating education with language but because I imagine that long after I got out he continued walking his tightrope of plausibility in that strange institution, leaving himself enough time and space to do what he felt really counted for the children he was teaching.

Developing at work

This experience disillusioned me deeply about how useful my contribution to the teaching of children in schools was likely to be should I find myself in a similarly powerless position in another institution that did not live up to the hype. An offer from the British Council answered a need I was feeling as a result of Birmingham – to be able to communicate with and support other teachers and perhaps one day be heard beyond institutional boundaries. In autumn 1974, I started working in the English Teaching Information Centre (ETIC), which ran a language teaching library and resource centre. Among the resources, I identified a set of materials that became key to my future professional life. During my PGCE, the term communicative language teaching (CLT) had not figured but this material provided many reference points for my particular take on CLT when the time came. Concept 7–9 (Schools Council, 1972c) was a set of boxed kits of game and puzzle materials for pairs and groups of seven- to nine-year-old children with communication tasks designed to integrate language and concept development. The activities were largely visual – drawing figures, tracing routes, identifying pictures – and in order to meet the challenges the children had to use language to overcome the fact that their partners' pictures or other materials were kept deliberately hidden. These are the first published information gap activities I am aware of and lie behind many of the developments in the ELT communication game/task movement. Standbys such as find the difference and picture dictation came to ELT ultimately via Concept 7–9.

After time spent teaching on a British Council English for specific purposes (ESP) project in Saudi Arabia, a posting followed in the British Council English Language Teaching Institute (ELTI), in Portland Place, London. This was mainly a materials and methods experimentation centre. The language courses we ran, although important, were seen more as a proving ground for innovations in materials and methods than as ends in themselves. So now I was being paid to write new materials and try them out and then publish the ideas via booklets and films.

One project I undertook was a publication and a film about communication games. This was unfinished business by the outgoing director of ELTI, that very Donn Byrne whose teaching materials I had admired while in Rome. Authoring the publication jointly with him (Byrne and Rixon, 1979) made up in a small way for the disappointment at missing him as a direct mentor. It was a chance to work out precise principles and categories for classroom games, and Donn's editorial and other advice (largely by phone) provided a unique apprenticeship for me as a new writer.

In teaching terms, one critical incident set me off on a path of investigation, experimentation and finally further formal study. One of the means used to collect samples of students' English at the beginning of courses was a short dictation. At the beginning of a course for British Council scholars, newly arrived from all over the world, I was puzzled why, in the tutorials held after this procedure, so many students said they had failed to recognise some words, such as 'teachers', that they realised later were very familiar. Analysing their work, I saw that in some cases 'teachers' had been rendered with an initial cluster /st/ (e.g. 'steeches', 'stiches') and realised that this was their attempt to account for my unfamiliar received pronunciation (RP) accent with its heavily aspirated initial /t/. The first edition of Gillian Brown's *Listening to Spoken English* (1976) appeared with perfect timing. This classic and very accessible work helped me address this teaching puzzle and so many more. Brown's book not only is lucid in its account of the phenomena of rapid English speech but also clearly explains its classroom consequences for listening comprehension. As a result of this incident and this book, I focused for the years to come on creating listening materials that took account of the 'fabric of the language' (how it sounded) within a framework of all the undoubtedly important more top-down strategies that could also be brought to bear on it.

When ELTI was abruptly closed down, I was given the opportunity of further study. It was Pit Corder's and Gillian Brown's presence at Edinburgh University that influenced my choice of master's course.

Conclusion: a brief statement of my beliefs/values about language and about learning languages

From this point onwards, my career was skewed more towards teacher education, as well as a great deal of administrative work, and my teaching interventions have become rarer. I was back in Italy for five years, mostly working with groups of state school teachers and renewing my interest in younger learners when the Italian government announced its intention to make a foreign language compulsory in primary schools. I returned to the British Council UK Headquarters in 1987 to a weird combination of responsibilities for materials development and for ELT in Middle Eastern and North African countries. In 1991, I entered university life as a teacher educator. My comments today should therefore be seen through the optic of a largely 'ex' language teacher, though I still work with children in voluntary work in schools.

My firm belief is that, while being a competent and if possible charismatic handler of people and their concerns may be a *sine qua non* of successful teaching, there are areas of learning that intuition, goodwill and interpersonal warmth alone cannot cater for. Although I have learned much from watching, moving and experimenting in the classroom and reflecting on the outcomes, there is a body of skills and knowledge that require rational engagement and study. The usefulness of their application has always seemed clear to me. Technical skills in planning and 'dosing' significant encounters with the language and a grasp of phonology are cases in point. Although my developing practices may have been in line with prevailing trends, especially during the exciting early times of activity development for CLT, I have always kept some secret corners of conviction and practice that did not quite fit any fashionable template. I would guess that this is true of most teachers. Some of what I encountered and learned may seem out of date by now but if there is one insight that has come out of this exercise in memory, it is that I do not actually care as long as it seems plausibly to fit the needs of the people in the class.

Finally, there remains a so far unmentioned elephant in the room. In my career I have floated on the convenient down-blast of being a native speaker. In terms of my skills set, I am now struck by how hard I have worked on consolidating my own knowledge of how English works and its consequences for learners. One of my major core beliefs turns out to be that 'living the language' and having the odd intuition is simply not enough. The ability to engage in analysis of what should be taught is as valuable for a native speaker teacher of a language as it is for any other teacher.

References

Alexander, LG (1967) *Practice and Progress: An Integrated Course for Pre-Intermediate Learners*. Harlow: Longman.

Broughton, G (1968) *Success with English: The Penguin Course*. Harmondsworth: Penguin.

Brown, G (1976) *Listening to Spoken English*. Harlow: Longman.

Bruner, JS (1966) *Toward a Theory of Instruction*. Cambridge MA: Harvard University Press.

Byrne, D (1970) *Intermediate Comprehension Passages*. Harlow: Longman.

Byrne, D and Rixon, S (1979) *Communication Games*. London: The British Council. Available online at: http://englishagenda.britishcouncil.org/research-publications/milestone-publications/elt-guide-1-communication-games

Carter, R (1987) Vocabulary and second/foreign language teaching. *Language Teaching* 20/1: 3–16.

Corder, SP (1967) The significance of learners' errors. *International Review of Applied Linguistics* 5: 161–169.

Corder, SP (1983) 'Strategies of communication', in Faerch, C and Kasper, G (eds) *Strategies in Interlanguage Communication*. New York: Longman.

Gardner, G (2001) Unreliable memories and other contingencies: problems with biographical knowledge. *Qualitative Research* 1/2: 185–204.

Hawkins, E (1999) Foreign language study and language awareness. *Language Awareness* 8/3: 124–142.

Hutchinson, T and Torres, E (1994) The textbook as agent of change. *ELT Journal* 48/4: 315–328.

Hutchinson, T and Waters, A (1987) *English for Specific Purposes: A Learning-Centred Approach*. Cambridge: Cambridge University Press.

Lortie, DC (1975) *Schoolteacher: A Sociological Study*. Chicago: University of Chicago Press.

Munby, J (1978) *Communicative Syllabus Design*. Cambridge: Cambridge University Press.

Myles, F, Hooper, J and Mitchell, R (2008) Rote or rule? Exploring the role of formulaic language in classroom foreign language learning. *Language Learning* 48/3: 323–364.

Nation, P (2015) Principles guiding vocabulary learning through extensive reading. *Reading in a Foreign Language* 27/1: 136–145.

Schools Council (1969) *Scope: Stage 1*. English for Immigrant Children Project. London: Longmans.

Schools Council (1972a) *Scope: Stage 2*. London: Longmans.

Schools Council (1972b) *Scope: Stage 3*. London: Longmans.

Schools Council (1972c) *Concept 7–9*. Leeds: EJ Arnold for the Schools Council.

Sinclair, J and Coulthard, M (1975) *Toward an Analysis of Discourse: The English Used by Teachers and Pupils*. Oxford: Oxford University Press.

Svalberg, AML (2012) Language awareness in language learning and teaching: a research agenda. *Language Teaching* 45/3: 376–388.

Wray, A (2013) Formulaic language. *Language Teaching* 46/3: 316–334.

For CPD activities, visit e-file link: www.teachingenglish.org.uk/sites/teacheng/files/e-file.pdf

15

Finding my own way

Malu Sciamarelli

Introduction

I have now been teaching English here in Brazil for more than 25 years. I never planned to be a teacher – it just crept up on me. And for the first decade or so, I had no formal training. That only came later – and by then I had accumulated a personal 'theory' of teaching that I could then match against the training I underwent.

That is why I strongly believe that when building a career in language teaching, Prabhu's (1987) concept of 'the teacher's sense of plausibility' is essential. Training is undoubtedly important and necessary, but as stated by Maley (2016), teachers build their personal theories of teaching and learning through a continuing process of reflection on their lived experiences; they adapt the training they have received to fit their reality. This process is what makes them grow personally and professionally. This has certainly been my own reality.

Early experiences of language learning and education

We as teachers are highly influenced by our beliefs, which in turn are closely linked to our values, to our views of the world and to our understanding of our place within it. Many of our beliefs about language teaching and education are formed long before we are trained to become teachers. Here I will confine myself to describing only some of the experiences that have had the most impact on me.

In Brazil, the pre-tertiary education structure is as follows:

- *Educação infantil* – before six years old
- *Ensino fundamental* – from six to 14 years old
- *Ensino médio* – from 15 to 17 years old.

Typically, students start to learn English in *ensino fundamental* when they are ten years old; however, in some private schools, English classes start in *educação infantil*. I was lucky enough to be exposed to English very early in my life.

- I started *educação infantil* at a nursery school when I was only two and a half years old. Although I was extremely young, I still remember some experiences very fondly from this period in my life.

  My older brother was studying at a small school near our house in the town where I was born. I used to walk him to school together with my mother and was always interested to know what was behind the school walls. One day I asked to go in and did not want to leave – I was fascinated by what I found inside and so I begged my mother to let me stay.

It was the English teacher who caught my attention. I had English classes once or twice a week and it was the high point for me. There were games, riddles, storytelling and songs. How I loved the songs! Not only did I sing them, but I also drew the stories and told them at home. Learning a foreign language was great fun.

- I had the same English teacher in *ensino fundamental*. The classes were fairly similar to those in *educação infantil* with the addition of formal tests. However, the tests reflected what was learned in the classes and were not standardised. So even doing tests was fun. At the same time, I started learning a third language at school, French. All the students, including me, used to mix languages at the beginning – Portuguese, English and French. Nonetheless, our French teacher never criticised us; it was quite the opposite. With role plays and drama techniques, she encouraged us to notice the nuances of each language we were studying at any one time. I used those techniques when I studied Italian and Spanish at university, and I have adapted some of them with my own English students.

- When I was ten years old, the English teacher changed and so did the classes: there were no speaking or listening activities at all, only written grammar and reading comprehension activities. The classes were silent as we were not allowed to speak. That was when my ability to communicate in a foreign language shrank and I became insecure. By contrast, at the same time, my Portuguese teacher introduced us to the Brazilian writer Machado de Assis and to a whole new world of reading and writing and, just like Machado, studying languages on my own.

- All my classes in the last three years of *ensino médio*, including English classes, had the same objective: prepare students to sit the pre-entry university tests. There were standardised tests every week, memorisation and competition among students. Needless to say, not much real learning happened in those three years of my life. But I did get into university.

So, before I started the English language, translation and interpreting undergraduate programme at university when I was only 17 years old, I already had strong beliefs and preferences about foreign language learning and education in general.

Places

At 21, as a newly fledged translator, I was ready to translate the world. However, to satisfy my grandmother, I agreed to teach some English classes for just three weeks at what was then called Anglo Germânica English School in my hometown, Jundiaí, in the state of Sao Paulo, Brazil. The weeks became months and then years. I worked there for 15 years! I had no experience of teaching at all when I started, but the owners and fellow teachers supported me and trusted in my skills. There I learned not only practical classroom teaching, how to use coursebooks and how to prepare students for standardised tests, such as Cambridge English for speakers of other languages (ESOL), but also the power of improvisation, creativity and fun learning. With one colleague, I also revisited the use of stories and reading aloud in the classes, which had shaped my own learning as a very young, pre-school girl. I also learned to accept advice and suggestions from more experienced teachers while they also encouraged me to share my opinions, beliefs and teaching practices. This equality of sharing had a big impact on my professional development.

My time there was interrupted in 1999 when I married and moved to Porto Alegre in the state of Rio Grande do Sul in the deep south of Brazil. For the first time in my professional life, I experienced prejudice and discrimination. Not for being a non-native speaker of English, but for not being a local teacher. I applied for many teacher positions, but only one offered me a place. There I was free to use the methodology that suited each group in the best way, from teenagers to seniors, but there was not much interaction with other teachers. I then realised that working alone comes with a certain amount of risk, mainly not developing professionally.

Moving back to my home town in 2000, I came back to Anglo Germânica, which had made a partnership with the Centro Britânico. We were used to sharing experiences informally at Anglo Germânica, but at Centro Britânico professional development was more formally organised. There was an internal convention once a year with presenters ranging from internal teachers to international speakers; monthly workshops and seminars; and weekly meetings at our local branch. I had always participated in conferences since I started university in 1988, but it was at Centro Britânico that I decided to become a presenter myself.

At the same time, I was invited to work as a primary and secondary English teacher at my old school, Divina Providência. I stayed for six years and decided to leave because I disagreed with their ways of teaching in the later years. My own experience showed me what real learning is, but there I had to follow strict rules and use mainly standardised tests. When I tried to introduce creative practices in the classes it was not accepted, so I left.

Frustrated by this experience, I decided to acquire more formal teaching qualifications. Thus, I accepted the invitation to work at Inova Centro de Línguas in Campinas and undergo certificate in teaching English to speakers of other languages (CELTA) training in Sao Paulo at the same time. This training brought more routine in my classes, but also more awareness of the validity of what I had been doing for more than 15 years based on my own classroom experience. It also introduced me to applied linguistics publications, which had not been available in my undergraduate course.

After two years at Inova, I was assigned a teaching position at a software company. This helped familiarise me with technology, but once again I worked alone and felt there was not much interaction with other professionals in my area. When searching for professional associations, I discovered and joined TESOL, IATEFL and Braz-TESOL and had a chance to interact with many ELT professionals.

I changed schools again when I was invited to work at a local school in Campinas. This new school has a solid reputation in Brazil, but it was a complete disappointment for me as a teacher. The classes were standardised, so teachers had to strictly follow guidelines from the academic department. In addition, classroom observation and peer feedback, which should be teaching practices aiming at professional development, were moments of terror. Most teachers and mentors would criticise teachers in negative ways, causing great distress. Once I was criticised for not following the script and for being 'too creative' because I had improvised when I considered it necessary. While working there, I presented for the first time at an IATEFL conference. Upon my return from the UK, the branch manager informed me that I could not participate in international conferences any more. That was when I decided to leave.

I was then invited to be a Cambridge ESOL and University Press freelance speaker and teacher trainer and started to present in many schools in the state of Sao Paulo and Rio de Janeiro, which gave me more important insights into language teaching. At the same time, I started to work at Seven Idiomas in Vinhedo, where I have now been working for 11 years, mainly because of the motivation and inspiration. At Seven, there is a balance between routines and standards in the classroom, and creativity, improvisation and fun. I can develop my own classroom projects based on my experience and make use of routines based on teaching methodologies I have encountered. I have also been allowed to participate and present at conferences worldwide, volunteer to work for teacher associations, write in several ELT journals and contribute to ELT publications. This has been by far the place I have thrived most as a teacher due to their constant support and encouragement.

Since then, I have been a conference presenter in many places around the world: Brazil, England, Scotland, France, Hungary, Greece, the UAE, Indonesia and Japan.

People and ideas

This is a selection of the many people who have influenced me personally and professionally and have offered me ideas that have helped form my beliefs and practices.

- My first English teacher, Maria Teresa Pontes Nogueira Rezende, was my first role model. She encouraged play in the classroom, acknowledged its value and developed activities for children to be actively engaged when learning a language. I owe my passion for learning languages to her.

- My French teacher, Madame Ivete, showed me that a supportive emotional and social environment can be just as important as the physical environment. Students learn better when they feel secure, happy, valued and listened to. This is central to any learning experience.

- My Portuguese and literature teacher, Cleide da Costa e Silva Papes, instilled in me the love of reading and literature. She taught me that stories can help us understand the world we live in, teach us about where we came from and help us see possible futures. She also introduced me to the Brazilian writer Machado de Assis who was a self-taught speaker of several foreign languages. Inspired by him, I went on to learn other languages too.

- My first boss and co-worker, Paulina Kristina Abramczuk, opened my eyes to several creative ways of teaching a foreign language. She also showed me the power of reading aloud in a foreign language class. What I have learned from her is that reading stories aloud improves listening skills, vocabulary acquisition and the understanding of common themes and structures that will impact students' learning. But it has to be done well.

- The several encounters with the Portuguese writer Maria Adelaide Amaral in my first year at university showed me the power of storytelling in the learning process. Based on my own experiences in the classes with her, I have seen that students love to hear their teachers telling stories and this helps develop a positive attitude towards the learning process.

- My co-worker at Seven Idiomas Vinhedo, Catherine Ross-White, has been an inspiration for sharing classes, information on students and strategies for teaching. She has been a source of inspiration for writing articles, publications and stories, and creating activities for my classes. She showed me that peer encouragement is extremely effective in professional development.

- Barbara Hoskins Sakamoto invited me to present with her twice in Japan for the Japan Association for Language Teaching (JALT) congress. In our second presentation, she supported me to start my own project of teaching children with mascot-inspired projects based on project-based learning. This project became a chapter in the British Council publication *Creativity in the English Language Classroom* (Maley and Peachey, 2015).

- Chuck Sandy invited me to join the International Teacher Development Institute (iTDi) and to start writing for its blog. This was when I started to write more ELT blog posts and articles, and discovered their power as a source of professional development.

- It was also thanks to Barbara and Chuck that I met John Fanselow in Japan. In a series of informal meetings and conference workshops, I have learned that simple changes may cause a huge impact in teaching practices. His books *Try the Opposite* (2013) and *Small Changes in Teaching, Big Results in Learning* (2016) express his ideas very well.

- Alan Maley has been a major influence in my personal and professional life. He has always inspired me to believe in myself and overcome my limits. His creative ideas and the use of literature and creative writing in the foreign language classroom have fuelled my own ideas. It was also thanks to him that I joined the project Asian Teacher-Writer Group as an associate member and started to write poems and stories to use in my classes; I also joined the C Group (www.thecreativitygroup.weebly.com) and met many more like-minded professionals in the area.

Each time I go somewhere, I meet new colleagues, face new challenges and embrace new ideas. I truly believe this is essential in personal and professional development.

Important publications

Every book that I read has an impact on me. However, the ones selected below have had an immense impact on my personal and professional development:

- *Memórias Póstumas de Brás Cubas* ('The Posthumous Memoirs of Bras Cubas', Machado de Assis, 1982), especially the chapter 'The Black Butterfly'. This chapter is a profound reflection on themes such as racism and freedom.

- *A Hora da Estrela* ('The Hour of the Star', Clarice Lispector, 1998). An intriguing novel about the human condition, but also about the exercise of writing and the role of the writer.

- *Pedagogia do Oprimido* ('Pedagogy of the Oppressed', Paulo Freire, 2017). This book has inspired the movement for critical pedagogy, which seeks to reconstruct both schools and society.

- *Creative Schools* (Ken Robinson, 2016). Its main idea is that education should foster diversity and curiosity through creative teaching.

- *How Children Learn* (John Holt, 1995). This offers insights into the nature of learning: learners are creative and know how to learn. We need to nurture and encourage this ability, not stifle it.

- *Try the Opposite* (John Fanselow, 2013). Fanselow suggests that, if we carefully examine what we habitually do in our classes and then try to do the opposite, we may stumble upon some interesting new ways of proceeding.

- *Creativity and English Language Teaching: From Inspiration to Implementation* (Alan Maley and Tamas Kiss, 2017). This innovative book shows how creativity can be channelled into the teaching and learning process using not only theoretical ideas but useful practical advice and recommendations.

- *The Language Teacher's Voice* (Alan Maley, 2000). This opened my eyes to the importance of the voice for language teachers and raises awareness of the valuable asset that we put to daily use.

- *About Language – Tasks for Teachers of English* (Scott Thornbury, 1997). It invites teachers to comment on the learning value of what they are doing, and thus discuss and reflect on different ways of teaching and learning.

- *Second Language Acquisition* (Rod Ellis, 1997). This was a powerful tool in opening the door to the SLA field and easing me into an understanding of key ideas.

Critical incidents

Successful students

Some years ago, I started teaching a class of teenagers who were preparing for an international English language test. I felt that they needed much more than just curricular activities, so I risked bringing global issues into their lessons, as well as teaching their more restricted syllabus.

I raised the topic of how poverty affects migration choice. At first, the students were not interested, but when I asked them to do a project about our own country and our ancestors who migrated years ago, they became engaged and committed. The results exceeded my expectations. Both their language skills and their cultural awareness increased considerably.

What I have learned: when students and teachers care deeply about an issue it leads to better learning.

Teachers' support

Teachers must trigger students' imagination and desire to learn and then help channel their creativity. This must happen when teachers are working together with students or with other teachers. Once when I delivered a Literature in the English Class workshop at IATEFL Hungary 2015, the teachers were so motivated that they set up a follow-up group online to support and develop the work in their classrooms.

What I have learned: teachers' support is very important; teachers should create their own resources when these are not available.

Themes emerging from the chapter

These are the major themes that have always been central for me and have shaped who I am today as a person and as a professional.

Creativity

Creativity has always been present in my life – personal and professional. My first English teachers encouraged creativity in their classes and since I became a teacher myself, it has been a major interest in my classroom. In 2014 I joined the C Group (www.thecreativitygroup.weebly.com). I am the current co-ordinator, having the chance to network with like-minded professionals from all over the world. The study of creativity theory and practices has also been central to my own development. I contributed a chapter to the British Council publication *Creativity in the English Language Classroom* (Maley and Peachey, 2015) and in 2017 I contributed another chapter to *Integrating Global Issues in the Creative English Language Classroom* (Maley and Peachey, 2017).

Literature (including storytelling, music, art and drama)

I have been exposed to the aesthetic learning of languages ever since I was a little girl. The contact with literature in my own language especially has made me realise that when I was studying literature and arts in English, I could make interesting and thought-provoking comparisons, thus enhancing language acquisition. This is exactly what I bring to my classes. To bring my own experiences and theory more closely, I have become an active member of the IATEFL Literature Special Interest Group.

Creative writing

Writing stories and poems has always been a central part of my life. I used to make them up in my grandmother's garden when I was just a little girl. This was then encouraged by my language teachers; but only later in my professional life did I start to use them to teach a foreign language. However, it was only when I decided to present in conferences that I started to use my own stories and poems in the classroom. This professional practice was enhanced when I joined the Asian Teacher-Writer Group (https://flexiblelearning.auckland.ac.nz/cw/index.html) in 2014 as an associate member and learned with and from other professionals.

Reading

In my view, there is no better way to acquire, develop and keep the language fresh than reading (Maley, 2008). The benefits of extensive reading have been broadly listed by many professionals in the area. Not only do students benefit from reading, but so do teachers. Based on my experience, I also believe that teachers should read widely beyond professional literature. Reading outside the professional canon will bring more vibrancy to the classroom and more discussion about any topic. It will also help maintain teachers' level of language.

Global issues

Growing up and living in a country such as Brazil, with a diverse population of people from all over the world, with different backgrounds, races, religions and cultures, I am exposed to global issues on a daily basis. I always bring these issues into my classes. From my point of view, teachers have the responsibility not only to teach a language, but also to make students understand how their decisions or actions affect others globally.

Play

I have always believed that real learning is enhanced when students are enjoying themselves. One way of making learning fun is by using play. The value of play and playfulness is increasingly recognised by researchers and within the policy arena, for adults as well as children, as the evidence mounts of its relationship with intellectual achievement and emotional wellbeing (Bateson and Martin, 2013; Whitebread, 2012). The chapter I contributed to *Integrating Global Issues in the Creative English Language Classroom* (Maley and Peachey, 2017) uses the 'playfulness approach' to discuss global issues.

Teachers' associations

Being a member of teachers' associations, participating in conferences and having the opportunity to network face-to-face are some of the best ways to share knowledge, skills, theories, practices, materials, experiences and new trends in ELT. I can honestly say that I have developed in many ways since I joined and started to participate in events.

Conference presentations and journal articles

Gaining new knowledge, presenting their classroom practices and research results, and staying current are some primary reasons why teachers should attend conferences. From my point of view, there are many other benefits from attending conferences as a professional development tool: practising communication skills, networking, finding future collaborations, coming in contact with new ideas, finding new strategies and new approaches – to name a few. Writing articles is also a valuable way to facilitate reflection and encourage teachers to express feelings regarding their experiences.

Beliefs and values about language and language learning and teaching

My beliefs about language

- Learning a language leads to a new way of thinking and so helps keep my brain active.

- The more languages I learn, the easier it becomes.

- It is very important to keep my language fresh and vibrant (Maley, 2012). In my case, reading and writing creatively are the best ways for doing so.

- I can teach myself another language, but the interactions with peers and the support and encouragement of teachers and mentors are inestimable. It is also much more fun.

- Reading extensively is one of the most effective ways of acquiring, maintaining and developing a foreign language (Day and Bamford, 1998).

My beliefs about language learning and teaching

- The more I teach, the greater my own need to learn both professionally and personally.

- Planning lessons is important, so is being prepared to respond spontaneously in the moment (Maley and Underhill, 2012; Underhill, 2014).

- My own passion for teaching and learning languages can ignite others to follow their dreams.

- Making learning stimulating with motivating tasks that protect and build students' self-esteem is vital not only to make initial motivation flow, but also to sustain it. With this practice, it is possible to increase students' satisfaction and help them continue to reassess individually what drives their learning.

- Successful language learning can be achieved when students have the opportunity to receive instruction, and at the same time experience real-life situations in which they can acquire the language. In my opinion, a main way of doing so is to use projects in the classroom.

- Play can help foster a desire for lifelong learning in our students as well as an ability to adapt throughout their lives. It provides the base for our students to be able to explore better opportunities to create and develop their own future in a global age.

- Creativity should be central for language teachers, as creative communication is both needed and crucial in today's world.

- The use of literature is an effective way of encouraging creativity in language classes. It generates an environment of possibilities that offers choices and encourages students to play with ideas and words.

- Most teachers do not encourage creativity because they think that only special people can be creative. They also think creativity is just wild chaos. These are myths: everyone has creative capabilities that can be encouraged and developed (Robinson, 2016) and constraints and discipline within the realm of creativity are very important (Maley, 2012).

- Teachers have the responsibility to encourage creativity, engagement and critical thinking. These skills will help students adapt to their changing world.

- As a profession, language teaching should take into account the social responsibility of creating internationally aware students. Discussing global issues transforms the classroom into a real-life environment. You take students out of their textbooks and into conversations and scenarios that they are likely to encounter daily.

- One important point in teaching is to know our students, so that we can meet their needs and create a pleasant and supportive atmosphere in the classroom. When the students know the teacher is getting to know them, they will know that the teacher cares; they know that the teacher is teaching people and not the subject matter. 'They don't care how much you know until they know how much you care.'

- The fundamental premise of being a language teacher is not only to teach language, but also to add value to the learning of each student in our classroom.

- I believe teachers' lives become examples and inspirations for students to follow. We can be the models for our students' futures.

Concluding remarks

Brazil is well known for its spontaneity. However, in the educational field it is exactly the opposite. With pre-entry university tests that are extremely competitive and demand extensive memorisation for limited university places, Brazilian educators face a dilemma: they know what they would like to do in the classroom but feel the constraints of the system. They know that it is important and more efficient to prepare students to pass these tests, but this is far from learning for life.

In order to fill this gap in learning English for real communication, many students have turned to language schools. Yet to become more competitive, these schools have become more test-oriented too. I understand that in this fast-paced world, results are crucial; however, learning is not always measured by just one number. Creativity is important in the classroom but must be justified when questioned by students, administrations and parents. Additionally, teachers need to seek like-minded school systems because there are always choices. An unhappy teacher is not facilitating learning.

It is this situation that makes it so important to empower teachers, through making them aware of the ways they can develop their individual 'senses of plausibility' and develop a resistance to the dulling effects of conformity.

References

Assis, M (1982) *Memórias Póstumas de Brás Cubas*. São Paulo: Abril Cultural.

Bateson, P and Martin, P (2013) *Play, Playfulness, Creativity and Innovation*. Cambridge: Cambridge University Press.

Day, R and Bamford, J (1998) *Extensive Reading in the Second Language Classroom*. Cambridge: Cambridge University Press.

Ellis, R (1997) *Second Language Acquisition*. Oxford: Oxford University Press.

Fanselow, JF (2013) *Try the Opposite*. Charleston: John Fanselow.

Fanselow, JF (2016) *Small Changes in Teaching, Big Results in Learning*. Tokyo: iTDi TESOL.

Freire, P (2017) *Pedagogia do Oprimido*. Rio de Janeiro/São Paulo: Paz andTerra.

Holt, JC (1995) *How Children Learn*. Boston: Da Capo Lifelong Books.

Lispector, C (1998) *A Hora da Estrela*. Rio de Janeiro: Rocco.

Maley, A (2000) *The Language Teacher's Voice*. Oxford: Heinemann/Macmillan.

Maley, A (2008). 'Extensive reading: maid in waiting', in Tomlinson, B (ed) *English Language Learning Materials: A Critical Review*. London/New York: Continuum, 133–156.

Maley, A (2012) Creative writing for students and teachers. *Humanising Language Teaching Magazine* 14/3.

Maley, A (2016) The teacher's sense of plausibility revisited. *Indonesian Journal of English Language Teaching* 11/1: 1–29.

Maley, A and Kiss, T (2017) *Creativity and English Language Teaching: From Inspiration to Implementation*. London: Palgrave Macmillan.

Maley, A and Peachey, N (eds) (2015) *Creativity in the English Language Classroom*. London: British Council.

Maley, A and Peachey, N (eds) (2017) *Integrating Global Issues in the Creative English Language Classroom: With Reference to the United Nations Sustainable Development Goals*. London: British Council.

Maley, A and Underhill, A (2012) Expect the unexpected. *English Teaching Professional* 82/September, 4–7.

Prabhu, NS (1987) *Second Language Pedagogy*. Oxford: Oxford University Press

Robinson, K (2016) *Creative Schools*. London: Penguin.

Thornbury, S (1997) *About Language – Tasks for Teachers of English*. Cambridge: Cambridge University Press.

Underhill, A (2014) Training for the unpredictable. *The European Journal of Applied Linguistics and TEFL* 13/2: 59–69.

Whitebread, D (2012). *The Importance of Play*. Report commissioned by Toy Industries of Europe (TIE). Available online at: www.importanceofplay.eu/IMG/pdf/dr_david_whitebread_-_the_importance_of_play.pdf

For CPD activities, visit e-file link: www.teachingenglish.org.uk/sites/teacheng/files/e-file.pdf

16

Learning to teach English

Fauzia Shamim

Introduction

Reflecting on the rich tapestry of people, places, publications and ideas in my development as an ELT professional has been a humbling experience. At the same time, it has reaffirmed my belief in teacher agency to use the given opportunities, and create openings where none existed, often against the odds! I feel lucky to have had such a rich array of experiences both at home and abroad, and met and learned from some really wonderful people and professionals in the ELT world. All of them have played a major role in my development as an ELT professional.

Learning English (and other languages)

When my father, an army officer, went to the war front in 1965, our mother packed up and took her four kids to live with our grandparents in a small town. I was just finishing my Grade 3 at that time. In our new home town, we were enrolled in a small primary school – the best of the few available. The medium of instruction in the school was Urdu. I had a reasonably good knowledge of English due to my early schooling (Grades 1 to 3) but discovered that English was a low asset in this 'new' linguistic market (Bourdieu, 1991). For the first time, it also dawned on me that not knowing a language, Urdu in this case, well enough as a language of literacy and classroom discourse, could become a major impediment to my progress as a student. Thankfully, the war ended a year later, and my father was posted to a city with very good English-medium schools. Our mother wasted no time in enrolling us in the best convent school to learn English for improving our future life chances. As a young adult, she had faced major challenges when her medium of education shifted from Urdu to English in higher education, and she did not want her children to go through the same language barrier (English in this case). My sister and I were admitted to this 'elite' school mainly because they could not turn away the children of an army officer who had fought in the recent war. Interestingly, during our more than one year of schooling in the Urdu-medium school, I had almost forgotten English, so on the first day in my new school, I required help from a translator to talk to the head teacher.

I was in Grade 5 now. We were immersed in English in our convent school and were able to pick up the language quite quickly, as it was a matter of survival in that environment. The educated-English-speaker-in-Pakistan accent came as an added advantage. It was much later in life that I could actually appreciate the socio-cultural and political value of this 'asset'.

Experiencing more than one language of literacy in my early years – English, Urdu and then English – made me believe that the best way to learn a language was through the immersion method (Cummins, 1983). It was only later, when I trained as an English language teacher, that I was able to consider other ways of learning English, particularly in under-resourced and acquisition-poor environments.

A more recent experience of learning a foreign language – Arabic, while working in Saudi Arabia – was less successful. Despite my almost seven-year stay in the country, I was only able to learn very basic Arabic. Working in the English Language Centre, I could easily get help from English-Arabic bilingual colleagues for interacting with Arabic monolingual administrative staff and for filling the forms and so on in Arabic. By contrast, my son, who was in high school, rapidly started speaking fluent Arabic, mainly to blend in with other predominantly Arabic-speaking learners in his school. This brought home to me that learning another language requires not only extensive exposure to the language in the environment but also a compelling, and probably immediate, purpose to learn the language, as this governs the learners' investment in their language learning (Pierce Norton, 1995).

My trajectory as an ELT professional

Learning to teach English

When I graduated with a master's in English literature, I was proud that I knew the classics so well that I could recite the soliloquies from Shakespeare's plays almost faultlessly. However, in my very first class, I realised that just knowing English or appreciating the classics was not sufficient to teach English. In fact, I needed to know *how to teach* English as a second or foreign language. This realisation drove me to seek out opportunities to learn to teach English as a language. I attended all available workshops, and read teachers' magazines in my effort to 'learn' to teach English. However, the day when I decided to experiment with a technique I'd read about in *Forum* magazine is unforgettable. I tried to use group work in a large class where the students were only familiar with teacher-fronted lectures. More importantly, I lacked the skills to introduce, monitor or manage group work. As a result, there was complete chaos in the class. The students quickly realised that the teacher did not know how to teach, took advantage of this and started having fun instead of doing the assigned task. I came back from class in tears, fully convinced that I could never teach English and should resign from my job. Fortunately, the chair of my department had more faith in my skills than I did. He encouraged me to continue, and later played a crucial role as a mentor in my personal, professional and career development. Soon after, I got the opportunity to undertake a four-month intensive residential training course in teaching English as an international language organised by the then University Grants Commission in the capital. This provided me with the breakthrough I was looking for. I absorbed everything taught on the course like a sponge and came top of the class, and this led to a scholarship from the British Council for an MA in Linguistics for ELT at Lancaster University.

Finding my voice!

Studying in the master's programme at Lancaster proved to be a major turning-point in my life. Being accustomed only to the traditional way of learning in teacher-fronted classrooms, the one-year programme at Lancaster with its focus on student-centred pedagogy was initially a rollercoaster ride. During the course, we were constantly engaged in discussion and debate with peers and tutors. However, being pushed into the deep end, I began to develop critical-thinking skills but, more importantly, gained the confidence to analyse and critique theories, and expand my intellectual horizon through open discussions with my 'gurus' as well as fellow learners. This encouraged me to question received knowledge and learn to think independently. The essence of this experience, however, was finding my own voice, which I have tried to develop in my students since then. Furthermore, this experience gave me the necessary confidence to develop as an ELT professional!

On return to my institution, I tried to introduce changes both in my ESL and applied linguistics courses. Equipped with my repertoire of techniques, and strong in my belief that student-centred pedagogy is necessary for in-depth learning to take place, I felt more confident to re-design my courses and introduce innovative methodology in my classroom. More importantly, when things did not go as planned, I could now reflect on the critical incidents in my class and look for ways to address the issues identified (Shamim, 1996). Several times, I heard derogatory remarks from colleagues who felt that this was a passing phase and I would soon get over it. As I asserted my new teacher role (as equal co-participant in the classroom), I was also confronted by the learners: 'Do you want to change this place into Oxford University?' This time, I did not cry when my learners challenged my new ways of teaching-learning; instead I reflected on the reasons for their resistance to innovative methodology. I was often asked 'What can you teach us in one semester when we haven't been able to learn English until now?' (after six to 12 years of studying English in school). During discussion with the students, it emerged that they felt frustrated that they had failed to learn the language during their school years. This led to current low motivation levels. Hence, they were sceptical of any new experiences in the English classroom.

Founding SPELT – taking a problem-solving approach
I felt an urgent need to share and discuss my successes and challenges with like-minded people in a supportive learning environment. While discussing this with some colleagues I met at an ELT conference in 1983, the first of its kind in Pakistan, it became clear that a platform was needed for teachers to discuss, debate and dialogue, to change the curriculum, pedagogy and assessment methods in ELT. Also, in order for new ELT ideas to germinate and grow, we needed to engage extensively in teacher education activities, and national and international networking. Subsequently the Society of Pakistan English Language Teachers (SPELT) was formed in 1984 to provide English language teachers in Pakistan the much-needed platform for professional and personal growth and development (for details see www.spelt.org.pk). SPELT also helped develop my leadership skills and I feel proud to have represented it at national and international forums.

SPELT is 35 years old today and faces several challenges to continue to empower English language teachers in Pakistan (Shamim and Sarwar, 2018). Despite these challenges, my work in SPELT has strengthened further my belief in learning with and from colleagues in a supportive environment.

Mentors and students

I have been fortunate, from my first day in the classroom until now, to have had amazing mentors for my personal and professional development. Starting from the chair of my department in my alma mater to my professors at Lancaster, my mentors have guided me to become an autonomous and lifelong learner. Similarly,

Hywel Coleman, my PhD supervisor at Leeds University and Professor Zakia Sarwar, also known fondly as 'Mother SPELT', have constantly encouraged and supported me to develop my full potential as a teacher and teacher educator and in emerging leadership roles in the ELT profession. I am also inspired by my students to be passionate about my teaching, and energised constantly when I meet former students several years later and see them successful in life. They appreciate the fact that I always had high expectations of them, which urged them to do their best in class and outside. This emphasises for me the need for us, as teachers, to set high benchmarks for our students. However, at the same time, we need to be sensitive to their need for support and provide relevant and interesting scaffolding activities, as and when required.

Key ideas I have encountered that have helped form or change my beliefs and practices

Communicative language teaching (CLT), and the way it was practised by some of its pioneers at Lancaster University, Christopher Candlin and Michael Breen in particular (Breen and Candlin, 1980), left an indelible mark on me both as a person and as a teacher. 'Doing' CLT in their courses was a 360-degree turn for me, both in terms of my beliefs about how learning can take place and in my own development as an ELT professional. My professors' complete trust in students' capacity to learn independently and in collaborative pairs and small groups, led them to use a pedagogy that was unnerving to start with, but left lasting impressions on my pedagogical beliefs and classroom practice.

Soon after completing my master's in 1986, I began conducting short-term teacher education programmes from several platforms including SPELT. However, I only became a full-time teacher educator on joining the Aga Khan University's Institute of Educational Development in Karachi a few years later. There I was introduced to ideas on educational reform and change (Fullan, 1991/2016; Fullan and Hargreaves, 1992) and also had the opportunity to become acquainted with other educational research, particularly on teacher knowledge and teacher learning (Freeman and Richards, 1996; Shulman, 1987). I also realised that, as an ELT professional, I was ignorant of all the ground-breaking work being done in general education, particularly in educational change and management (Hall and Hord, 2001/2014), and teacher learning and effectiveness. Other formative influences during this period were the significance of teacher knowledge in both education and ELT (Shulman, 1987; Freeman and Johnson, 1998), the recognition of the central role of reflection in teacher's professional development (Schon, 1983) and action research as a strategy for continuing professional development. Reading theoretical and research literature in these areas (e.g. Kemmis and McTaggart, 1988) widened my horizons and I felt more equipped to help teachers-in-training undertake action-research projects in their own classrooms as part of their degree requirement. Since then, I have found Ann Burns' book on action research in ELT (Burns, 2010) a very teacher-friendly and stimulating resource and have used it extensively in teacher education and development programmes for English language teachers.

A few important publications have also impacted my beliefs and given me the confidence to find my own voice in the ELT profession in Pakistan and abroad. Kachru's work on World Englishes (1982) changed the way I looked at English.

It gave me ownership of English and confidence in myself as a non-native speaker of Pakistani English. Holliday's work on the need for a 'thick description' in introducing change (Holliday, 1991, 1992) and subsequently his focus on context-appropriate methodology (1994a, 1994b) helped me critically analyse my earlier failures as a novice teacher and undertake situation analysis before introducing innovative methodology in my classroom. His subsequent work on subcultures has been a constant source of enlightenment for me when considering strategies preparing for and introducing change in traditional educational settings.

Norton's idea of learner investment (1995) helped me analyse the apathy shown by students in learning English. In Pakistan, students normally reach a plateau after several years of learning English language in a less than conducive or acquisition-poor environment. When they have to study English as a compulsory subject in higher education programmes, they typically feel that even if they work hard, they cannot improve much in English. In contrast, if they put in equal effort into learning other subjects, they can improve their grades significantly. So, despite wanting to improve their English language skills, learners in higher education settings are not motivated to invest in learning English due to poor expected returns on their investment.

Critical incidents/epiphanies in my life

Two critical incidents as a novice teacher were instrumental in helping me articulate and critically examine my teaching strategies and the beliefs underlying them. The first happened during my year at Lancaster. As I mentioned earlier, some of our professors wanted us to experience CLT in their classes. Hence, we were encouraged to take responsibility for our own and our peers' learning. This ran counter to my earlier beliefs about teacher/learner roles that were entrenched in my previous educational experiences. I decided to challenge the 'lecturer' (in the same way as I often get challenged by my learners) and forcefully asked him to give us a lecture summarising the main ideas and principles of CLT, and findings of major studies in that field. The lecturer calmly replied that if he did that, it would be his view and interpretation of research findings only. He invited me to go through the required readings and form my own opinion instead, which could then be tabled for discussion in class. Until then I had viewed the ideas presented by the 'gurus' as almost written in stone and that it would be disrespectful to question them. However, here I was being invited to read, analyse/interpret these ideas and engage in a critique of them if required, not only to gain in-depth understanding but also to form my own ideas and develop them further through debate and discussion in the classroom. This was a major challenge for me but once I accepted it, it brought about a lasting change in my beliefs about teacher and learner roles and ways of learning. A related incident at Lancaster was my horror on receiving a handout questioning the single-best-method paradigm in language teaching. Once again, until then I had been raised to believe that there was ONE best method for language teaching. However, questioning the relevance of these beliefs and the basis for them was a transformative experience. More importantly, it helped me gain confidence in using an eclectic methodology in my future teaching assignments. Larsen-Freeman's *Techniques and Principles in Language Teaching* (2000) was of major help in fully understanding different methods in language teaching. This has an accompanying video, which I later used extensively with my graduate students to help them clarify differences between various methods and select and/or adapt the 'best' principles for their own teaching-learning context.

The second incident took place when I returned to my country (and institution) after completing my MA at Lancaster and started introducing student-centred methodology in my classes. One day, the students staged a protest against what they considered were my 'new' ways of teaching. In their view, these meant that the teacher was abdicating her responsibilities and transferring the burden of learning onto them. An analysis of their resistance to using innovative methodology made me realise that it was caused by their lack of understanding of the need for change, the change process and what it involved in both the short and long term – but also by views about 'authority' in their social context (Shamim, 1996). This helped me initiate a dialogue with the learners on the respective role(s) of the teacher and learners in the learning process. As a result, they were more willing to engage in classroom activities and participate in joint construction of knowledge with the teacher and their peers.

Finally, during my recent work in Saudi Arabia as a non-native English language educator, there was a stark realisation that while languages are central for communication, one's accent is a socio-cultural and political construct – an identity marker that can lead to inclusion/exclusion from a group (native and non-native speakers in this case). This is exemplified in the following conversation between myself and some students who had come to interview me for a class project:

SS: Where are you from?

FS: I'm from Pakistan.

SS: No, not originally. Where have you come from?

FS: Pakistan.

SS: No, no, where are you living, in America or England?

FS: No, I live in Pakistan, but I've studied in England.

SS: [with an obvious sigh of relief] Oh, that's why you've got such a 'good' [close to native-speaker] accent.

The questions asked about my nationality and their disbelief about my not being a resident of a native English-speaking country revealed two things: first, that the Saudi learners discriminated between native and non-native speaker English teachers on the basis of their accent; and second, that they were themselves not clear about differences in accents. Nonetheless, they had some shared sense of 'markedness' to distinguish between native and non-native speakers of English.

Lessons learned

The lessons learned from my trajectory as an ELT professional over a span of almost four decades mainly concern the processes of initiating, managing and sustaining innovations or change both at the systemic level and at the level of teachers' individual classrooms. This is probably because of the initial resistance I faced as a novice teacher to introduce innovative methodology to both my learners and my colleagues. As a teacher educator, I have tried to understand teachers' resistance to innovation (Shamim, 2013), and tried to build in an element of on-site support in designing teacher development programmes.

The major lessons learned are these:

1. Learners and teachers need to be equal partners in introducing any educational reform.

2. Teachers need to have high expectations of their learners.

3. Educational managers, supervisors and teacher educators must be sensitive to teachers' need for continuing support and find ways of providing it.

4. Continuing teacher support can be provided through encouraging dialogue and discussion about the need for change, the change process, etc. in a professional learning community within the school.

5. Teachers can find the required support for their continuing professional development by joining teacher networks such as language teacher associations.

6. No change effort can succeed unless teachers take ownership of the given educational reform. This requires a change in their beliefs in particular about how languages are learned, and how learners learn best.

7. Teachers also need a repertoire of skills and techniques to initiate, manage and sustain a change effort. These include skills to take a holistic account of change partners, as well as the potential impact of any reform effort or change at the systemic level; also required is the capacity, for example, to analyse contextual factors (both affordances and challenges or potential barriers to change). The development of these skills should therefore be included in professional development programmes for language teachers.

8. Reflection on both successes and challenges in classroom practice, particularly in translating theoretical principles into context-appropriate pedagogy, requires additional knowledge and skills that should be explicitly focused on in teacher development programmes.

9. Involving teachers in a situation-analysis and discussion on context-appropriate pedagogy helps them identify and articulate their own underlying beliefs and concerns regarding the success of the change effort. This also helps them recognise gaps in their knowledge and skills for successful implementation of the required change.

10. Finally, ELT professionals have a lot to learn from theory and research in *general* education. Hence, some fundamental ideas about educational change and innovation should be introduced formally during training programmes for language teachers.

To summarise, changing teachers' beliefs is essential for the successful implementation of an innovation at the classroom level. At the same time, teachers need to build the required knowledge and skills or the capacity to initiate, manage and, more importantly, sustain an educational reform. Finally, teachers need to engage in continuing reflection on their classroom practice and have opportunities to discuss their successes and challenges with peers and colleagues in a non-threatening professional learning community (DuFour, 2004; Lave and Wenger, 1998; Shamim et al., 2018).

My current beliefs and practices

Who am I? What are my current beliefs and practices as an ELT professional?

I strongly believe that our main job as teachers is to inculcate a love of learning among our students and to help them develop the required skills and capacity for lifelong learning. I normally do this by focusing on the four Cs: communication, collaboration, critical thinking and creativity. I try to go 'beyond the book' and include students' life experiences to help them relate their learning of English in the classroom to their everyday life. To achieve this, I provide the students with opportunities for expressing their feelings and sharing their ideas in pairs/groups in a supportive classroom environment, with appropriate scaffolding as and when required. I also encourage them to collaborate with each other through a range of out-of-class activities such as service learning and then reflect on their experience (Shamim, 2018). I invite them to debate, discuss and write about real-life issues to develop critical thinking skills. I am always looking for ways to increase their engagement levels, essential in my view for in-depth learning to take place. Finally, I believe that students' creativity can be developed through open-ended questions and activities and encouraging multiple responses to a given situation. I feel that if the students become autonomous learners, they will eventually be able to continue their learning beyond the specific course I am teaching. This requires a lot of patience, knowledge of a range of pedagogical approaches and related techniques, and, more importantly, a strong belief in your teaching-learning approach. Also, learner training is vital, in my opinion, for the success of any innovation at classroom level.

I consider myself successful in my teaching practice only when I feel I have been able to develop learners' interest in learning English beyond the requirements of their prescribed textbook and exam syllabus. Like Maley (2016), I am sceptical about the role of formal exams (and inflated grades in many institutions to get a neat-looking bell curve) in language learning success. I also believe in the power of context-relevant and engaging topics, tasks and activities for intrinsic motivation, which in my experience work better than the pressure to learn English for instrumental purposes, particularly when learners have many competing priorities.

My experiences of learning English, learning to teach English, teaching teachers to learn to teach English and my own classroom practice, spread over approximately four decades now, has reaffirmed my faith in learners' and teachers' capacities to excel when they are valued as individuals working within both personal and contextual constraints. Hence, teachers' ability to critically analyse both challenges and affordances in a specific teaching is crucial not only for a heightened understanding of their context, but also to select and adapt the strategies, techniques and materials to suit their learners' needs. More importantly, it makes them aware of their own strengths as well as gaps in knowledge and skills for future professional development.

Though I understand that linguistic ability is often loaded with social meanings such as background and status, often based on the speaker's accent (Levis and Zhou, 2018) (and the interlocutor's recognition of it for identity construction), I believe that both proficiency and professionalism are required for being an effective non-native English speaker teacher (Shamim, 2014).

I also believe that the role of teacher educators is central for teachers' continuing professional development. On the one hand, teacher educators need to provide teachers with opportunities to develop a repertoire of teaching techniques and practical classroom activities; on the other, they need to develop teachers' skills to critically examine the feasibility and usefulness of innovative pedagogy in various teaching-learning contexts. I have observed that, as teachers begin to experience, critique and discuss innovative pedagogy in their teacher education programmes, they begin to unpack and articulate their own underlying beliefs and reflect on them individually and collaboratively. Often, they are surprised by what they discover! However, overall, this helps them develop the confidence to question received knowledge and adapt it for their own needs as well as to create new, indigenous and context-appropriate knowledge (Kuchah and Shamim, 2018). I also believe that teacher agency is crucial, particularly in poor-resource environments, both to take advantage of training opportunities and to create learning opportunities within collaborative teacher groups and networks (Sheikh et al., 2018).

Finally, I firmly believe that the major role of a teacher is not simply to teach but to inspire the learners to continue learning long after the course or teaching programme is over. This can only happen if I as a teacher am open to new ideas and enjoy learning myself. Hence, I will announce my retirement the day I realise that I have ceased to learn!

References

Bourdieu, P (1991) *Language and Symbolic Power*. Cambridge: Polity Press.

Breen, M and Candlin, CN (1980) The essentials of a communicative curriculum in language teaching. *Applied Linguistics* 1: 89–112.

Burns, A (2010) *Doing Action Research in English Language Teaching: A Guide for Practitioners*. London: Routledge.

Cummins, J (1983) Language proficiency, biliteracy and French immersion. *Canadian Journal of Education* 8: 117–138.

DuFour, R (2004) What is a professional learning community? *Educational Leadership* 61/8: 6–11.

Freeman, D and Johnson, K (1998) Reconceptualizing the knowledge-base of language teacher education. *TESOL Quarterly* 32/3: 397–417.

Freeman, D and Richards, JC (eds) (1996) *Teacher Learning in Language Teaching*. New York: Cambridge University Press.

Fullan, MG (1991/2016) *The New Meaning of Educational Change*. Fifth edition. New York: Teachers College Press.

Fullan, M and Hargreaves, A (1992) 'Teacher development and educational change', in Fullan, M and Hargreaves, A (eds) *Teacher Development and Educational Change*. London: Falmer Press, 1–9.

Hall, GE and Hord, SM (2001/2014) *Implementing Change: Patterns, Principles and Potholes.* Fourth edition. Boston: Allyn and Bacon.

Holliday, AR (1991) *Dealing with tissue rejection: The role of an ethnographic means analysis.* Unpublished doctoral dissertation. University of Lancaster, UK.

Holliday, AR (1992) Tissue rejection and informal orders in ELT projects: collecting the right information. *Applied Linguistics* 13/4: 402–424.

Holliday, A (1994a) *Context-Appropriate Methodology.* Cambridge: Cambridge University Press.

Holliday, A (1994b) The house of TESEP and the communicative approach: the special needs of state English language institutions. *ELT Journal* 48/1: 3–11.

Kachru, B (1982) *The Other Tongue: English Across Cultures.* Oxford: Pergamon Institute of English.

Kemmis, S and McTaggart, R (1988) *The Action Research Planner.* Victoria, Australia: Deakin University Press.

Kuchah, H and Shamim, F (eds) (2018) *International Perspectives on Teaching English in Difficult Circumstances.* UK: Palgrave/Macmillan.

Larsen-Freeman, D (2000) *Techniques and Principles in Language Teaching.* Second edition. Oxford: Oxford University Press.

Lave, J and Wenger, E (1998) *Communities of Practice: Learning, Meaning, and Identity.* Cambridge: Cambridge University Press.

Levis, JM and Zhou, Z (2018) 'Accent', in Liontas, JI (ed) *The TESOL Encyclopedia of English Language Teaching.* New York: John Wiley and Sons, Inc. Available online at: https://doi.org/10.1002/9781118784235.eelt0002

Maley, A (2016) The teacher's sense of plausibility revisited. *Indonesian Journal of English Language Teaching* 11/1: 1–29.

Pierce Norton, B (1995) Social identity, investment, and language learning. *TESOL Quarterly* 29/1: 9–31.

Schon, DA (1983) *The Reflective Practitioner: How Professionals Think in Action.* New York: Basic Books, Inc.

Shamim, F (1996) 'Towards an understanding of learner resistance to innovation in classroom methodology: A case study', in Coleman, H (ed) *Society and the Classroom: Social Explanations for Behaviour in the Language Class.* Cambridge: Cambridge University Press.

Shamim, F (2013) 'Towards an understanding of teachers' resistance to innovation', in Ahmed, A, Hanzala, M, Saleem, F and Cane, G (eds) *ELT in a Changing World: Innovative Approaches to New Challenges.* Newcastle upon Tyne: Cambridge Scholars Publishing, 87–106.

Shamim, F (2014) *Proficiency and professionalism: Arab teachers' perceptions and experiences.* Paper presented at TESOL international conference, Portland, US, 26–30 March 2014.

Shamim, F (2018) *Service learning in TESOL: Case from a business university in Pakistan.* Paper presented at the Third Experiential Learning Conference, Institute of Business Management, Karachi, Pakistan, 27–28 October 2018.

Shamim, F, Khurram, BA, Rashid, U, Qayyum, K and Muslim, S (2018) Building a community of practice for implementing EAP curriculum in difficult circumstances. *ELF Annual Research Journal* 20: 23–38.

Shamim, F and Sarwar, Z (2018) Against the odds: setting up and running an English language teachers association in Pakistan. *SPELT Quarterly* 33/1: 2–15.

Sheikh, A, Coombe, C and Effiong, O (eds) (2018) *The Role of Language Teacher Associations in Professional Development.* Springer, Cham.

Shulman, LS (1987) Knowledge and teaching: foundations of the new reform. *Harvard Educational Review* 57/1: 1–22.

For CPD activities, visit e-file link: www.teachingenglish.org.uk/sites/teacheng/files/e-file.pdf

17

Found in translation

Jane Spiro

My beliefs/values about language and learning languages

I did not know what my beliefs were about learning languages until I was confronted with its opposite. At school, we learned French through humiliation and rules, yet a few nuggets of enlightenment stay with me today. The first was the day we learned the French song *Il était un petit navire*. I relished the gorgeous sounds of these new words that floated into meaning: the little sailor who had never sailed. To this day I thank him for launching me into the joys of language. The second realisation was when I spent the summer with a family in Provence, and realised that French was spoken by real people, sitting around large farmhouse tables as dusk fell, talking animatedly and effortlessly in this other code. It was never again just a school language, inside the hard green covers of our grammar book. The third moment of enlightenment was realising that there were word families from which you could build new words: so the *navire* couldn't *naviguez* nor in English 'navigate' though he might be in the 'navy'. Realising there was a system that joined things up, instead of random words floating in space, was exciting. From that starting point I began to build a language of my own, with different building blocks only I understood, but with systems of morphemes and compounds learned from English. My beliefs as a teacher sprang from these experiences as a learner:

- Language without meaning, music and imaginative reach is like food without taste or texture.

- Language learning needs crucially to be connected with the way it is lived and spoken, not just functionally, but socially and emotionally.

- Learning anything at all should bring out the best in the learner – their passions, talents, aspirations, capacities and uniqueness.

- Learning a language should be about opening up opportunities to travel, think and communicate in new ways.

- Learning a language includes an appreciation of its systems and structures as building blocks of new language.

Earliest experiences of language learning and education

My first explicit language learning experience was as a child, being tutored by a family friend in colloquial Hebrew with my sister, three years older. In these lessons I heard the terms 'masculine' and 'feminine' to describe words, and was too intimidated to ask what they meant. By deduction, I came to understand that they seemed to divide nouns into two groups, and there were patterns of word-endings that belonged to each group. This was my first realisation that the 'rules' of language were sometimes beyond meaning and logic, and that simply 'feeling' the language did not necessarily lead to accuracy. I think what I took away from this as a language educator was that there are some aspects of language that cannot simply be 'picked up' and that can be helpfully illuminated by a teacher giving them shape – classifying, labelling and providing the tools for 'noticing'. I may have stumbled upon these differences for myself, but being told there were two distinct groups, and noticing the shapes of words in each group, provided a framework that came to help with other languages too.

Most notably, when several years later we began French in school, the idea of 'articles' inflecting to introduce 'masculine' and 'feminine' nouns was familiar. In fact, it was a delight to realise that being open to one kind of system had opened my mind to many. It seemed that Latin too had this habit of dividing nouns, and there was a third category called 'neuter'. How interesting to discover that German had this third category too and, like French, all the articles changed to introduce their category: der, die and das. At 11 years old I recognised that languages had systems that could be learned and 'felt' and other aspects that were unpredictable and had to be remembered through many encounters. Those childhood Hebrew lessons were the first building blocks of a whole tower of Babel with its architecture revealed.

However, languages were just another school subject, until my first trip to France when it was possible to actually use the language learned in school. They were an intellectual discipline, and sentences were written out and practised because they were good for us, like spinach or fluoride toothpaste. But when, aged 15, I went to Provence with my school penfriend, the language transformed into a people, a culture, a landscape and a literature. During those long summer weeks in the Provencal countryside my 16-year-old penfriend was mostly off somewhere with her boyfriend, so I learned from everything and everyone I could to cope with the desertion: from her ten-year-old little brother who taught me 'argot' – the language of teenagers and children (not to try out with teachers on coming home). I listened to French songs by Charles Aznavour and Jacques Brel and learned to sing them myself; deciphered the extracts from Rimbaud and Sartre pasted all over the walls of the elder sister's room; and was thrilled to be called *ma belle* by the handsome visiting cousin with the equally handsome name, Roc. The feeling of French took me over by stealth and, when I came home after six weeks of that long summer, I had absorbed its music and amazed the French teacher. In my French oral exam the examiner commented that I sounded like a true *campagnarde* – a country girl; so in this process I had unknowingly also acquired a Provencal twang in my accent. My insight from that long summer is this: that the French learned in school for all those years bore almost no resemblance linguistically, functionally, emotionally or pedagogically to the French I actually came to learn, use and love in France. Everything learned in France came from an encounter, with music and song, with intriguing texts, with people, events and emotions, whereas learning French in school was not much different from learning maths – systematic, disciplined and applied to nothing very much.

Influences arising from places/institutions where I have lived and worked

Before training, or even choosing to be a language teaching professional, I was offered a teaching assistant job at the University of Liege, Belgium. I taught English language to large groups of students, alongside linguists who were thrilled by the mechanisms of the relative clause or the role of the comma. The enthusiasm in the Department of Philologie Germanique was sincere and contagious. The problem for me was how this scientific approach to language could ever make a difference to teaching it. The language teachers and the researchers belonged in different camps and, though they respected one another, they didn't expect to learn from one another. It gave me a thirst to grapple with the question of how research can make a difference to teachers, and vice versa. My very first piece of published academic writing was with Jacques Noel, looking at how multiple-choice items were ambiguous at worst, but at best could tease out appreciation of fine nuance. It was an interesting joint project that gave me an insight into compromise and collaboration: multiple-choice was not a testing method I much valued but it was one that could play to the fine-tuned research interests of my colleague, and to my interest in testing the subtleties of literary texts. But most of all, this experience confirmed that I firmly belonged in the teaching camp, wanting to do that work professionally and to the best of its possibilities. From a position of best practice, I could think about research only in terms of *What difference does this make for teachers?*

Returning from Liege, I began my teaching qualification at the London Institute of Education when ESOL was in favour in the UK: children with other first languages (EAL or English as an additional language) were supported by special government funding (Section 11) and there were EAL specialist co-ordinators in schools, well-equipped EAL resources centres in each educational region and dedicated EAL teacher-training qualifications awarded alongside all other state qualifications. It was a thrilling time to enter the profession; it had status, it met urgent social needs and it was making a positive difference to children and schools.

My first teaching practice with this qualification was in a London inner-city primary school. There were 30 children and a 'lockstep' approach to learning, at that time. One of my tasks as a novice teacher was to support Turgay, newly arrived from war-torn Cyprus. The experience of seeing the school through his eyes made me aware of the importance of non-linguistic activities as a starting point for language. Turgay was happy following movements in a dance ('Simon Says'), face-painting, building villages out of matchboxes, playing football, drawing portraits of others in charcoal and working with numbers and counters. It was through these activities he became loved and accepted and even something of a leader. I came to see the importance of non-linguistic activities and the other arts as a springboard for language learning, providing a safe haven in which learners with all kinds of different access to the language were equal.

This was not the only approach, however. At Bedford College, then a higher education college merged with a college of education, I worked in the centre for English asylum-seekers and new arrivals. It was a task fuelled by a mission and a passion. The centre, part of the college, worked from a spacious Victorian house in a side street, with a large sitting room on the ground floor where there were regular parties and social gatherings for both staff and students. Among those I taught were Vietnamese boat people newly arrived in traumatic circumstances, several so shocked by the cold English winter that they were reluctant to get out of bed. They were on the edge of depression and despair, and it was patently clear that the areas of language I could cover in one-hour lessons didn't come anywhere near the real needs of these people. How was I to understand what they had been through and what they now needed? How could my experience as a language teacher thus far give me the empathy for what it meant to cross worlds?

This was a watershed moment and I determined my experience would take me to the places where my students came from, so I would know what it was for myself to be newly arrived, to cross cultural borders and to negotiate a new language and life. This took me to India, Sri Lanka, China, Mexico, Egypt, Kenya, Japan and, after the Berlin wall came down in 1989, to the former Soviet countries: Poland, Russia, Romania and Hungary. These travels entailed multiple, different kinds of teaching: materials-writing projects in Kenya and Romania, literature for language teaching in India and Egypt, upgrading university language teachers in Mexico, test-writing in China and retraining Russian teachers in Hungary. But what I powerfully learned from these travels was that the deep learning from one culture will not necessarily transfer to another; it would never be possible to make assumptions about how one skill or method might translate into another setting. Every new setting entailed new learning, different conditions, different sensitivities, different needs. For each place, there would need to be a kind of forgetting to avoid comparison with other places; and a kind of remembering that this learning would take constant vigilance.

Key people who have left an enduring mark on my life, beliefs and practices

It would only be fair to start this section by explaining the enduring influence of my father whose first language, Polish, was a secret code he shared only with his mother and surviving siblings. He left Warsaw at the age of 16, travelling through Berlin on *Kristallnacht* 1938, on the last train to safety. Like other refugees who silenced their pre-flight stories, he spoke to us always and only in English, his second language (Wajnryb, 2001). It was only when my school friends who came to tea asked 'Why does your father have a funny accent?' that I noticed he spoke differently to them, and to me. His English was peppered with Polish and Yiddish words, usually highly colourful expletives that were untranslatable, and occasionally the names of myself and my sister would emerge from the miasma of his Polish. So we knew when we were being spoken about, and the rough mood of what was being said; but we developed a negative capability that simply accepted this was his family language and not ours. As I grew up and his story became real to me, I began to grieve (too late) that this language was never shared with us, and that we showed so little curiosity in learning it. In not growing up bilingual, I was driven towards the needs of children who were bilingual; my empathy for Turgay, the Turkish Cypriot boy at Downside School, was fuelled by empathy for my father who at that age had no one in the English school to help him navigate its language and culture. Helping Turgay was healing some of the isolation he must have felt, arriving at the age of 16 with not a word of English, dropped into a school in the suburbs of Newcastle, perhaps feeling, as did Hoffman (1989), that moving from his first language to English was like being 'lost in translation'.

For my own learning, there was as much to learn from the flawed teachers as the inspirational ones. They gave me a model of how I did, or did not, want to be as a teacher. Miss Macauley the English teacher was legendary. She read aloud all the literature we studied, from *Hamlet* to *Beowulf* to *Paradise Lost*. We were shaken awake by these theatrical lessons, and inspired by her passion for them. Yet on the other hand, she had a way of putting children down that made our English lessons complicated experiences of push/pull, towards and away from the subject. However, the lessons gave me an abiding love of literature that has never waned, and has carried me through life as a strong guiding star. Even now I remember the awe of hearing for the first time the opening lines of *Paradise Lost* – 'Of man's first disobedience / and the fruit of that forbidden tree'. My second degree was an MPhil in Cultural History in which I specialised in the education Milton gave himself, in preparation for writing *Paradise Lost*. In 2016 my first book of poetry was published, and it was her words I remember: 'One day I will see your name on the spine of a slim volume'. (I think that meant poetry, rather than slim volumes of teacher resources or ELT methodology!) Yet the main insight from learning with Miss Macauley was how even more powerful a teacher might be who could give that inspiration and belief in the future of each child, but without the undertow of bitterness. That would be the kind of teacher I would hope to be.

At University College London, where I studied English, Randolph Quirk's first lecture on everyday English was a revelatory moment. This was the first time I had considered everyday language as a focus for study; the difference between a sentence and an utterance, the architecture of spoken grammar as distinct from written grammar and the ways we change the sounds of English in fluent natural conversation. I didn't know then that this English department was at that moment collecting ground-breaking data of everyday language, with research students such as David Crystal, or that this would lead eventually to the corpus and a revolution in the way language would be understood and explained. But it did feel like a totally new and exciting way of hearing language, and re-calibrating what we should notice, learn and teach in language.

Max Morgan, my violin teacher at the Guildhall School of Music, was a different kind of inspiration. The teachers described above delivered knowledge from the front of the room, and it happened to resonate with me. The difference with a music teacher is that the teaching has no validity unless it has tangible results in the way the student performs. Max Morgan's genius was the way he carried his huge expertise with such lightness, focusing instead on the minutest measures of progress in my playing. He chose music that would stretch me technically but played to my strengths – work by Geminiani, Wieniawski and Vila Lobos, which I might not have found for myself. His attention to the fine details of music, and to courteous ensemble playing, informs my playing with other musicians to this day and wherever I live. Music, like language, requires 'feeling' alongside a scientific precision and accuracy. To have one without the other is to be limited, either as a musician or as a linguist. The parallels are clear: playing the violin is, among other things, social. It expresses itself most fully in practice with others, in duos, trios, quartets; just like language, which is also profoundly social.

I came to see that the link between language teaching and the other creative arts, and especially literature, was a critically important one for me; but that in this respect the mainstream ELT profession did not agree. However, there were several important allies who championed the language–literature union with brilliance and authority. The first was my supervisor, Henry Widdowson, at the London Institute of Education. He had the same way as Miss Macauley, of dramatically delivering the literary text so the tutorial room became a theatre, but was full of belief in his learners and never delivered a put-down in my hearing, unlike Miss Macauley. Then, as my line manager in my first full-tenured job at the University of Nottingham, was Ron Carter, for whom there hardly seemed enough hours in the day to produce all he did. He had such energy, grace and generosity that it seemed you could take away with you a little dusting of his genius as a gift after each encounter. It was Ron who brokered an introduction to Chris Brumfit, who published my four papers about literature teaching and assessment; and John McRae, who published my collections of stories for language learners in a new Thomas Nelson series. As a newly qualified teacher and writer, at the very start of my career, this generosity was beyond my wildest dreams. These were the people who made up for me a brief professional Garden of Eden. Others who were kindred in their vision of language, creativity and literature were Alan Maley and Jill Hadfield, who made generous and inspiring publishing decisions and changed the landscape for ELT writers and teachers; Rob Pope at Oxford Brookes University; and Amos Paran at the London Institute of Education (now University College London), all who became friends, mentors and co-facilitators.

The final crucial influence I have time to mention is the educator and action researcher, pioneer of living theories, Jack Whitehead. Jack has the passionate conviction that practitioners have a story to tell that deserves to be legitimated in the academic world. He has a genius for harnessing the messy realities of a working life, helping to tease out its inner consistencies and to shape it as doctorate-level writing. When I met him at Bath University as my doctorate supervisor, I spread out on the floor a *smorgasbord* of my written work: short stories for language learners, books of creative resources, childhood poems, a novel, two poetry manuscripts and articles on literature testing. Through a mixture of Socratic questioning, co-counselling methods of reaching self-disclosure and action-research guidance, seven years later a doctorate emerged that I feel truly represents the multi-layered professional I had become. Jack's way of being as a supervisor has been profoundly influential in my own practice, shaping the way I am now as an action researcher guiding creative practitioners to write about their own practice. I have characterised this is a story that is an allegory of two kinds of supervisor – thought-doctor and fellow-traveller – with the latter being the kind of supervisor Jack was and I try to be. I now run an action-research programme for creative artists at Oxford Brookes, and am doctoral supervisor to professionals in musical theatre, nursing and social sculpture.

Pivotal ideas that have helped form or change my beliefs and practices

Pivotal ideas that have formed or changed my beliefs fall into four categories: ideas about language itself; ideas about the language learner; ideas about the language teacher; and ideas about being a teacher in the world.

Ideas about the language

Since Randolph Quirk's lectures on everyday language, written and spoken corpora worldwide are now freely available online, defining the way dictionaries and coursebooks are written and changing the meaning of written and spoken accuracy. For me, availability of the corpus is the single most influential difference between teaching at the start of my career and the way I teach now. In other words, there is no need for artifice and guesswork. We can see how a word, a phrase or a structure is actually used, and measure the distance between this and prescriptive explanations. The books that set me on the path of corpus and the use of everyday language in teaching are numerous, but I shall cite here as significant Halliday (1985) and Carter and McCarthy (1996).

Ideas about language learning

Ideas about the holistic teaching of learners have also been an important influence. I welcomed the development within the profession that recognised language learning was about the whole person, and not just the language faculty. *Caring and Sharing in the Language Classroom* (Moskowitz, 1978) helped to endorse this view, and gave me some practical ideas for dealing with it. A holistic approach to learning has been on a long journey since then, and we have notions now of wellbeing in learning that are becoming almost mainstream. But it is satisfying to know that the ELT profession recognised its importance many decades ago, with books such as Arnold (1999) that helped me to make our classrooms more holistic.

Ideas about teaching

A concept that helped me in my own development as a teacher was that of the 'enlightened eclectic'. The enlightened eclectic does not follow any orthodoxy or fashion, but places the learner at the centre and draws on any ideas that suit the learner's needs. This was a liberating philosophy and one that I had unconsciously adopted; but it was helpful to have a language for explaining it. An inspirational book, leading the way for this philosophy, was *Beyond Methods* (Kumaravadivelu and Gass, 1997). Yes, this is what we were and there was a language and a literature to explain and endorse it. It was the teaching approach of the new century, and one that still inspires teachers as I introduce them to it today on teacher development programmes. It was the approach that gave teachers the mandate to think for themselves and be confident about their own teaching decisions.

Ideas about teaching in the world

I have also mentioned, as an important insight from teaching in different parts of the world, that insights from one setting cannot safely be transferred to another, and that there are limitations to both comparing and generalising. I found several books that opened up this problem and made me recognise it as essentially political. A fundamental publication was Hall and Egginton (2000) and in particular Pennycook's article within that (2000). It led me to question what I was doing as an educator in other countries and cultures, and to be more acutely sensitive to power roles and balance. I was able to look back with refreshed eyes at my experience retraining Russian teachers to speak English, or working with teachers in India to bring Indian literature into their language teaching.

What then can be done? Into the gap opened up by this question came the notion of 'intercultural competence'. Most inspiring was Byram's book *Teaching and Assessing Intercultural Competence* (1997). This suggests that learners might develop a set of *savoirs* or ways of knowing akin to a social anthropologist. These would include being open to each new culture without assumptions or judgements, noticing patterns and trends, and seeking out the appropriate and typical within any new situation. It has seemed an ideal competence to develop for my own purposes as a teacher, and to build into all the ways I work with teachers and students.

Critical incidents/epiphanies in life and work that have given me new insights

My very first teaching experience was in the summer holidays while I was a student at University College London. My belief at that point was that language teaching was something anyone could do, especially if you were studying English as I was. You simply talked about what you knew. The teaching was at a summer school in Poole, a seaside town in the south of England, and the children were mostly young teenagers from Europe, sent away by their parents to be kept out of mischief and improve their English over the summer. Thus the setting was not the best for motivating children; and my naivety and complete lack of experience made for a perfect storm. On one of these bad-teaching days a small group of the teenage boys voted with their feet when breaktime ended and refused to come back into the classroom at all. Instead they stayed out in the playground, playing football, shouting instructions to one another. I remember standing in the playground watching them, and had a series of insights. The first was that I did not wish to stop them, because they looked so thoroughly *happy* and engaged, in a way that nothing in class had made them. The second insight was that if I could generate this kind of engagement in my lessons, then real learning would start to happen. I had come to take for granted that real happiness, 'flow' and engagement happened somewhere else, not in language lessons; and this was simply unacceptable. My lessons thus far had been an ordeal for us all, because I had seen teaching as something different from 'the thing I most want to do with my time'. From that moment my aim in teaching was to generate that intense level of engagement, by many different means and methods; for example, by joining up my lessons with the thing my learners enjoyed most – seeking it out, extending it and bringing it into the classroom.

Another moment of insight was a lesson with international students in a language centre in Plymouth. I was using sentence frames to create poems through patterning, rhymes and repeated lines. One of the poetry lines was 'I used to ...' and a student from Mostar wrote, 'My city used to be beautiful'. The line shafted through my heart, because that week the city of Mostar had been bombed and its ancient bridge had been destroyed. Inside that past time-form lay a wealth of pain and loss. I remembered the line from Yeats, 'Tread softly for you tread on my dreams.' There is life beyond language that we need to handle with profound sensitivity as language teachers: there is more to what we do than language.

Referring back to contexts mentioned in the sections above also constituted critical moments. One was working with Turgay, the Turkish Cypriot child in Downside School. After six weeks of being his mentor and friend through his first weeks in school, my teaching practice was over and I was to leave. He had prepared for me two new words: 'Don't go.' In that moment I had another shaft of insight: yes, teaching language is more than language, and *we can make a difference*. At that moment I made a personal vow to commit my professional life to supporting learners like Turgay, as my father had done.

Themes emerging from my chapter

The following themes seem to me to recur in my stories and accounts.

Empowering the learner

Each of the sections above seems to bring out the capacity for language teaching to transform more than language. While I am deeply interested in language as a subject, all my teaching has revealed to me that good language teaching is a great deal more than this. It can build self-esteem, opportunity and new channels of thought. For this, the teacher needs to tread with sensitivity and caution, paving the way for change to take place responsibly.

Post-methods and the enlightened eclectic

Another theme that repays attention is that of the teacher as 'beyond methods', not following any orthodoxy but learning from each situation and fine-tuning their response, case by case.

Creativity and spontaneity

Connected with both the themes above is the capacity of the teacher to think 'out of the box', and to notice the quality of actions that are unplanned and intuitive. The critical incidents and many of the stories recounted above all open up the importance of unplanned responses, and thinking 'sideways' and laterally to take account of the unexpected. It is in these unexpected moments where most learning seems to have taken place, both for myself and for my learners.

References

Arnold, J (1999) *Affect in Language Learning*. Cambridge: Cambridge University Press.

Byram, M (1997) *Teaching and Assessing Intercultural Competence*. Clevedon: Multilingual Matters.

Carter, R and McCarthy, M (1996) *Exploring Spoken English*. Cambridge: Cambridge University Press.

Hall, JK and Eggington, WC (2000) *The Sociopolitics of English Language Teaching*. Clevedon: Multilingual Matters.

Halliday, MAK (1985) *Spoken and Written Language*. Oxford: Oxford University Press.

Hoffman, E (1989) *Lost in Translation*. London: Vintage.

Kumaravadivelu, B and Gass, S (eds) (1997) *Beyond Methods: New Perspectives in Second and Foreign Language Education*. Cambridge: Cambridge University Press.

Moskowitz, C (1978) *Caring and Sharing in the Foreign Language Classroom*. Boston: Heinle and Heinle.

Pennycook, A (2000) 'The social politics and the cultural politics of the language classroom', in Hall, JK and Eggington, WC (eds) *The Sociopolitics of English Language Teaching*. Clevedon: Multilingual Matters, 89–103.

Wajnryb, R (2001) *The Silence: How Tragedy Shapes Talk*. Crow's Nest, New South Wales: Allen and Unwin.

For CPD activities, visit e-file link: www.teachingenglish.org.uk/sites/teacheng/files/e-file.pdf

18

A sense of plausibility

Adrian Underhill

My understanding of 'a sense of plausibility' is the way teachers develop professionally and personally by building a personal theory of teaching action based upon their accumulated experiences – and reflection on them.

I am lucky to have been part of an exciting time in the development of ELT, and to have met and worked with so many extraordinary and wonderfully ordinary people in many countries. Such experience has taught me what I know about language learning and teaching, being in a great team, training teachers, managing a school, professional learning or having a voice in the world.

Some early experiences affecting my current views and practices

When I was eight our headmaster, Mr Kelly, took our class for one single lesson. He brought a poem to life. It was 'The Tyger'. He transported us through the 'word barrier' of unpromising lines into an imagined world of tiger, forest, life and immensity. I realised words were triggers that could make an internal world appear, even in the unlikely setting of a classroom, even without pictures, or indeed tigers.

Daydreaming
On the other hand school also taught me to daydream. It afforded an escape from non-negotiable boredom when my body, which ached to run around the woods across the road, was confined to my seat behind the desk. I became proficient at leaving my body where it was, and leaving the present moment behind.

However, I gradually learned that daydreaming, despite its advantages, sapped my energy and robbed me of the time that I could trade for experience. It was a kind of self-vandalism. It also meant I could not do the exercises that inevitably followed the explanations. I learned too that my attention follows personal meaning. Later I tried to avoid seeding such vandalism in my classes. Tyger woke me to that possibility.

For want of a sound a language was lost
My French teacher spoke French well, and taught it well, given the methods of the time. But he did not know how to enable us to say the French vowel in 'tu', which we replaced with the vowel in the English word 'too'. He made us repeat after him, but you cannot repeat your way out of a habit, so the result was the familiar lopsided game of ping-pong.

'Repeat after me: Tu...'
'Too...'
'Tu...'
'Too...'
'Good' (though we could all hear it wasn't).

If he had simply got us to prolong the vowel in the English 'see ...' while slowly rounding our lips, without moving the tongue, he would have got us into the zone of 'u ...' quickly, elegantly and forever, and opened the way for a number of other French vowels. Instead, we heard that we sounded not French, but kind of stupid. Our self-esteem plunged and we became reluctant to speak. This reduced our capacity to yield to the language. A different relationship with French sounds could have led a quite different way. For want of a sound, a language was lost.

Mr Jones

Physics A-level involved practical experiments using lab apparatus, making measurements, writing up results, making a mess and drawing conclusions. Mr Jones facilitated a lively and playful class atmosphere. When experiments went wrong he would laugh with us. Riding that laughter energy, he would take us right into the mess we had just made to see what we could learn from it (in terms of improvisation he 'accepted the offer'). He started from first principles so we did not need to remember anything. If we needed a certain formula to describe the passage of light through a lens, he would simply work it out on the blackboard by going back to what we did know and drawing it out from us, elegantly and quickly. He would say, 'It's no use remembering this stuff, you have to understand it. Then you won't need to remember anything ...'

What I learned from Mr Jones

I learned from Mr Jones that it's fine for both students and teacher to 'not know'. Learning lies in the act of inquiry, not in the act of banking the facts. The teacher needs to model the very learning he or she requires from us. With all subjects there is a detail that on its own requires a lot of memory. But there is also a bigger picture, which, as it develops, relieves the memory load as the detail finds its place in something larger.

Influences in the formative years

In 1972 I followed an introductory ELT four-week teacher-training course at International House London. I discovered the delight of looking at my own language from inside and outside, at its living operating system, which was more than the 'rules' of grammar we had studied at school. I read Thomson and Martinet (1969) from cover to cover like a thriller. The greatest impact was the discovery of a range of techniques for presenting and practising language and fitting it together into bigger bits. Though every lesson required long and careful technical preparation, the living lesson invited improvisation and participation as the human stuff unfolded.

I soon moved to Hastings to help set up an International House school in an old hotel overlooking the sea. That decade was vivid with professional excitement. Different educational theories and practices co-existed and teachers experimented with a variety of approaches such as the direct method, total immersion, grammar translation; so-called 'humanistic' and artisan approaches such as suggestopedia, community language learning and the silent way; and later the inner game, total physical response, inner track learning, and so on. From outside ELT came the voices of Steiner and Montessori, AS Neil's *Summerhill* (1960) and John Holt's moving accounts of the inner world of children's learning (*How Children Fail*, 1965). And Leila Berg's *Risinghill: Death of a Comprehensive* (1974). Tony Buzan's 'cult' series *Use Your Head* (1974) was being screened by the BBC. This reflected an extraordinary array of personal development approaches challenging us to view learning and living as a holistic activity, in particular Carl Rogers's person-centred approach (Rogers and Frieberg, 1994). All of this nourished the new International House school in Hastings, encouraged by principal Maurice Conlin, who challenged us not to toe the line but to make the line in the first place.

Against this backdrop several things unfolded for me: (1) doing the teaching diploma course; (2) encountering Dr Gattegno and *The Silent Way;* (3) opening, directing and teaching in an executive school; (4) studying and playing jazz improvisation; and (5) the publication of Earl Stevick's book *Memory Meaning and Method* (1976).

By the end of the one-year part-time diploma course I had read most of the available ELT literature (not extensive in those days) and as it settled I had the impression of seeing a kind of coherence through the talk and the walk of ELT. Yet, only two months later this rug was pulled from under my feet, when in July 1976 I attended a one-day teachers' seminar given by Dr Gattegno in London. Half of the 100 teachers recoiled in horror at the questioning of their sacred method, and the other half, including me, were lured beyond the edge of mainstream ELT territory by insights into learning and teaching that seemed richer, deeper and more practical, and which seemed to follow more closely the moves and contours of learning itself. This resonated with my own feeling that something was missing from the theory and practice we had studied the previous year.

Next day I introduced some of the practical insights into my teaching. That was my first taste of enabling learners to take pronunciation further than considered possible, and exploring emergent syllabuses while still following pre-selected syllabuses. Students and colleagues responded positively, and I arranged with Dr Gattegno for his deputy Cecilia Bartoli (an extraordinary teacher and trainer for whom learning was a transformational process, wider than the topic being taught) to give two consecutive weekend workshops in Hastings.

Thereafter I and many others met Dr Gattegno for three days every November until he died in 1988. These workshops were hosted by David Berrington-Davies at his school in Bristol. I found that my hard-earned mainstream insights were still on target, but now seemed clumsy, and rather distant from the learning they claimed to facilitate.

Dr Gattegno's impact altered the trajectory of my teaching, my personal theories and my career

1. It is possible in his phrase 'to put on spectacles that see learning' to go beyond a learner-centred focus and towards a learning-centred focus.

2. Classroom learning can engage not only the cognitive, problem-solving mind, but also intuition, hunch, pattern-seeking, insight and other human attributes suited to the complexity of language.

3. Don't 'teach' learners what they can find out for themselves.

4. Below every 'group lesson' a class consists of many private lessons taking place alongside, and in interaction with, each other.

5. The need for self-expression may be prior to the need to communicate.

6. We can focus on a single structure while remaining open to any other structure that might be needed for self-expression, thus allowing for an emergent syllabus.

7. *Mistakes are the syllabus,* a gift to the class. Mistakes are not a nuisance, but an indication of where the students are and what I need to do next.

8. In teaching, as in conversation, spontaneity is indispensable in order to make use of the movements of learning as they occur, and to find the 'teachable moments' (when a new item is taken in without need for 'teaching').

9. Preparing oneself is as important as preparing the lesson: 'You teach who you are' (Parker Palmer, 1997).

We also experimented with community language learning based on a simple and profound approach to derive the entire syllabus from the learners, to perform a dialogue of their own creation 'at a level far above their level' and gradually to inhabit that performance as the benchmark for every further utterance.

Executive teaching at International House Hastings

I was asked to start an 'Executive School' for professionals – scientists, doctors, diplomats and business people. This involved working with individuals or groups of two. Without the clamour of a larger class, I could broaden my attention to the learner, to the person behind the language and to their learning. I began to see their individual learning moves, as if I were somehow 'closer to the action'.

Jazz improvisation and my teaching

I cannot separate jazz improvisation from my development as a teacher. I was playing jazz, which is complex, creative, rule-based and improvisational – just like language. I did not read music. My inspiration and learning came from studying phrases and passages from the great jazz players through intensive listening to their recordings – the way most jazz musicians learn.

I would select a short passage I wanted to learn, listen repeatedly to one phrase, a note at a time, and gradually work out the sequence of notes, the phrasing and timing. Then I would replicate that bit of melody with my voice, and then play it on the guitar. Once I could play the right notes in the right order, I could practise the phrase for speed, fluency and articulation. I had the exhilarating experience of leaping from receptive incomprehensibility to productive fluency within a few minutes.

In language terms this was like attending to the vocabulary and the grammar of an authentic utterance by taking it apart, and then putting it all together into a single whole or flourish by attending to the pronunciation, the unstressing, the linking, the assimilation and intelligible prosody.

This seemed transferable to my learners of English, giving them a visceral experience of listening and speaking like a fluent speaker, at a much higher quality of connected-speech pronunciation than they thought possible, or than conventional methods expected. Though this achievement applied only to that phrase, it engendered the expectation that this could be transferred to any other utterance they made. This for me was also the beginning of *Demand High* (Scrivener, 2014).

Earl Stevick's *Memory Meaning and Method*

Stevick posed his famous riddle: 'You have two quite different methods, Method A and Method B, based on different assumptions about how people learn. Yet one teacher gets excellent results with A, and another with B. How is this possible?' Stevick further asked: 'Why is it that Method A or B sometimes works so beautifully and at other times so poorly?' He suggested that each method, regardless of its surface methodology, can fulfil a set of other requirements that *goes beneath and beyond any of the methods*. He proposed that *the deeper the source* of an utterance within the student's personality, *the more lasting value* it has for learning the language. 'This same depth factor ... is *more to be reckoned with than technique, or format, or underlying linguistic analysis* ...' (1976: 110).

This resonated strongly with my feeling that something was missing from ELT teacher thinking, a 'Factor X' – another zone of great importance beyond and beneath our methods – and it gave me ideas about where to look. We experimented with emergent syllabuses alongside the prescribed ones. For some time my students' materials consisted simply of an intermediate learner-dictionary and a class reader – from which we derived story, meaning, four skills, improvised dramas, re-writing, and all the grammar and vocabulary we needed, at the point of need. By constantly rephrasing things, we extended structure and vocabulary sideways, and by extending the story into other domains students had opportunities to speak from the heart, and to engage in meaningful connected speech. Coursebooks were not needed, and the learning appeared joyful and lasting.

I was appointed director of in-service training in about 1982. The first thing we did was invite anyone interested to attend a 20-hour introduction to Rogerian counselling at the local college. It was two hours per week over ten weeks and focused on the practice of listening and understanding people without judgement. It was very popular and brought a certain quality to the school culture, and helped create a context in which 'people had time for each other'. Staff still talked about this 15 years later.

TD group

During the 1980s there was growing interest in the development of personal and interpersonal skills in teaching, though this remained outside the remit of formal training courses – and still is. In 1985 I and others started a teachers' interest group to run with this theme. Rod Bolitho suggested the term *teacher development* to describe this focus. This was a new term in ELT at that time! At the 1986 IATEFL conference, the chair, Peter Strevens, proposed starting Special Interest Groups in IATEFL and suggested the TD Group become the first one. Thus, a new focus and purpose was legitimised within ELT. If we want learning from our students, we too need to show learning, not just before and after a lesson, but during it, at the same time as the students. In Gattegno's words, 'Teachers need to be on the same side of the learning fence as the students'.

Facilitation styles

Mainstream methodology was and is largely focused on language and techniques for language learning. But I discovered that a discipline of *facilitation* already existed, based on humanistic values about learning and growth, practised through well-developed sets of intervention skills and in trainable format. However, this was not included in any ELT certificate, diploma or master's programme at that time or now.

I attended a week-long experiential programme on facilitating groups and discovered a developmental skill set that could be imported into ELT. The programme facilitator, John Heron, had founded the Human Potential Research Project (HPRP) at the University of Surrey, which ran personal and professional programmes, and their flagship was a two-year postgraduate diploma in facilitator styles. I embarked on this programme in 1986. It was part-time with a major focus on facilitating experiential learning. Participants were from many sectors and on this programme I learned that:

1. Group dynamics, people processes and interpersonal skills form a coherent field of skilful practice, much needed in English language teaching and teacher training. It was learnable by any motivated person, though probably not from training manuals.

2. It clearly articulated its ethical base, its assumptions about human learning and its purpose: to develop confident lifelong learners, to foster fundamental worth and equality of humans, and to raise self-esteem and the capacity for self-direction.

3. This was based on Carl Rogers' three fundamental teacher qualities essential for learning to take place: authenticity, non-judgemental acceptance and empathy.

4. With my colleagues at International House Hastings, we could develop a new range of teacher training courses to offer through our International Teacher Training Institute, of which I was now director, incorporating person-centred facilitation skills that we felt were missing from ELT. And that is what we did.

5. I qualified as a trainer of *Six Category Intervention Analysis* (Heron, 1990), which we offered as a 25-hour intensive experiential programme, packed with practical intervention skills for teaching, training, learning and feedback.

Pivotal ideas that have helped form my beliefs and practices

By the mid-1980s we had developed five departments at International House Hastings: The Executive School, Teacher Training, The Summer School (in 25 centres), Special Contracts and, of course, General and Exams English. Staff could gain experience and develop their careers in any department, teaching executives, running a summer school, leading in-service sessions, becoming a trainer, speaking at conferences and participating in the wider world of ELT by, for example, writing materials or helping launch or run an IATEFL SIG. Year-round teacher-training courses meant all teachers were used to being observed by trainees and peers, and chatting with observers afterwards. I began to feel that the whole school itself was like an adventure play park, conducting its primary business while at the same time learning through doing it.

This led very naturally towards the concept and practice of the *learning organisation*, new in the UK and US at that time, from which I learned:

1. The idea that just below the surface of everything we do there is potential for a layer of learning, which can continuously transform the organisation.

2. That human capital is not about having smart people, but having smart people *connected up* … and that connecting people up actually allows people to be smarter.

3. That an organisation that encourages individual professional learning is not a learning organisation unless that individual learning is connected up.

4. In such a setting it becomes normal to try out new ideas and learn new skills, and for everyone to get to hear about it; for people across departments to know what each other needs and how to help each other, and to see that learning and contribution count for as much as position and status.

5. That *learning itself* is a way of doing things, and that *learning your way* into and out of a situation has the potential *to change the situation itself.*

6. Living as learning gets to the heart of what it is to be human.

7. A natural extension of this is the intent to grow a learning community embracing all staff and all learners.

From 1999 my trajectory continued but as a freelance, self-employed trainer and consultant. In that year I also started a master's course and became Vice-President of IATEFL (and thus President the following year). To get real refreshment from a master's meant to follow my heart and to feed my new freelance career, so I enrolled on a two-year Master's in Responsibility and Business Practice at the Centre for Action Research in Professional Practice (CARPP) at Bath University, which was deeply rooted in action-based justice for people and the planet, through responsible commerce and business. Commerce may look like the cause of many of the serious problems, but could it also be the solution? This programme and the community around it had a big impact on my professional and personal practice. For example:

1. I was introduced to *systems thinking*, which is a science of the whole, while conventional science is perhaps a science of parts. Both are needed, in balance. It's about connecting with the bigger picture, the interconnected context in which we are embedded and which frames our seeing, thinking, feeling and actions.

2. I learned how to advocate and facilitate the art of *open space technology*, which is about holding creative and forward-looking discussions with large groups of people, addressing spontaneously whatever is most important at the time. Based on principles of self-organisation, it has a contemporary and democratic immediacy about it. I was able to introduce *open space* in my ELT practice including to IATEFL.

3. *Sustainability.* There is a business opportunity in acting responsibly towards people and the planet. Most individuals and organisations have more power than they realise to influence sustainable practice *upstream* by opting for suppliers who can show sustainable credentials for their own production and impacts, and *downstream* by critiquing the sustainability of their own practices. For me, a new question arose: 'What is sustainability in ELT?'

4. *Reflective practice* as a life discipline at individual, team and corporate level was what enabled all the other ideas to flow. Inquiry is the essential core to any transformational activity and needs to become integral to the operating system of any team or organisation.

Leadership in complexity: the Bath master's gave me a new way of viewing and practising leadership, and I started to offer workshops on new paradigms of leadership for teachers, managers and school leadership. In my consultancies with schools the problems I was asked to deal with often proved to be systems – that is, the problem lay in *the context* within which the problem was presented, rather than with the problem itself. To bring about change one had to work with the *context*, not necessarily with the *problem*.

I was invited to become a facilitator on Leaders UK, a UK cabinet office initiative aiming to develop new forms of inclusive leadership in and between government ministries, to get them to operate less as separate silos, and more as part of a single connected-up intelligence. For six years, I and ten others facilitated action-inquiry groups of middle and senior civil servants, each lasting two years and meeting for a day or two every month or two. The aim was to develop new leadership skills and strategies through action and reflection cycles. What I learned about leadership was that:

1. The activity of leadership is essentially about getting things done through people.

2. When you unhook *leadership activity* from *the person of the leader,* you find that anyone at any place in any organisation can engage in leadership activity from where they are, whether back-office assistant or the visible CEO.

3. New concepts of leadership focus more on drawing leadership activity out of everyone, distributing leadership through the system, and creating a more coherent organisation than is possible while leadership and control resides solely at the top.

4. People want to take their values to work rather than sacrifice them in order to go to work. This requires a culture of leadership that serves people, not just itself.

5. The vision of a school needs to be guided by values that include the values of the staff. Our energy and intelligence are almost boundless when we do what we feel is deeply worthwhile.

Four epiphanies in my work

Student mistakes as a gift to the class
After ten years of classroom teaching, right in the middle of a class, I suddenly realised I was no longer afraid of my students' mistakes. Whatever happened, I could find a way to turn their mistakes to learning advantage. I had been acting as if my job was to get learners to be correct, treating mistakes as a nuisance that slowed down our progress, to be eradicated in order to 'get on with the lesson'. I saw the immense waste of psychological energy this involved.

Teaching one-to-one in a group
After teaching one-to-one and small groups for a few years, I returned to larger classes, and immediately had the vivid impression that even with 18 students I could still have a close one-to-one relationship with each learner. I saw that my job was not to teach *one group*, though it might look like that, but to teach 18 private lessons (19 including my own) that were contained in one group. It was as if there was a thread between me and each student and my job was to keep it taut, to gently maintain each learner at their learning edge.

Removing the ceiling
Following from that, I became aware that whatever an individual student was working on, could, if I made it visible somehow, be engaging for the rest of the class, both as a mini-drama of learning happening in front of their eyes, and as proxy-learning for them.

Acting as if all my thoughts are visible to the student

One day it suddenly became obvious that I could not pretend in front of learners. I could not pretend to be patient if I was not, non-judgemental if I was not or listening attentively if I was not. There was only one solution: to listen, to be patient and not to judge. This became not a destination, but a direction of travel.

My three quick 'modifications' for teacher training

Based on all this, my three quick 'modifications' for teacher training might be:

1. *Reduce input.* Essential input such as different skills lessons can be made available through a library of videos of classes in action.

2. *Increase teaching practice,* whether with 'real' students or with peer trainees, but in particular use *peer-teaching* to help trainees to develop their own ways to connect with people and deal creatively with the events that happen in groups. It is about identifying and practising core facilitation skills that develop relationships in and between people. Once there is connection, everything flows differently, not just better.

3. *Attend to playfulness, spontaneity and improvisation.* Teaching is a performance art.

My beliefs/values about language and learning emerging from this experiential pathway

What emerges from my experience is a pattern of connected but fluid beliefs and values. Underneath that is something less transitory that I still cannot articulate fully. This is my current position:

Language and learning: language, especially grammar, is a system and needs to be learned in a primarily systemic or holistic way, for which humans are supremely well equipped. Teaching grammar broken down into rule-abiding parts is probably useful and necessary, but is not the whole story since it utilises only the cognitive, problem-solving part of our brains. I have come to trust the more-than-cognitive human learning attributes such as intuition, instinct, pattern-seeking, noticing, experimenting, playfulness and indeed the learning power of the self-esteem people feel when they are learning what is worthwhile and meaningful to them. Humans are capable of much more than we and our teachers imagine. Believe in the unbounded capacities of learners, and something else happens.

I see *self-expression and personal meaning* as a primary function of language, perhaps prior to the need for communication, and probably with more learning value. Self-expression does not mean saying something about yourself, though it might. It means being oneself in the world, having a voice in the world. I think we'd have a different methodology if we took self-expression rather than communication as our starting point, and this could open up transformational, not just transactional language learning.

Where am I in all this? As a teacher and trainer I am first a learner. I can only hold open a learning space when I am learning alongside my students. Learning evokes learning. I feel that there are always two things going on, teaching the past simple (i.e. the topic), and something else wider and bigger (exercising learning). The former is the reason we think we are there, to get hold of enough language for our purpose. The latter exercises the humanising gift of learning itself, regardless of content. The former is *transactional*, the latter is *transformational*. The former is on the syllabus and in the test. The latter is not, though it appears unexpectedly in 'good lessons' the world over. I think it is about self-expression, personal meaning and having a voice in the world. It is about becoming, and learning to feel OK with ourselves. That is why teachers are VIPs. Their impact does not stop at the classroom walls.

References

Berg, L (1974) *Risinghill: Death of a Comprehensive.* London: Pelican.

Buzan, T (1974) *Use Your Head.* London: BBC.

Heron, J (1990) *Helping the Client: Six Category Intervention Analysis.* London: Sage.

Holt, J (1965) *How Children Fail.* London: Penguin.

Neil, AS (1960) *Summerhill.* London: Pelican.

Palmer, P (1997) *The Courage to Teach.* New York: John Wiley and Sons.

Rogers, C and Freiberg, HJ (1994) *Freedom to Learn.* Third edition. New York: Merrill.

Scrivener, J (2014) *Demand-high teaching.* European Journal of Applied Linguistics and TEFL 3/2: 47–58.

Stevick, EW (1976) *Memory, Meaning and Method.* Rowley, MA: Newbury House.

Thomson, A and Martinet, A (1969) *A Practical English Grammar.* Second edition. Oxford: Oxford University Press.

Suggested further reading

Bolton, R (1986) *People Skills*. London: Prentice-Hall.

Boal, A (2000) *Theatre of the Oppressed*. London: Pluto Classics.

Brandes, D and Ginnis, P (1986) *A Guide to Student-Centred Learning.* Oxford: Basil Blackwell.

Capra, F (1997) *The Web of Life*. London: Flamingo.

Fanselow, JF (1987) *Breaking Rules*. New York: Longman.

Field, J (aka Marion Milner) (2011) *A Life of One's Own*. London: Routledge.

Freire, P (1970) *Pedagogy of the Oppressed*. New York: Continuum.

Gattegno, C (1971) (republished 2010) *What We Owe Children.* Toronto: Educational Solutions Worldwide Inc.

Gattegno, C (1976) (republished 2010) *The Common Sense of Teaching Foreign Languages*. Toronto: Educational Solutions Worldwide Inc.

Head, K and Taylor, P (1997) *Readings in Teacher Development*. London: Heinemann.

Heron, J (1989) *The Facilitators' Handbook*. London: Kogan Page.

Leonard, G (1969) *Education and Ecstasy.* New York: Delacorte Press, Penguin/ Random House.

Lewin, R and Regine, B (2001) *Weaving Complexity and Business: Engaging the Soul at Work*. Knutsford: Texere.

Nachmanovitch, S (1990) *Free Play: Improvisation in Life and Art*. New York: Tarcher/Putnam.

Pedlar, M and Aspinwall, K (1998) *Concise Guide to the Learning Organization.* London: Lemos and Crane.

Senge, P (1990) *The Fifth Discipline.* New York: Doubleday.

Sinclair, B (1998) *Doing Leadership Differently.* Melbourne: Melbourne University Press.

Torbert, W and Associates (2004) *Action Inquiry: The Secret of Timely and Transforming Leadership.* San Francisco: Berrett-Koehler.

Young, R and Messum, P (2011) *How We Learn and How We Should be Taught: An Introduction to the Work of Caleb Gattegno* (Volume 1). London: Duo Flumina.

19

Becoming a language teacher

Tessa Woodward

My earliest experiences of language learning

My mother spoke English. My father spoke Welsh and English. My parents had come well adrift of each other by the time I was three years old. From the start then, I understood that different languages were possible and that they could be a cause of strife. For one thing, a person who doesn't speak a foreign language can then feel isolated and excluded when in the company of those who do speak it.

After my mother left my father and had nowhere much to go, she knocked on the door of a Roman Catholic convent asking for accommodation. The nuns took us in, on one condition: that I attended their convent school. There, I became friends with a little French nun called Sister Bernadette. She kindly peeled my oranges for me, in the breaks. Sister Bernadette taught me some French words and, I realise now, looking back that, from her, I learned that liking a person who speaks a different language from you can also endear their language to you.

In the convent school, we had a few beginner French lessons. We kept two language vocabulary lists. I can still see them in my mind's eye.

La table   *the table*
Le pupitre   *the desk*
La fille   *the girl*

We also had daily retrieval practice: 'Please say/write the French word for girl.'

I took my vocabulary notebook, my tangible word store, with me when transferring to my next school. There, I was the only pupil in class who had done a little French before. Thanks to all that practice I could answer questions, such as, 'Does anybody know the French word for *girl*?' Those little successes made me feel good.

I have since learned to add to the basic idea of the two-language list, by recording collocated phrases rather than single words, using codes such as F (for formal), I (for informal) and N (for neutral) to indicate register and by marking the primary stress. I have also learned to vary regular retrieval practice with differing prompts. But I have never abandoned the humble practice itself as it got me on my way with French. I have also never scorned simple repetitive drills, practised later in secondary school, since those moments of reciting *Je le, tu le, nous le, vous le, je la, tu la, nous la, vous la* have stood me in great stead! I have simply made drills a bit more fun by varying their speed, volume and intonation.

Sadly, although I was on my way with French, I was not on my way with Welsh. I now lived in England, so had little contact with Welsh speakers. Once I'd left home, however, I did join a Welsh language class. When the teacher asked, 'Does anybody know any Welsh words?' I happily offered a few that I had learned from my *mangu* (Welsh grandmother). I had been in this situation before with French and I looked forward to some appreciation. But instead, I heard incredulous laughter from the teacher! Apparently, I sounded like a yokel. She taught me the 'proper' way to say my words, BBC Welsh style. It dawned on me that if I spoke to my dad her way, he would laugh at me for sounding posh. If I spoke to her his way, she'd laugh at me for sounding like a country bumpkin. Either way, it wouldn't work. So that was that. From this I learned that strong emotions can be aroused, not just in someone who is surrounded by a language that they cannot speak, but also in people who speak the same language but in different ways. Pronunciation, I learned, is dynamite.

And, of course, there was Latin. At school we translated texts such as *Gallia est omnis divisa in partes tres*. We conjugated verbs such as *amo amas amat*. But, despite the meaning of that verb, there was no love. No conversation either. I found it tedious. Latin has, however, been super useful for my vocabulary learning the rest of my life. The point here, for me, is that lessons can stultify and yet turn out to be useful!

Places in which I have lived and worked

The first place I ever did any teaching was in a college of further education in London in the 1970s. Once a week, I 'taught' 30 day-release,15-year-old post-boys. They hated school and loved motorbikes. But, to leave school and become motorised postal workers, they had had to agree to a day a week in college. I was supposed to teach them English and sociology. I had no training, no induction and was myself on day-release from a postgraduate course, desperate to earn some money. It was ghastly. Chairs were thrown, floor tiles were jemmied up, people arrived late, left in the middle and shouted. (Students, not me, by the way.) I simply stared in amazement at the boys' antics and endeavoured to get through the day unscathed. From this, I learned that being in the role of teacher can be an appalling experience and that it is probably a good idea to get some training!

Once I had got some, I had the good fortune to work in a small staffroom with colleagues who helped and shared, with a mentor, a supportive boss, decent resources and even a trade union membership. I thought staffrooms would be ever thus. Not so.

Anyway, I have had the great fortune to live and work in many different countries but often for short periods. I will thus choose the places where I have stayed longest.

I worked in Tokyo for about three and a half years and lived in Kamakura, one of the old capitals, a seaside town, one hour south by train. I had chosen to go to Japan because I had found the Japanese students in my London language classes so interesting. Their gestures, surprise noises, attitudes, handwriting, doodles, ways of counting things on their fingers ... all were different from other international students. Once in Tokyo, standing in front of classes of 55 students, it took a while for my eyes and ears to adjust and then for me to be able to learn about the people, the language and their attitudes to learning.

Most of the people I had prolonged contact with worked for a living. Most were learning something in the evening or at weekends. English yes, but also *ikebana*, tea ceremony, dance, archery, puppetry or golf. No matter what they were learning, they all seemed to have teachers that they saw regularly, who in turn saw older more senior teachers regularly, who themselves saw even older teachers. An intermediate calligraphy student could thus be taught by a qualified, experienced *Sensei* who might in turn be taught by someone in their eighties and nineties. The learning was never considered to be complete. Such commitment to further learning, such dedication, stamina and humility were new to me. I had, up to then, apart from a set of six horse-riding sessions, never had a private lesson in my life.

And the students in my own language classes did not seem to expect to understand easily or quickly. They expected, instead, relentless practice and hard graft. Sometimes they would take the same course with identical content over and over again. Not for them the eager request to be moved to a higher-level class. From them, and from watching my friends doing their brush and ink calligraphy, their *ikebana* or *aikido* moves, I learned about perseverance and the pursuit of perfection. I learned to slow down, attend, take care and be realistic about the length of time it takes to learn anything to a reasonable level of skill.

A very different experience occurred when I was travelling on a train in China. Word went down the compartments of the train that English speakers were on board and, as a result, a small group of Chinese students came to find us. They proceeded to act out units from the popular English language television show in China at the time, *Follow Me!* I could not think of any Japanese students I knew at the time who would put themselves forward in such a public situation, in English. The students performed the units, word-for-word. The interesting thing was that they had no interest whatsoever in using the language to actually communicate with us in English. This, despite the fact that the language being performed contained phrases such as 'What's your name?' and 'Where are you from?' The students were happy just to perform the skits *at* us. Once they had finished, the Chinese passengers in the train carriage applauded and the students vanished, leaving us somewhat perplexed.

From these encounters I found out that learning a language can be used as a stalling method, a way of structuring your life with pleasant hobbies. Or it can be used as a display device that has nothing whatsoever to do with communication. Language students have their own motives and intentions!

Another place I was lucky enough to work was the German-speaking part of Switzerland. I taught a few English language classes of my own there and also ran a diploma-level training programme for well-trained, experienced Swiss German teachers who wanted to further their qualifications in and through English.

There, I learned how shy most young Swiss Germans were about writing things down in their own language, and about how unwilling they were to speak High German. I was struck once again by the strong emotions that can be triggered within and between languages.

But one particular set of events surprised me. I was invited to meetings where colleagues from different parts of Switzerland and thus with Swiss German, Italian and French mother-tongues were present. My own first language brought the number of languages in the meetings to four. 'How was this going to work?' I wondered. It was simple. Everyone who wanted to say something did so in their own first language so that they could express themselves fully. The others listened to the foreign language and asked clarification questions in their own language if necessary.

So, passive skills often do outstrip active ones! I came out of the meetings exhilarated, not just at how much I had understood of languages I didn't think I was any good at, but also at how alert my brain felt, even before coffee!

Key people

At every step of the way over 40 years in this profession, I have been fortunate to have had people to learn from, whether they were teacher trainers, language students, colleagues, employers, authors or professionals from other fields.

It is thus very difficult to single individuals out. Should I choose my secondary school French teacher who, in a sea of strict, older teachers, was the only one to wear bright colours and have real verve and a sense of humour? She showed me that a teacher could dare to be herself in class.

Perhaps I should mention my Royal Society of Arts diploma trainer, who, by the relaxed way she dealt with latecomers to her language class, showed me that classrooms did not have to be punitive places.

The principal of my first language school wrote each member of staff a Christmas letter, mentioning positive things we had done during the year. That showed me what a real difference support could make to a starter teacher!

And how could I forget Elayne Phillips who, with imaginative warm-up exercises, plunged a group of experienced teacher trainers into a profound learning state of mind at the start of a course.

Next, I want to mention Bernard and Marie Dufeu. I met them on a British Council course. I had never before seen anything like the work they were doing. I attended many of Bernard's courses on psychodramatic language learning in the years following. His use of space, objects, masks and shadowing was so inventive, so imaginative, it blew apart my limited understanding of how a language might be learned, of what could happen in a language classroom and the amazing places that people could go to in their memories and imagination (Dufeu, 1994).

It seems then that, after a childhood and education of tight discipline, strict rules and straight lines, the people I remember most are the ones with humour, warmth and different ways of being that did not involve straight lines.

I could mention many more who had flair and verve. But for real, lasting impact, I will choose two people in this section and cheat by mentioning others in other sections!

In Japan, I fetched up in a staffroom full of genial American teachers, one of whom became my best friend. Whereas I had come from a non-academic family, my new friend came from a family of teachers and university professors. He knew about writing articles and bibliographies, and what the word 'citation' meant in practice. This was not, as you will guess, the sort of thing we talked about as we first got to know each other (and later married!). But, when I would come home from class over the years, relating some idea I had just dreamed up that had worked a treat in class, he would say, 'Why don't you write it up?' and then would explain what that actually meant. In other words, he put the idea of getting published into my head. He knew the ins-and-outs of submission, rejection, revision and resubmission. He knew what was broadly acceptable within an academic community and what was not. He supported me through the various trials of thesis writing and presentation. Since the early days, I have had the luck to publish articles, chapters in books and whole books. But it all started with that first little idea and the person who said, 'Why don't you write it up?'

Now for my second person. When I wrote a personal letter to the Director of Studies of a fully booked British Council specialist course begging to be squeezed in, I discovered that Mario Rinvolucri, the Course Director, didn't just write about humanistic approaches, he lived them too. I got on the course. And so began a long friendship. It is not just the many creative workshops of his that I have enjoyed attending, the many phone conversations, the books and articles of his that have sparked my interest. Mario invited me to work at his organisation, to run a workshop for Pilgrims trainers, pushed me to write my first book, to take book proposals to major publishing houses, to start a journal for teacher trainers, and then start an IATEFL Special Interest Group for teacher trainers and travel abroad to do workshops, and keep learning, keep teaching, keep writing and keep being surprised by his unusual take on absolutely everything.

Key ideas I have encountered and connected publications

Above, I have reflected on my early language learning experiences, on influences arising from places I have worked and on some key people who have left an enduring mark on me. Below I will mention a few ideas that still appeal to me as being reasonable or likely to be true in the matter of language learning and teaching. Further ideas that still seem plausible to me will pop up in later sections.

1. Difficult students can make things hard for everyone. Interest in people, and warmth towards them, seems to help the language learning process (Moskowitz, 1978).

2. The students are the ones who (or whose parents or sponsors) are paying to learn. They need the language practice and a chance to speak and learn about interesting things (Ashton-Warner, 1966). Teacher explanations should thus be very short.

3. If we want to learn about our students but have large classes, we can still gain one-to-one time with students by having a correspondence with them using interactive dialogue journals (Peyton and Staton, 1993). The written feedback, including simple rephrasing, may be more effective than oral feedback.

4. The errors that language learners make can tell us how they are working out the new language. The errors are thus informative rather than simply 'wrong' or to be avoided (Corder, 1967).

5. Regular retrieval practice is fundamental to learning new material (Brown et al., 2014).

6. Music, poetry, art, movement, drama, colour, literature, film, mind maps, thinking frameworks, nice things to read, routine plus variety – all these support language learning (Buzan, 2009; De Bono, 1985; Maley and Duff, 1978; Stevick ,1980; Woodward, 2001, 2006).

7. It takes skill to help a group to form, norm, storm, perform and mourn. It is thus important for teachers to keep on learning, not just about the English language and pedagogy but also about group dynamics (Houston, 1990) and about ourselves as fellow members of the group (Dufeu, 1994).

Critical incidents in work that have given me new insights

In a Saturday morning class in Japan, the adult students worked hard all week in their normal jobs. The language class was called English Conversation. The students got on fine with each other. On paper, their level was intermediate. They were attending because they needed to speak more English in their jobs. However, they were so afraid of making mistakes and so shy of speaking in English that, no matter what I tried, I could not encourage more than about two words out of any of the students. They looked interested. They listened attentively. But they did not speak much at all.

I tried every type of material and prompt I knew. After several weeks, in desperation, I went to my director of studies to talk it over. He listened carefully and then gave me an article to read. It was from a practical teaching magazine and was all about community language learning (CLL).

I read the article. It described a process where students sit in a circle facing each other. The teacher sits outside the circle and has no eye contact with the students. There is a recorder on a table in the middle of the student circle. Once the students are told how to proceed, the teacher does not initiate anything. The students decide what they will talk about in the session. A student then tries to formulate whatever they want to say, in English. If unsure, they turn to the teacher outside the circle, to check that their utterance is correct. The student turns to the others, picking up the recording device and, speaking into it, says what they wish to say to the others. The recorder is switched off again until another student wishes to say something to the group, possibly after whispered help from the teacher and some practice. There is a lot more to the process than this but those are the basics (Curran, 1976).

I was so desperate that, though the idea seemed weird and utterly different from anything I had experienced up to that point, I decided to try it. The article had prepared me for the fact that I had to be patient and wait out the silences, especially at the beginning. I was to avoid initiating, interrupting or making eye contact with students while they faced each other in the circle and had to start. I toughed it out and the first time we tried it, it sort of worked. I kept it up and, after a few weeks, it was really working. The students were deciding on their own topics and talking to each other, if haltingly.

From this experience, I learned that I could ask for help with my teaching, that there were magazines full of ideas for teachers, that I didn't have to be the central figure in the classroom and that silence in the teacher was OK. I could try different ideas out and some might work. I could run experiments in my own classroom. And that last was the epiphany. I was free at last! Free from my own experiences as a student and as a teacher in training, free simply to define a puzzle in my work, hypothesise, experiment and adjust.

Themes emerging from my chapter

I have been considering what influences there have been on my own teaching of English to speakers of other languages (TESOL). I've been gradually discovering, over the years, what I can about how teaching leads to learning. Having thought it through thus far, it seems that I may have emerged from the strict, straight lines of my early education, gradually making a transition to something a little more humane, colourful and creative. I have perhaps moved towards a model of greater participation by all in the language class and of greater teacher-ownership of the process of discovery and of experimentation with what goes on in class.

Starting in Japan, however, while resolutely keeping one foot in the language classroom, I have also been working with teachers of TESOL. I have thus also been trying to understand how the teaching of teachers leads to teacher learning. There have been fresh influences from people and publications on this area of my work too. That would perhaps be a subject to explore in a different chapter or another book! One issue of relevance, however, is that I have worked with pre- and in-set teachers who, unlike me, save for my very first teaching setting, have had an extremely lax experience so far in terms of class discipline, language accuracy and an accompanying and almost exclusive focus on speaking and listening skills and on creativity and communication without clear parameters. For these teachers, the longed-for transition is often towards *more* structure in all its manifestations rather than less.

The learning point thus would seem to be that it is vital for us teachers to uncover our own influences, to see what they have caused in us and to check out whether the ensuing beliefs, values and practices still seem plausible to us, likely to be true and reasonable. If not, we need to adjust. The activities I propose in the CPDs (see e-link below) may help with this exploration.

A brief statement of my beliefs about language and about learning languages

I will now go back and scoop up all the beliefs I have mentioned so far that have arisen from my experiential pathway. The following thoughts still seem to me to be plausible:

- Growing up in a setting where different languages are spoken primes a person to accept that different languages exist and are real.

- It also gives the hint that strong emotions can be aroused by different languages and by differences of use within the same language.

- Meeting a person you like who speaks a different language from yours can make their language seem friendly to you.

- If a language learning activity helps you personally to learn a language, then you will want to offer the technique, albeit with adaptations, to others once you are a teacher yourself.

- Pronunciation is a sensitive area and needs subtle and sensitive treatment.

- Language lessons can be very boring and yet their contents can turn out to be extremely useful.

- We need to be realistic about the length of time it takes to learn a language to a reasonable level of skill.

- People have their own motives for attending language classes and may do unusual things with what they have learned!

- Passive skills often outstrip active ones.

- As a teacher, I can dare to be myself in a class.

- Classrooms do not have to be punitive places.

- A bit of support can make a real difference to a starter teacher!

- Imaginative warm-up exercises can ease a group into a profound learning state of mind.

- Getting an idea published is quite possible if we learn the basics of article submission, rejection, revision and resubmission.

- If people give us chances, and we take them, interesting things can happen.

- There are many different ways to learn a language and many interesting things that can happen in a language classroom.

- As a teacher I can experiment by framing puzzles, informing myself, trying things out, considering the results and then framing new puzzles.

- It is essential to keep learning a language or learning something else, so we can empathise with the learners we work with and understand the cognitive processes involved in engaging with the new.

- We can learn a lot from colleagues, students and those who teach subjects other than English.

References

Ashton-Warner, S (1966) *Teacher*. London: Penguin.

Brown, P, Roediger III, H and McDaniel, M (2014) *Make it Stick: The Science of Successful Learning*. Cambridge, Mass.: Belknap Press of Harvard University Press.

Buzan, T (2009) *The Mind Map Book: Unlock Your Creativity, Boost Your Memory, Change Your Life*. London: BBC Active.

Corder, SP (1967) The significance of learners' errors. *International Review of Applied Linguistics in Language Teaching* 5: 161–170.

Curran, C (1976) *Counseling-Learning in Second Languages*. Illinois: Apple River Press.

De Bono, E (1985) *Six Thinking Hats*. Boston: Little Brown.

Dufeu, B (1994) *Teaching Myself*. Oxford: Oxford University Press.

Houston, G (1990) *The Red Book of Groups: And How to Lead Them Better*. Third edition. Rochester, NY: Rochester Foundation.

Maley, A and Duff, A (1978) *Drama Techniques in Language Learning*. Cambridge: Cambridge University Press.

Moskowitz, G (1978) *Caring and Sharing in the Foreign Language Classroom*. New York: Longman ELT.

Stevick, E (1980) *Teaching Languages: A Way and Ways*. Boston: Heinle/Cengage.

Woodward, T (2001) *Planning Lessons and Courses*. Cambridge: Cambridge University Press.

Woodward, T (2006) *Headstrong: A Book of Thinking Frameworks for Mental Exercise*. Elmstone, UK: TW Publications.

For CPD activities, visit e-file link: www.teachingenglish.org.uk/sites/teacheng/files/e-file.pdf

Suggested further reading

Asher, J (2012) *Learning Another Language Through Actions*. Seventh edition. Los Gatos, CA: Sky Oak Productions.

Clark, C (2001) *Talking Shop: Authentic Conversation and Teacher Learning*. New York: Teachers College Press.

Cosh, J (1998) Peer observation in higher education – a reflective approach. *Innovations in Education and Training International* 35/2: 171–176.

Fanselow, JF (1987) *Breaking Rules: Generating and Exploring Alternatives in Language Teaching*. New York: Pearson.

Huberman, M (1989) The professional life cycles of teachers. *Teachers' College Record* 91/1: 31–57.

Huberman, M (1991) 'Teacher development and instructional mastery', in Hargreaves, A and Fullan, M (eds) *Understanding Teacher Development*. London: Cassells, 171–195.

Maley, A and Prabhu, NS (1989) Interview. *The Teacher Trainer* 3/3: 28–30.

Peyton, J and Reed, L (1990) *Dialogue Journal Writing with Non-Native English Speakers: A Handbook for Teachers*. Alexandria, VA: TESOL.

Peyton, J and Staton, J (eds) (1991) *Writing our Lives: Reflections on Dialogue Journal Writing with Adults Learning English*. Englewood Cliffs, NJ: Regents/Prentice Hall and Center for Applied Linguistics.

Peyton, J and Staton, J (1993) *Dialogue Journals in the Multilingual Classroom: Building Language Fluency and Writing Skills through Written Interaction*. Norwood, NJ: Ablex.

Tripp, D (2012) *Critical Incidents in Teaching: Developing Professional Judgment*. London: Routledge.

Weintraub, E (1989) Interview. *The Teacher Trainer* 3/1: 7–8.

Woodward, T (1991) *Models and Metaphors in the Foreign Language Classroom*. Cambridge: Cambridge University Press.

Woodward, T (1997) Working with teachers interested in different methods. *The Teacher Trainer* 11/3: 7–9.

Woodward, T (2004) *Ways of Working with Teachers*. Elmstone, UK: TW Publications.

Woodward, T (2011) *Thinking in the EFL class*. Rum, Austria: Helbling Languages.

Woodward, T (2015) Professional development late in a teaching career. *The Teacher Trainer* 29/3: 2–3.

Woodward, T, Graves, K and Freeman, D (2018) *Teacher Development Over Time*. New York: Routledge.

Woodward, T and Lindstromberg, S (2014) *Something to Say*. Rum, Austria: Helbling Languages.

20

Meanings that matter to the user

Andrew Wright

Introduction

During my 60 years in language teaching and language teaching materials production 'meaningful' use of language has been held up, mainly during conferences and in academic papers, as a tenet for 'good' language teaching.

The argument has rested on two ideas: a meaningful use of language shows respect to the learner and makes it easier to learn because it engages the whole brain. However, my own experience of being taught has been that 'meaningful' has rarely meant 'meaning that matters to me'.

In this chapter I will describe some of the experiences that have been meaningful to me and contributed to my personal and professional development. I will also highlight the key concepts in this development and suggest how they might be incorporated into teacher development.

Meanings that mattered in my childhood

In this section I describe examples of my experiences that were developmental to me in holistic terms. I highlight the role of verbal language wherever it is relevant.

My war years: the experience of war

I was two years old at the beginning of the Second World War. I learned the meaning of a wailing siren. I learned that the anti-aircraft guns would only start firing when two searchlight beams crossed on one German plane. I learned fear and I learned the power of caring love from my mother.

My toy clockwork car stopped working. I asked my mother to take it to the shop to repair it. She turned it over and showed me the words 'Made in Germany'. She read the words out to me in a regretful, reflective voice. 'Made in Germany,' she said. 'We should be mending children's toys and not fighting wars.'

I learned that verbal language contains information of a material kind but that the voice and the accompanying body communication can contain deeply felt emotions and the expression of complex values and perceptions. I learned that letters on the bottom of a toy car could combine to convey the information that my toy car was made in the same country as the planes that were trying to kill us each night.

Key concepts: non-verbal meanings – sirens, body language, voice quality.
The written word.

My war years: curiosity and excitement

My mother took me on walks. We looked at birds through her binoculars. Once we saw a golden oriole near Whitby in the top of a horse-chestnut tree. It was a male, with a bright yellow body and black wings. At home we looked it up and saw it came from South Africa: we looked at an atlas. My mother was thrilled. She shared her excitement and her driving curiosity with me.

We went into caves inhabited in Neolithic times. We lit a fire and toasted flour and water to make bread. And the smoke was in my eyes as the warm bread melted in my mouth. My uncle, a farmer in Derbyshire, gave us pre-historic flint tools that he had unearthed with his plough. My mind was stretched back in time.

Key concepts: curiosity, observation, analysis, hypothesis, research, revision of hypothesis. And human sharing, co-operation, communication. Historical and geographical concepts.

My war years: books

My mother read Rupert Bear books to me (Bestal, 1940–45). She read the rhyming verse beneath each picture. I was entranced by the visual beat of repetition and by the beat of rhyme. Form not only illustrated but also enhanced the content.

At the age of eight I read the whole of *David Copperfield* by Charles Dickens (1858): all 515 pages of it! My mother told me that I asked her who writes stories and draws pictures. She explained this to me and I told her, 'One day I am going to write and illustrate stories.' She replied, 'Begin whenever you feel like it.'

About this time I joined the church choir and sang the hymns and psalms with lusty joy, revelling in their rhythms and in my role as part of a choir.

The rhyming verse of Rupert and the majesty of the psalms gave me a feeling of the sound of language and how it can be more of an immediate reality than the content the words refer to. I came to love the potential of language to sound and to live.

And Dickens introduced me to the idea that we can vividly create people through writing companions: these bubbling, simmering, breathing words.

Key concepts: the potential of language for expression as well as naming and describing.

Secondary school: verbal language study

With Dr Macgrar we drily translated a Maupassant story word-by-word, so myopically that when we came to the end of a sentence we teetered on the last syllable of the last word before the full stop, giddy at the gap between us and the new sentence.

A few years later a new headmaster heard about the direct method and hired a teacher who pointed at the door and said, in French, 'This is a door.' I felt dismayed by the surrealism of these lessons – just as Magritte's painting of a pipe dismays me because he wrote on the painting that it was not a pipe.

The teacher believed that pointing at a door was more meaningful than the sentence we had to translate in Latin: 'The soldier left by the South Gate.' Why did the soldier leave by the South Gate? By himself? Why? Who was he? Why the South Gate? South Gate of where? We swept past any potential meaning that might have mattered to me.

But! I learned *amo, amas, amat, amamus, amatis, amant*. I have written these words from memory for the first time in 70 years!

I was thrown out of the Latin class and I failed my public examinations in English and French. Did I fail or was I failed? In later life I went on to publish several hundred books, individually or as a co-author or team member. Was that failure?

In language studies at school the only meaning that mattered to me was the rhythmic repetition of sets of words in the Latin lessons and the occasional contact with poetry in the English lessons; for example, Thomas Hardy – the notion of language as a potentially living creature in its rhythms and chiming and rhyming.

Key concepts: we flourish in different ways. My intelligence and caring were not engaged ... except occasionally when the sound of the language sang to me like a bird from outside the classroom window. The potential of language to come alive and not only be used for instrumental purposes.

Secondary school: drawing and painting
All the teachers in the school chose what we should study. Study was largely based on the three Rs: reading, remembering, regurgitating.

In the art lesson it was utterly, utterly different. My art teacher put me in front of nature and expected me to draw it ... he looked at my drawings and said very little. One day I drew a wintery tree outside the classroom window battered by a northerly wind. He looked at it for several moments twitching his eyebrows and pulling his moustache and then he rumbled deeply, 'Bones! Bones! Wright, bones!' He then stood up and marched around the classroom, hands behind his back, uttering the same word at various pitches and volumes, 'Bones! Bones! Bones!'

For the last 68 years I have been wondering what he meant. I think he was telling me that the tree was deep rooted and solid enough to withstand the battering winds and that my drawing had not conveyed this. I think ... His voice and his words still ring in my mind. He has made me think for 68 years!

Sometimes we need to be put into challenging situations and given little or no help ... just presence and caring.

I went to the postgraduate Slade School of Fine Art directly from school. In four years all they did was tell me to look and look again and find whatever paths through infinite complexity I could. And I did try: again and again and again.

Key concepts: responsibility for choice. Searching for meaning in complexity. Not trying to remember beak-fed, ready-digested pills of pap, worthless to a growing mind. Caring.

France: English teaching assistant

I didn't want to become an art teacher immediately. I felt I didn't know enough about the world. I got a job as an assistant teacher of English in a school in France. My interviewer found out immediately that I couldn't speak French but told me that drawing was my second language (language teachers please note) and she was going to send me anyway. Little did she know that I would spend the next 60 years involved in the teaching of English! (I am now 82 and still teaching.)

For the first month I had no money, so I stayed in a hostel for young men. The other young men in my dormitory were bored when I arrived but finding I couldn't speak in French, they decided to teach me and have fun doing it. They decided to teach me slang and refused to let me speak with my English high, upper-throat delivery but to speak from the chest and to combine it with all the French body communication available ... even a heightened version of it, because they found that more hilarious. I was alone and urgently needed to be really accepted by this group. Every effort I made was greeted with cheers, slaps on the back and glasses of Cointreau, which I became very fond of.

I wanted to belong to the group and to be accepted. I was rewarded by getting it right and disappointed by getting it wrong or not good enough. And I knew I had got it right by their delight and laughter, not by their neutral approval or disapproval. Contrast that with the reward of getting high or low marks at school! Very different motivation! Even now, after all these years I can startle French native speakers with my oral fluency with no foundation in the written word.

Key concepts: social belonging, working together to achieve, emotionally charged motivation and emotionally given and received feedback. The power of non-verbal language accompanying and complementing every speech act.

Working as a materials producer: *En Avant* and *A Votre Avis*

After the Second World War and the disbanding of the British Empire, the guaranteed markets of the UK disappeared and it was not as clear as it is today that English would soon be the world language.

It was decided that the UK must take the teaching of foreign languages seriously. The Nuffield Foundation offered the money to establish a research team at the University of Leeds to draft and trial materials for teaching French to all children whatever their academic ability from the age of eight in the UK (Nuffield/Schools Council, 1963–72).

The national purpose of promoting international understanding and trade, etc. led to the teaching of French to all children in the country. The reason for choosing French was not educational enrichment. It was chosen partly because it was the only foreign language some primary school teachers might know! The methodology was chosen to cater to all abilities not just the 15 per cent of grammar school children who it was assumed could learn French by translating it or looking at doors and naming them.

The development of the audio-lingual approach in the US and the audio-visual approach in France provided a basis for the 'new' methodology to be adopted by the Nuffield team.

The team started work in the early 1960s, and I was appointed as a team member mainly responsible for producing the many pictures that would be needed by the methodology. Later I became a full team member, contributing to the writing of the material.

The team wrote stories and created games to appeal to the interests of eight-year-olds but there was still the underlying influence of Skinner and his ideas about the importance of repetition based on training rats (Skinner, 1957). The stories were trivial and far from offering 'meaning that mattered' to them.

My epiphany came in 1967 when Julian Dakin and Tony Howatt of the Department of Applied Linguistics in Edinburgh were employed to examine our material and evaluate it. Among many other things, they pointed out that the children using our materials virtually never used the first-person subject pronoun to refer to themselves! The children only used it to act out their roles in the story dialogues! This was simply shocking!

In 1968 Europe and North America exploded socially, particularly in universities, with the demand for change in order to recognise the importance of the individual rather than the authoritarian guidance of rational social behaviour. The notional and functional description of language, based on what people want to do with language rather than solely on the grammatical form, was developed by David Wilkins, John Trim, Jan Van Ek and Louis Alexander. This was description of language not a methodology, though it was highly influential.

In the late 1960s in *A Votre Avis*, the secondary extension of *En Avant*, it was Michael Buckby who was the driving force in creating activities on highly engaging topics and forms of participation. It was Michael who hired a journalist from a teenage magazine in Paris to join our team. Michael's argument was that, as a journalist who made his living by engaging teenagers, he should know how to do it!

Key concepts: the potential influence of national and cultural values in determining what and how language is taught. The rise of 'humanism' in Europe and North America and its influence on language teaching.

Working as a materials producer: *Kaleidoscope*

In 1972 I was employed by the University of York as director of a production team of a course for the teaching of English as a foreign language to primary school children aged eight to 11: *Kaleidoscope*. My colleagues were David Betteridge and Dr Nicolas Hawkes.

We were determined to produce materials in *Kaleidoscope* that were a genuine alternative to other published material. The course helped the teacher to engage the children in activities that they cared about with the prospect of intellectual, creative and social development. This would fit in with any 'progressive' concept of primary education. We assert that our course, *Kaleidoscope*, was the beginnings of what would become CLIL!

We did not begin with a fixed language curriculum, though we had various options in the background, including informal copies of the notional and functional description of language by David Wilkins dated 1972, later to be published (Wilkins, 1976).

We began as authors by brainstorming hundreds of activities we thought classes of young children might enjoy doing with a teacher in a classroom. We noted the English they would need to understand and the English they would need to use in order to take part. Nicolas Hawkes then put these activities into a language-learning and development sequence based on his experience of teaching English. In other words, we began with what children might enjoy doing but finished up with a structural syllabus!

In writing the material, we were acutely conscious that the teacher was much more important than we were. The teacher was part of the 'medium'. We had to assume that the teacher was positive towards the idea of, above all, creating a learning environment in the language classroom in which curiosity, personal responsibility and willingness to 'have a go' were paramount. And, of course, a teacher with sufficient linguistic skills to provide a good model of the language. *Kaleidoscope* was piloted in eight countries (University of York, 1976).

Key concepts: the full orchestration of communicative instruments and the deep-rooted driving force in the teacher as a creator of events that engage the learner and in which the target language has 'meanings that matter to the learner'.

Humanism took off in the mid-1970s

Driven by the same current of cultural change so noticeably sparked by *les evenements* in 1968, this 'humanism' stirred individuals to demand a methodology that was genuinely engaging rather than the existing tokenism related to everyday topics.

Kaleidoscope was certainly a response to this 'humanistic' demand. In 1976 I wrote my first handbook for teachers, *Visual Materials for the Language Teacher.* In this book I expressly went beyond pictures and included timetables, maps, tickets and anything visual that could be part of an engaging activity (Wright, 1976). In 1979 David Betteridge, Michael Buckby and I published *Games for Language Learning*, continuing the theme of finding engaging activities that develop a variety of language skills and awareness (Wright et al., 1979).

A year earlier, Alan Maley and Alan Duff had published *Drama Techniques in Language Learning* (1978), a perfect example of bringing into the world of language teaching some of the involving activities from professional actor training.

Mario Rinvolucri made even dictation into *meaning that matters* in his wonderful book, *Dictation* (Davis and Rinvolucri, 1988). And later, among many other teachers' resource books by Mario, *Once Upon a Time* (Morgan and Rinvolucri, 1983).

These books were the beginning of a 'golden era' of resource books offering many ways of 'making meaning matter' in the classroom.

International teacher training

Since 1968 my work in writing teaching materials has overlapped with my work with teachers and sometimes students in 55 countries. I can only select from this huge richness: first, we can say that in spite of our many different values, perceptions and behaviours, we language teachers do have much in common. At the same time, I have learned that some values and perceptions that I hold about learning and teaching and that are evidenced in this short chapter are not shared with many of my teacher colleagues in other countries. Here is just one anecdote to illustrate that assertion.

In one country, I was talking to the local trainer during a coffee break in a teacher-training course. He asked me about my ideas and I told him how fundamental it was for me to see my learners as fellow humans, each with experience and talents different to mine and a potential treasure-house for the creation of meaningful events. He listened to me for several moments, his body becoming more tense and distancing himself. Suddenly, he drove his cigarette into the ash-tray with a savage twist, stood up and uttered in a deep, hard monotone, 'When I walk into a classroom I represent two thousand years of learning and expect total respect!'

Key concepts: the values, perceptions and behaviours held by the teacher and students are the most important factor in what actually happens in the classroom, whatever may be said in conferences or published in books.

Travelling as a storyteller, story-maker and book-maker

I have worked with literally thousands of students in many countries as a storyteller, story-maker and storybook-maker. I have learned so much but here is one highly relevant anecdote from my travels. I was in Klagenfurt in Southern Austria. A woman stopped me in the street. She asked, 'Are you the storyteller working in the local school?'

I told her I was. She replied, 'I have something I want to tell you. My son is 15. All his life he has been difficult to get out of bed in the morning for school but this week he has been setting his alarm in order to go in to school one hour earlier in order to work with his friends on the book they are making in your class.'

He cared. Meaning mattered for him. He and his friends wrote and illustrated because the book was not going to be marked. It was going to be shown in the local library and his grandma could get a copy.

Stories are a fundamental part of the everyday life of adults as well as children. Even the news is presented as 'story': 'The top stories today ... ' To help teachers to use stories within the classroom and to retain the students' involvement with them I have written three books (Wright, 1997, 2008; Wright and Hill, 2008).

Key concept: student activity for social reasons rather than for the teacher's marks. The teacher as an agent, a supporter, a consultant not a receiver and a judge.

Conclusion

Experiencing and studying language both have their parts to play. But if we have two legs, why hop? This chapter has focused on the leg less used – experience. Learning English, it is argued, is a by-product of experiencing meanings that matter combined with more traditional study. YOUR experience! THEIR experiences!

Eat the peach and then plant the stone in your garden.

References

Bestal, A (1940–45) *Rupert Bear Annuals.* London: Daily Express.

Davis, P and Rinvolucri, M (1988) *Dictation.* Cambridge: Cambridge University Press.

Dickens, C (1858) *David Copperfield.* London: Chapman and Hall/Bradbury and Evans.

Maley, A and Duff, A (1978/2005) *Drama Techniques in Language Learning.* Third edition. Cambridge: Cambridge University Press.

Morgan, J and Rinvolucri, M (1983) *Once Upon a Time.* Cambridge: Cambridge University Press.

Nuffield/Schools Council (1963–72) *En Avant* and *A Votre Avis.* Leeds: EJ Arnold.

Skinner, BF (1957) *Verbal Behavior.* Acton, MA: Copley Publishing Group.

University of York (1976) *Kaleidoscope: English for Juniors.* London: Macmillan.

Wilkins, DA (1976) *Notional Syllabuses.* Oxford: Oxford University Press.

Wright, A (1976) *Visual Materials for the Language Teacher.* London: Longman.

Wright, A (1997) *Creating Stories with Children.* Oxford: Oxford University Press.

Wright, A (2008) *Storytelling with Children.* Second edition. Oxford: Oxford University Press.

Wright, A, Betteridge, D and Buckby, M (1979) *Games for Language Learning.* Cambridge: Cambridge University Press.

Wright, A and Hill, D (2008) *Writing Stories.* Innsbruck: Helbling Languages.

For CPD activities, visit e-file link: www.teachingenglish.org.uk/sites/teacheng/files/e-file.pdf

Suggested further reading

Wright, A (2015) 'Medium: companion or slave?' in Maley, A and Peachey, N (eds) *Creativity in the English Language Classroom.* London: British Council, 14–23.

Biographies

About the authors

Robert Bellarmine served the British Council Division, South India, as English Studies Officer for 11 years, until he voluntarily retired in 1997. He continued his part-time service for the British Council Division as examiner and examiner-trainer for the Cambridge ESOL examinations. Since 2013 he has been devoting his time to academic lectures, translating Tamil books, voluntary work and his family. Before joining the British Council Division, he served the Central Institute of English and Foreign Languages (CIEFL), now re-named the English and Foreign Languages University (EFLU), in Hyderabad. He came to the CIEFL after working as a teacher of English for 11 years and as a demonstrator in chemistry for three years. He received his MSc in Applied Linguistics from the University of Edinburgh, his postgraduate diploma in Teaching English as a Second Language from CIEFL, his MA in English from Kamararaj University in Tamil Nadu and his BSc in Chemistry from Madras University. His publications include *Hello English*, a series of 23 books for English-medium students in India, *Provocations: Teaching English Literature in the Universities*, book reviews and articles in British Council Division's *Focus on English*.

John F Fanselow is Professor Emeritus at Teachers College, Columbia University, and a faculty member of the International Teacher Education Institute (iTDi). His main interest has been observation and analysis of interactions, both inside and outside of classrooms. His publications reflect this interest. In *It's Too Damn Tight!* he illustrated major differences in how we talk about objects inside and outside of classes and used some common spoken words for the first time in the *TESOL Quarterly. Beyond Rashomon* and *Let's See*, two of his seminal articles in the *TESOL Quarterly,* led to *Breaking Rules* (Longman, 1987) and *Contrasting Conversations* (Longman, 1992). *Small Changes in Teaching, Big Results in Learning – Videos, Activities and Essays to Stimulate Fresh Thinking about Language Teaching and Learning* (iTDi, 2017) illustrates practices he has been exploring since his first teaching job in 1961 in Nigeria. In addition to teaching and writing, he has been active professionally, serving as second Vice-President and President of TESOL and President of New York TESOL. In 2005, John received the Distinguished Alumni Award from Teachers College, Columbia University.

Thomas SC Farrell is Professor of Applied Linguistics at Brock University, Canada. Professor Farrell's professional interests include reflective practice and language teacher education and development. Professor Farrell has published widely in academic journals and has presented at major conferences worldwide on these topics. A selection of his books include: *Teaching Practice: A Reflective Approach* (New York: Cambridge University Press, 2011, with Jack Richards); *Reflecting on Teaching the Four Skills* (Ann Arbor: The University of Michigan Press, 2012); *Reflective Practice* (TESOL, US, 2013); *Reflective Writing for Language Teachers* (Equinox, 2013); *Reflective Practice in ESL Teacher Development Groups: From Practices To Principles* (Palgrave McMillian, UK, 2014); *International Perspectives on English Language Teacher Education: Innovations From The Field* (Basingstoke, UK: Palgrave MacMillan, 2015); *Promoting Teacher Reflection in Language Education: A Framework for TESOL Professionals* (Routledge, 2015); *From Trainee to Teacher: Reflective Practice For Novice Teachers* (Equinox, 2016); *Reflecting on Critical Incidents in Language Education* (with L Baecher, Bloomsbury, 2017); *Preservice*

Teacher Education (TESOL publications, 2017); *Sociolinguistics and Language Teaching* (TESOL publications, 2017); *Research on Reflective Practice in TESOL* (Routledge, 2018); and *Reflective Language Teaching: Practical Applications for TESOL Teachers* (Bloomsbury, 2018). His webpage is: www.reflectiveinquiry.ca

Claudia Ferradas is based in Buenos Aires, Argentina, where she graduated as a teacher of English and has taught language and literature for many years. She holds an MA in Education and Professional Development from the University of East Anglia and a PhD in English Studies from the University of Nottingham. She teaches on the MA programme in Literatures in English at the Universidad Nacional de Cuyo, Mendoza, and is an affiliate trainer with Norwich Institute for Language Education (NILE), UK, where she teaches on professional development courses and on the MA in Professional Development for Language Education, validated by the University of Chichester. She has also taught on the MA programme in TEFL at the Universidad de Alcalá de Henares, Spain. She often works as a consultant and trainer for Oxford University Press, the British Council and Trinity College London. She has co-chaired the Oxford Conference on the Teaching of Literature (Corpus Christi College) on five occasions. She has published numerous academic papers, has contributed to books and intercultural ELT materials, and is a member of the editorial boards of *Argentine Journal of Applied Linguistics (AJAL)* and *Children's Literature in English Language Education Journal (CLELE)*.

Christine Goh is Professor of Linguistics and Language Education at Singapore's National Institute of Education, Nanyang Technological University. She is a qualified English language teacher with more than 30 years of experience in language teaching and teacher education in school and university contexts. She is interested in second language speaking and listening and the role of metacognition in language learning. She derives great satisfaction when her ideas can help teachers teach oracy effectively. Christine also publishes extensively. Her recent books are *Teaching Speaking: A Holistic Approach* (with Anne Burns, Cambridge University Press, 2012) and *Teaching and Learning Second Language Listening: Metacognition in Action* (with Larry Vandergrift, Routledge, 2012). *Teaching Listening in the Language Classroom* (RELC, 2002) has been translated into Chinese and Portuguese. She also co-edited *Language Learning in New English Contexts: Studies of Acquisition and Development* (Continuum/Bloomsbury, 2009). Her most recent book, *Teaching English to Second Language Learners in Academic Contexts* (Routledge, 2018), was a collaboration with Jonathan Newton, Dana Ferris, William Grabe, Fredricka Stoller and Larry Vandergrift. Her weekends are spent mostly with her family and their two cats. She is also involved in a weekend community story-reading programme that encourages young children to love books and imagination.

Yueguo Gu, MA, PhD, Dr Lit. honoris causa (all from Lancaster University), is a research professor and the Head of the Corpus Linguistics Department, the Chinese Academy of Social Sciences. He is also the holder of Special Title Professor, Director of China Multilingual Multimodal Corpora and Big Data Research Centre, Beijing Foreign Studies University, and Director of Aging, Language and Care Research Centre, Tongji University/CASS. His research interests include pragmatics, discourse analysis, corpus linguistics, rhetoric and online education. His latest publications include *The Routledge Handbook of Pragmatics* (co-edited, 2017), *The Encyclopedia of Chinese Language and Linguistics* (co-edited, 5 volumes,

Brill, 2016). He also has three separate titles, all published by Foreign Language Teaching and Research Press in Beijing: *Using the Computer in ELT* (2006), *Pragmatics and Discourse Studies* (2010) and *Chinese Painting* (2015). He is the winner of five national top research prizes, and was awarded a KC Wong Fellow of the British Academy in 1997. He is a holder of many honorary posts, most noticeably special professorship of the University of Nottingham, Adjunct Professor of West Sydney University, Visiting Lecture Professor of Peter the Great St Petersburg Polytechnic University, and Distinguished Research Fellow of Sydney University. Personal website: www.multimodalgu.com

Dr Jennifer Joy Joshua is the Director in the Office of the Director-General for the National Department of Basic Education (DBE) in South Africa. The DBE manages policy development and its implementation in all South African public schools in the country ranging from birth to Grade 12. Dr Joshua has held this position since August 2016. Prior to this, she was the Director for Curriculum Development and Quality Improvement (Grades R–9) in the DBE. Other roles she has held within the DBE include the Director for Learning and Teaching Support Materials and the Director for Foundations for Learning, which was the flagship programme of the DBE. Her qualifications include a Doctor of Education degree in Language Policy Implementation from the University of KwaZulu-Natal in 2008, and a Master of Education degree specialising in second language teaching from the University of South Africa in 1995. In 2014/15, as a recipient of the AS Hornby scholarship, she obtained a Master of Arts degree with distinction from the University of Warwick, specialising in English for young learners. Dr Joshua has a passion for education in the early grades and language learning and teaching in particular.

Kuchah Kuchah is Lecturer in Language Education at the University of Leeds, UK. Previously, he worked as an English language teacher, teacher trainer and policymaker in his home country, Cameroon, before moving to the UK in 2009. He has also been involved in a range of teacher education and materials development initiatives in Sub-Saharan Africa, South East Asia and Europe. More recently, he has served as a consultant for the Council of Europe, Windle Trust International and the British Council. In 2016 Kuchah was recognised by TESOL International Association as one of '30 upcoming leaders' in ELT globally. He is currently President of the International Association of Teachers of English as a Foreign Language (IATEFL) and member of the British Council English Language Advisory Group. His research interests include teaching English to young learners, English-medium instruction, language teacher education and CPD, as well as language education in difficult circumstances, and he has published extensively in these areas. His recent co-edited book, *International Perspectives on Teaching English in Difficult Circumstances* (Palgrave Macmillan), was published in April 2018.

Dr Phuong Le is currently based at Phu Yen University in Central Vietnam. After graduating in English at Hue Education College in Vietnam, she won various grants for postgraduate education overseas (postgraduate in TESOL and MA in Applied Linguistics in Australia and a course in culture and literature at Keble College, Oxford University). Her Doctor of Education thesis was recognised as the best thesis of the year at La Trobe University in Australia in 2008. In the following year, she was at the University of South Florida, US, doing research as a Fulbright Scholar. She has also received further grants/awards for conferences in South Korea, Australia and

Malaysia. As an ESL teacher educator and language assessor for almost 40 years in various tertiary contexts in Vietnam, she has also worked as an interpreter/translator for different projects conducted by UNDP, FORD, UNICEF, UNAIDS, Doctors without Borders and the Social Science Research Council. As a researcher, Dr Phuong Le has published and presented extensively on various ESL topics in international journals and conferences besides serving as a journal reviewer. Her current research interests include developing ESL learners' interest, autonomy and creativity.

Péter Medgyes, CBE, is Professor Emeritus of Applied Linguistics and Language Pedagogy at Eötvös Loránd University Budapest. During his career he has been a schoolteacher, teacher trainer, vice president of IATEFL, vice rector, deputy state secretary and ambassador of Hungary to Syria. He has been a plenary speaker in more than 50 countries and is the author of numerous articles and books, including *The Non-Native Teacher* (Macmillan, 1994), winner of the Duke of Edinburgh Book Competition; *The Language Teacher* (Corvina, 1997); *Laughing Matters* (Cambridge University Press, 2002); *Golden Age: Twenty Years of Foreign Language Education in Hungary* (National Textbook Publishing Company, 2011); and *Reflections on Foreign Language Education* (Eötvös Publishing House, 2015). His most recent book is the updated and revised third edition of *The Non-Native Teacher* (Swan Communication, 2017), shortlisted for the Ben Warren Prize. His main professional interests lie in language policy and teacher education, with a special emphasis on non-native English speaker teachers.

Freda Mishan is course director of the Structured PhD TESOL at the University of Limerick, Ireland, where she lectures on both the PhD and MA TESOL. Her research interests and publications include blended learning, ESOL and materials development. Her publications include *Designing Authenticity into Language Learning Materials* (University of Chicago Press, 2005), *Materials Development for TESOL* (co-authored with Ivor Timmis, Edinburgh University Press, 2015) and two co-edited books on materials development, *Practice and Theory for Materials Development in L2 Learning* (Cambridge Scholars Publishing, 2017) co-edited with Hitomi Masuhara and Brian Tomlinson, and *Perspectives on Language Learning Materials Development* (Peter Lang, 2010) co-edited with Angela Chambers. Contributions to recent edited volumes include chapters in *Authenticity in Materials Development for Language Learning* (Maley and Tomlinson, 2017), *The Cambridge Guide to Blended Learning for Language Teaching* (McCarthy, 2016) and *Developing Materials for Language Teaching* (Tomlinson, 2013). Publications include the edited volume *ESOL Provision in Ireland and the UK: Challenges and Opportunities* (2019) and a co-authored book (with Tamás Kiss) *Developing Intercultural Language Learning Materials: From Principle to Practice* (forthcoming 2021). Freda Mishan is editor of the Materials Development Association journal *Folio*.

Jayakaran Mukundan, PhD, is Professor at Universiti Putra Malaysia. He retired at 60, in 2016 (mandatory) and has continued on contract ever since. He started work as a school teacher and served in remote rural areas in Pahang; the Jengka Triangle (where teachers get their lives sucked out and dried); and in Raub Pahang where the communist insurgency was very much alive and thriving (and if you didn't die in accidents on the timber-lorry tracks, the bandits got you!). He started teaching at Universiti Putra Malaysia in 1990 and worked right through to retirement. He was a teacher trainer for many years. His main interests are in materials development and writing. His MA is in Writing and his PhD on Materials Development. He developed the first *Composite Framework for Materials Evaluation* and the first *Online Textbook Evaluation Checklist*. Two of his materials evaluation software packages won international awards, at the British Invention Show, London, UK, and at IENA, Nuremberg, Germany. In 2013, he won the National Award for Academic Excellence.

Chrysa Papalazarou is an English teacher in a state primary school in Greece. She holds a BA in English Language and Literature with a minor in Greek studies from the University of Athens. She also has a joint MA in Comparative Education and Human Rights from the University of London (Institute of Education) and the University of Athens. She is interested in art, visuals, thinking and creativity in ELT and learning. She blogs about her classroom insights and practice in her blog Art Least. She has shared her ideas in conferences in Greece and abroad. She is one of the authors in the British Council publications *Creativity in the English Language Classroom* (2015) and *Integrating Global Issues in the Creative English Language Classroom: With Reference to the United Nations Sustainable Development Goals* (2017). She is also one of the authors in *The Image in English Language Teaching* (2017) ELT Council publication. She is a member of the Visual Arts Circle, the C Group and FILTA. Chrysa is a keen self-taught photographer.

NS Prabhu has a Master's degree in English Literature from Madras University and a Master's as well as a Doctoral degree in Linguistic Science from the University of Reading. He taught English in undergraduate colleges for about ten years, and then did a year's Diploma in Teaching English at the Central Institute of English, Hyderabad. He went on to work at the British Council in Madras for the next 20 years giving advice and short courses on teaching English at undergraduate colleges in Southern India, before going on to teach applied linguistics at The National University of Singapore for ten years. His best-known publications are *English Through Reading* (Macmillan Education, 1974) and *Second Language Pedagogy* (Oxford University Press, 1987).

Shelagh Rixon studied Classics at Newnham College, University of Cambridge. She started teaching English while in Italy for study purposes and this eventually became her chosen profession. She was a career officer with the British Council between 1974 and 1991, working in a range of countries including Saudi Arabia, Italy, China, Israel and Malaysia. She then moved to the University of Warwick as a lecturer in the Centre for English Language Teacher Education (later Department of Applied Linguistics) before her retirement in 2010. She holds a Postgraduate Certificate of Education in TESOL, a University College London Certificate of Proficiency in English Phonetics, an MSc in Applied Linguistics from the University of Edinburgh and a PhD from the University of Warwick. She is the author of English language textbooks and books for teachers and an editor of and contributor to academic works on primary English language teaching. Currently she is a governor in two UK primary schools.

Malu Sciamarelli has been a teacher and teacher trainer in Brazil since 1993. She has also been an active member of a group of teachers dedicated to increasing the amount of creativity found in language classrooms throughout the world. She has been the co-ordinator of the C Group (Creativity for Change in Language Education) for two years and has published book chapters on project-based learning with puppets for young learners (British Council, 2015) and the importance of creativity and play in language learning (British Council, 2017). She has also published articles in several ELT journals all over the world. In addition to teaching students of all ages and levels, training teachers and writing book chapters and articles, she writes poems and short stories for language learners. She is also part of a movement in ELT that uses blogs and other social media to quickly disseminate new ideas in the area. Furthermore, she is a conference presenter, having presented in many countries, including England, Scotland, France, Greece, Hungary, UAE, Indonesia, Japan and Brazil, as well as many online conferences. She is also an active member of IATEFL, being the Literature Special Interest Group Web Manager.

Dr Fauzia Shamim is Professor and Dean, Faculty of Liberal Arts and Human Sciences, Ziauddin University, Karachi, Pakistan. She has worked as a teacher, teacher educator, researcher and teacher-leader in several higher education institutions both in Pakistan and abroad. Dr Shamim has taught EFL/ESL and trained English language teachers in a variety of settings in Pakistan and internationally. She also has vast experience in developing and teaching applied linguistics courses at undergraduate and postgraduate levels. Dr Shamim has presented, as invited speaker, at numerous conferences in Pakistan and several countries in Asia, Africa, Europe, the Middle East and the US. She has published widely in peer-reviewed journals and books, and co-edited three books. She is on the editorial and advisory boards of both national and international journals. She is also the recipient of the best NNEST paper award (TESOL, 2014) and TESOL's leadership mentoring award (2016). Dr Shamim is a founder member and President of the Society of Pakistan English Language Teachers (SPELT). Currently, she is also the Chair of TESOL International's Research Professional Council (US). Her current research interests include teacher development, programme development and evaluation, large-class teaching and English as medium of instruction.

Jane Spiro began teaching at school, directing her own short plays and helping the younger children to read. She has degrees in English Language and Literature, Cultural History, Applied Linguistics and Philosophy of Education. She has taught EAL children and asylum-seekers in the UK; Russian teachers retraining to English teaching in Hungary; teachers in Mexico and Switzerland upgrading qualifications; and short courses for the British Council in Japan, India, Kenya, the Czech Republic and many other locations. Her publications include *Creative Poetry Writing* and *Storybuilding* (Oxford University Press, 2004 and 2007), *Changing Methodologies in ELT* (Edinburgh University Press, 2013) and *Linguistic and Cultural Innovations in Schools* (with Eowyn Crisfield, Palgrave Macmillan, 2018). She has published two poetry collections, a novel and several collections of learner literature stories. She is committed to creative education both inside and outside language learning, and been involved in projects such as poetry on the Oxford buses, poetry in the park and retelling refugee stories (*Testimony of Flight*, Palewell Press, 2019). She is Reader in Education and TESOL at Oxford Brookes University, research lead for Applied Linguistics and a founder member of the C Group. In 2010 she won a prestigious National Teaching Fellowship for teaching excellence.

Adrian Underhill started teaching in 1972 after receiving a five-minute teacher training talk over the phone – in lieu of any interview – from a school principal he had never met, whose English teacher had just walked out. He started the next morning, but did not meet him for another week. Later he trained at International House and moved to Hastings, becoming director of the International Teacher Training Institute. He has a postgraduate degree in Facilitation Styles from Surrey University and a Master's in Responsible Business Practice from Bath University. From 1999 to 2003 he was Vice-President and then President of IATEFL. Since 1999 Adrian has worked internationally as an independent ELT consultant focusing on teacher training, professional and organisational development, and school leadership. He runs teacher training programmes for Oxford University on their ELT Summer Seminar, at Homerton College, Cambridge for The Bell Teacher Campus, and at International House in London. In recent years he has followed courses in storytelling, clowning and improvisation. He has a jazz band and has played regularly in pubs and bars and private parties since his teenage years. Aside from that, one of his hobbies is organic gardening, mainly stuff to eat.

Tessa Woodward, a teacher, teacher trainer and the Professional Development Co-ordinator at Hilderstone College, Broadstairs, Kent, UK until August 2016, still edits *The Teacher Trainer* journal for Pilgrims, Canterbury, UK. She is a Past President and International Ambassador of IATEFL, founded the IATEFL Special Interest Group for Teacher Trainers (now the SIG T Ed/TT) and is on the NILE advisory board. She is the author of many books and articles for language teachers and for teacher trainers. Her latest book, written with Kathleen Graves and Donald Freeman, is *Teacher Development Over Time* (Routledge, 2018). Tessa is also the founder of The Fair List, UK (www.thefairlist.org). In 2018, she was awarded the British Council ELTons Innovations Lifetime Achievement Award.

Andrew Wright trained as an artist at the Slade School of Fine Art, University College, London. After working as an 'assistant' in French Lycee and a year travelling in the Middle East, he was employed by the Nuffield Foundation and the Schools Council in a team producing materials for teaching French in the UK at the University of Leeds and then at the University of York (1963–72). He also worked freelance as story-writer and illustrator for West German TV. He was employed by the University of York/MacMillan Education to produce a primary school course for the teaching of English as a foreign language (1972–76). *Kaleidoscope* was the first topic-based course and pre-cursor of CILT. He moved to the Metropolitan University of Manchester as a Principal Lecturer (1976–87) to set up a degree course for the design of educational materials, Design for Learning. Along the way he published many influential books, including *Storytelling with Children* (Oxford University Press, 2008) and *Five-Minute Activities: A Resource Book of Short Activities* (with Penny Ur, Cambridge University Press, 1992). He has lived in Hungary since 1992, working as freelance author, storyteller, teacher trainer and teacher in 55 countries. His latest collections of stories are *Beggar of Bogota* and *Larger than Life*.

About the editor

Alan Maley worked for the British Council from 1962 to 1988, serving as English Language Officer in Yugoslavia, Ghana, Italy, France and China, and as Regional Director in South India (Madras). From 1988 to 1993 he was Director-General of the Bell Educational Trust, Cambridge. From 1993 to 1998 he was Senior Fellow in the Department of English Language and Literature of the National University of Singapore, and from 1998 to 2003 he directed the ELT graduate programme at Assumption University, Bangkok. For 20 years he was series editor for the Oxford University Press *Resource Books for Teachers* series. He has published more than 40 books and numerous articles. From 2006 to 2014 he worked with the Asian Teacher-Writer Creative Writing Group, publishing original stories and poems in English for use with students in the Asia region. He was Vice-President then President of IATEFL from 1988 to 1992. In 2014 he co-founded the C Group (Creativity for change in language education). He was given the British Council's ELTons Lifetime Achievement Award in 2012.